New Zealand's Responses to the 1916 Rising

Peter Kuch AND Lisa Marr

EDITORS

CORK UNIVERSITY PRESS

First published in 2020 by
Cork University Press
Boole Library
University College Cork
Cork
T12 ND89
Ireland

Library of Congress Control Number: 2020934753
Distribution in the USA: Longleaf Services, Chapel Hill, NC, USA

British Library Cataloguing in Publication Data
A CIP record for this book is available from the British Library.

ISBN: 978-1-78205-401-6

Printed in Poland by BZ Graf.
Print origination & design by Carrigboy Typesetting Services, www.carrigboy.com

Cover image: Lance Corporal Finlay McLeod (NZ), Private Edward Waring (NZ), unknown
(South Africa) and Private Michael McHugh (Australia), leaving front gate, Trinity College,
Dublin, April 1916. On leave in Ireland, they had been ordered to reinforce the defence of Trinity
College, ©Imperial War Museum (IWM 194 — screenshot at 7:20. LIC-24114-B2Q3Z8).

www.corkuniversitypress.com

Contents

Acknowledgements

Several of the essays included in this volume were first delivered as papers at a conference entitled 'Yet no clear fact to be discerned', which was jointly convened by the Centre for Irish and Scottish Studies at the University of Otago and Toitū Otago Settlers Museum, Dunedin. The programme can be accessed at https://www.otago.ac.nz/easter-rising-1916/. Some speakers chose not to submit papers; some offered essays that were different from the papers they had presented. Unfortunately, there were no contributions analysing the Māori or the New Zealand Scottish response to the Rising even though such were requested. The conference, which ran for two days, was attended by over one hundred people from all parts of New Zealand and Australia. The conference organisers and the contributors to this volume are very grateful for the generous financial support offered by the Eamon Cleary Trust, the Faculty of Arts at the University of Otago, and the Cultural Relations Committee of the Department of Foreign Affairs of the Irish government through the Éire/Ireland 1916/2016 *Clár Comórtha Céad Bliain* Centenary Programme. They are also grateful for the willing support of the Honorary Consul General of Ireland, Auckland, and the staff of the Embassy of Ireland, Canberra, Australian Capital Territory.

Abbreviations

A	*The Argus* (Melbourne)
AJHR	*Appendix to the Journals of the House of Representatives*
AS	*The Auckland Star*
AWM	Australian War Memorial
BA	*Bendigo Advertiser*
BMH	Bureau of Military History, Military Archives, Dublin
C	*The Colonist* (Nelson)
CP	*The Catholic Press* (Sydney)
D	*The Dominion* (Wellington)
EP	*The Evening Post* (Wellington)
FS	*The Feilding Star*
FJ	*The Freeman's Journal* (Sydney)
GR	*The Green Ray* (Dunedin)
IW	*The Irish World* (New York)
MW	*The Maoriland Worker* (Wellington)
NA	National Archives (New Zealand)
NAA	National Archives of Australia
NZH	*The New Zealand Herald* (Auckland)
NZPD	*New Zealand Parliamentary Debates*
NZT	*The New Zealand Tablet* (Dunedin)
ODT	*The Otago Daily Times* (Dunedin)
OW	*Otago Witness* (Dunedin)
P	*The Press* (Christchurch)
SC	*The Southern Cross* (Adelaide)
SMH	*The Sydney Morning Herald*
SRSA	State Records of South Australia
TCD	Trinity College Dublin
TDN	*Taranaki Daily News* (New Plymouth)
WC	*Wanganui Chronicle*

Introduction

PETER KUCH

Emeritus Professor, University of Otago

This selection of essays provides the first considered account of New Zealand's responses to the 1916 Rising. The word 'responses' is key, because it draws attention to the more nuanced reaction to and the more measured participation in what had taken place in Ireland at the height of the First World War in contrast to the reaction of its neighbour and fellow dominion, Australia. In part, the New Zealand responses were due to a shared perception that there were more emigrant Irish and more people of Irish descent in Australia who were sympathetic to Irish independence than there were currently in New Zealand.[1] There is some evidence to support this view. According to the 1916 New Zealand census (taken on 15 October), only 3.40 per cent of the population of 1,097,841 – of which 27.66 per cent had been born overseas – were native-born Irish compared with 12.84 per cent English, 4.73 per cent Scottish, and 4.15 per cent Australian. Another way of indicating the contrast is to consider religion, although, of course, not all Irish were Catholic. In New Zealand in 1916, Roman Catholics or Catholics comprised 14.17 per cent of the population compared with Anglicans at 42.90 per cent and Presbyterians at 24.36 per cent. Unfortunately, no figures are given in the New Zealand census for those identifying as Irish by virtue of Irish descent.[2] The Australian census closest to 1916 is the 1911 census. No figures are given for those living in Australia who were Irish-born or who claimed Irish descent. In respect to religion, however, where 4,274,414 people in a total population of 4,455,005 professed their Christianity, 1,710,443 were Anglican and 921,425 were Catholic. The next main groupings were Presbyterian (558,336) and Methodist (547,806). These numbers translate to Anglican 38.39 per cent, Catholic 20.68 per cent, Presbyterian 12.53 per cent, and Methodist 12.29 per cent.[3]

There are, however, three important refinements to these raw figures. As Rory Sweetman points out in Chapter 6, the New Zealand Catholic Church was less powerful, less politically active, and less influential than its Australian counterpart. And 'early twentieth-century political developments in Ireland', as Seán Brosnahan has convincingly shown in Chapter 7, 'made relatively little impact in New Zealand'. However, Malcolm Campbell contends in the final essay in this volume that there was an 'unforeseen measure of understanding shown' by New Zealanders for the 'motivation' of the Irish insurgents, a 'mild empathy' for the 'plight' of the local population, and a notable absence in the press of those 'racial stereotypes' that had characterised many nineteenth-century accounts of the Irish. When the Rising was first reported, and even when it was subsequently analysed, as all the essays in this collection show, it was initially described as an ill-conceived and unjustified rebellion; and it was viewed as a challenge – to loyalty, to Englishness, to Empire, and to victory in the First World War. Over time, however, as we will see, a number of distinctive New Zealand responses emerged.

Underpinning and to some extent shaping these responses was New Zealanders' attitude to military service and their expressed desire, as early as the Boer War, to blood themselves as a nation in defence of the Empire.[4] Like England, New Zealand implemented conscription; like Ireland, Australia resisted it. Like England, New Zealand was harsh on conscientious objectors and on those who avoided the call; like Ireland, Australia became a safe haven for anyone who refused to serve. That New Zealand was more anxious than its fellow dominion to defend the Empire was signalled by its eagerness to match the United Kingdom's National Registration Act (15 July 1915) with its own National Registration Scheme (October 1915).[5] When the government introduced the scheme, which required every man aged between seventeen and sixty to register, it promised that it was 'not a precursor to a conscription', claiming that 'the object was to assess how many men were available for service with the New Zealand Expeditionary Force' at a time when volunteer numbers, as with the British Army, were in decline. But in early 1916, when the number of volunteers 'fell below requirements', the government changed its mind and in August introduced the Military Service Act 1916 (7 GEO. V. 1916, No. 8).[6] Using the 'personal schedules' collected by the 1915 national registration as a database, the government required all men aged between twenty and forty-five to ensure they had registered, with the first ballot drawn on 15 November 1916 and subsequent ballots held almost every month until October 1918.[7] This is not to claim that the Rising prompted conscription; it is to show how intent this most remote of all the dominions was on remaining unquestioningly loyal to the mother country and how keen it was to forge a national identity through war.[8]

By contrast, legislation for compulsory military service was introduced by the new Commonwealth government of Australia shortly after Federation (1900–1) with the Defence Act of 1903, which gave the government power to conscript for the purposes of home defence but not for services overseas. This act was followed by the Universal Service Scheme of 1909, which passed into law in 1911, but two attempts to introduce conscription by Prime Minister William (Billy) Hughes via plebiscites on 28 October 1916 and 20 December 1917 were defeated.[9] As Jeff Kildea has emphasised in Chapter 1, all of the Australians and New Zealanders who found themselves in Ireland in Easter 1916 were volunteers. But once conscription was introduced, as Seán Brosnahan has shown in Chapter 7, many New Zealanders, who for personal, principled, or political reasons refused to fight, either went 'bush' or slipped across the Tasman. Although both plebiscites in Australia were conducted after the Rising, posters such as *Australia's Triumph Under Voluntaryism Puts New Zealand Under Conscription to Shame*, published by the Trades Hall Council of Melbourne in 1917,[10] and Harry Holland's *N.Z.'s Appeal to Australia. VOTE NO* (1917) reveal how both countries took cognisance of one another's domestic affairs.[11]

In fact, so close were New Zealand and Australia in 1916 – despite different political systems, climates, topographies, patterns of settlement, relations to the indigenous, gender politics, attitudes to religion, and sense of place in the world – that it is difficult to talk about one without taking account of the other. From first settlement there was a constant flow, rising or falling according to circumstance and fortune, of people backwards and forwards across the Tasman. While the 1851 Victorian gold rush drew a significant number of New Zealanders to Australia, the 1861 discovery of gold in Otago proved irresistible to many Australians.

Approximately 20,000 New Zealanders sought employment in Australia in the decades following the gold rush; a comparable number of Australians crossed the Tasman following the industrial turmoil that preceded the collapse of the Australian banking system in the 1890s.[12]

Nevertheless, when the eastern colonies of Australia invited New Zealand to consider federation in the late 1890s, the Liberal Seddon government declined, preferring to preserve a distinct identity and to foster a Pacific sphere of influence.[13] Seddon's successor, the conservative William Ferguson Massey (1856–1925), New Zealand's second-longest-serving prime minister, augmented this distinctiveness by aggressively promoting the idea that his country was an equal participant in Empire. Massey, who was born into a Protestant farming family in Limavady, in the north of Ireland, emigrated to New Zealand in 1870. Known for his sympathies for the British Israelites – he was also a member of the Orange Order and of the Oddfellows and Freemasons – Massey entered politics in 1894 and served as prime minister from May 1912 to May 1925.[14] His Australian counterpart, William Morris Hughes (1862–1952), was also an emigrant, having come to Australia in 1884, but that, and a common commitment to conscription, is where the comparison ends. The son of a London carpenter who worked in the House of Commons, Hughes' cultural heritage was English and Welsh and his religious influences, Anglican and Baptist. Active in the trade union movement and influential, as a journalist and politician, in advancing the Labor Party, Hughes was prime minister of Australia from 1915 to 1923.[15]

As mutually aware of one another and as different as the two countries were, the First World War nevertheless saw old commitments strengthen and further bonds develop. So, when discussing the role of dominion troops in the Rising, it is important to pay close attention to the nationality of those who took part, for, as Jeff Kildea has shown in Chapter 1, any simple recourse to the acronym ANZAC elides the distinctive contribution made by the New Zealand troops and the complex relationship that had developed between the New Zealand and Australian forces following Gallipoli. The surviving images of troops marching out the front gate of Trinity at the end of Easter Week, featured on the cover of this book, reveal all three soldiers wearing the slouch hats of the Australian Imperial Force, but two of the three are

New Zealanders, so it would be misleading to read the image solely in terms of the military uniform.[16]

Despite the role played by their troops and the significant coverage given to the Rising in the local press, it is noteworthy that most of the general histories of New Zealand are silent on 1916 or only refer to it in passing. Aside from Richard Davis' pioneering specialist study *Irish Issues in New Zealand Politics, 1868–1922* (1974), Barry Gustafson's *Labour's Path to Political Independence* (1980), and Brad Patterson's edited collection of essays *The Irish in New Zealand: Historical contexts and perspectives* (2002), the sole allusion in Paul Moon's *New Zealand in the Twentieth Century* (2011) occurs in the context of the 1922 trial of Bishop James Michael Liston for sedition and then as simply one of several indications of the bishop's questionable loyalties.[17] Michael King's *The Penguin History of New Zealand* (2003) does mention 1916, although as only one issue that provoked a virulent reaction from the Protestant Political Association.[18] But that reaction and its impact on New Zealand culture and society, as Brad Patterson has shown in his carefully researched essay in Chapter 9, was far more violent, far more pervasive, and far more enduring than is generally recognised.

Most general histories of New Zealand do not mention the 1916 Rising at all. James Belich's *Paradise Reforged: A history of New Zealand from the 1880s to the year 2000* (2001) and *Replenishing the Earth: The settler revolution and the rise of the Anglo-world* (2009) argue for sources of New Zealand identity that do not lie in Gallipoli or in Ireland or in the First World War but in the complexities and challenges of nineteenth- and early twentieth-century settlement that, while comprising pockets of Irishness, are predominantly Anglo-Scot rather than Anglo-Celt, Anglo-Irish, or Irish.[19] The Rising is not mentioned in Keith Sinclair's *A History of New Zealand* (1959–2000); or Tom Brooking's *Milestones: Turning points in New Zealand History* (1988, 1999) or his *The History of New Zealand* (2004); or Philippa Mein Smith's *A Concise History of New Zealand* (2005); or in either of the Oxford histories, W.H. Oliver with B.R. Williams (eds), *The Oxford History of New Zealand* (1981) and Giselle Byrnes (ed.), *The New Oxford History of New Zealand* (2010); or, for that matter, in Ian McGibbon (ed.), *The Oxford Companion to New Zealand Military History* (2000).

The ten essays that comprise *New Zealand's Responses to the 1916 Rising* offer a unique insight into a shared Irish–New Zealand history, which, despite being overlooked for nearly a century, possesses a significance that has seen an exchange of ambassadors, the establishment of an Irish embassy in New Zealand and a New Zealand embassy in Ireland, and a recent state visit by the Irish president to New Zealand.

In broad terms, these essays follow a trajectory from the particular to the general and from the initial reaction to a more considered response. Beginning with Jeff Kildea's careful analysis of the roles played by New Zealand and Australian troops in the fighting that took place in Dublin during Easter Week, the volume concludes with Malcolm Campbell's insightful transnational and comparative study that relates New Zealand's responses to the general reaction of the Empire and America. In keeping with the proposition that any informed discussion of a New Zealand response needs to take account of an Australian reaction and an Australian of a New Zealand reaction, Dianne Hall examines the ways Irish women who participated in the Rising were depicted in the Australian and New Zealand press. The counterpoint is Lisa Marr's detailed examination of the reactions of New Zealand women, focusing on the responses of Katherine Mansfield, Jessie Mackay, and the 'sterling' republican women of the West Coast. Chapter 4, by Peter Kuch, discusses the Dunedin theatre, where a performance of *Cathleen ni Houlihan* just prior to the Rising was countered by an Empire play subsequent to the Rising only to be countered in turn by a national tour of Sara Allgood playing the title role in *Peg o' My Heart*. Like Chapters 2 and 4, Chapters 5 and 8 by Jim McAloon and Stephanie James respectively reprise the reciprocal relations between New Zealand and Australia – Jim McAloon offering a detailed account of the Australian-born editor Harry Holland's synthesis in *The Maoriland Worker* of the arguments advanced by nationalist and Marxist historians for Irish self-determination, and Stephanie James proposing that any informed analysis of the Catholic press in Australia, and particularly in Adelaide, needs to take account of its exchange arrangements with its New Zealand counterpart. As with Chapter 1, Rory Sweetman's account of Bishop Henry William Cleary's investigation of the North King Street murders in Chapter 6 looks closely at a New Zealand response that took place in Dublin, on this occasion an enquiry into the killing of fifteen civilians by British forces during Easter Week. Finally, both Seán Brosnahan's extensively researched account in Chapter 7 of the New Zealand-Irish response to conscription, touted as proof of allegiance to the Empire, and Brad Patterson's carefully argued analysis of the bitter sectarian controversy provoked by the Protestant Political Association in Chapter 9 return readers to two issues that have left deep scars on the New Zealand body politic – prejudice and sectarianism. The final chapter, Malcolm Campbell's nuanced analysis of the reaction to the Rising throughout the Empire and in America, provides an international context for New Zealand responses and a way of calibrating their significance.

CHAPTER I

'The Empire Strikes Back': Anzacs and the Easter Rising 1916

JEFF KILDEA
(University of New South Wales)

As dawn broke across New Zealand and then Australia on 25 April 1916 heralding the first Anzac Day, a day that commemorates what some regard as the defining moment in the birth of these two nations, Irish rebels who had seized the General Post Office (GPO) in Dublin the day before were fighting to establish a nation of their own. When the British government marshalled its forces to strike back, dominion soldiers on leave in Ireland were called on to help put down the Rising.

Many of those dominion soldiers were Anzacs, mostly veterans of Gallipoli who had been evacuated sick or wounded to England and had decided to spend their Easter leave in Ireland. By that time, the first Anzac Corps had arrived on the Western Front and had begun to face the horrors of modern industrialised trench warfare. But for those on leave, Ireland was meant to be a haven far removed from all that. Yet, for them, Ireland itself soon became a battle front. Anzacs, who had enlisted to fight Germans in the fields of France, were given rifles and ordered to fight Irishmen in the streets of Dublin.

Their involvement was recorded in contemporary commentary on the Rising as well as in their own diaries and letters, some of which were published in newspapers in their home countries. Some of the men's accounts are reflective, revealing an ambivalence as to the duties they were ordered to perform; others are full of bravado and hyperbole – ripping yarns of derring-do.

This chapter describes the experiences of some of the Anzacs caught up in the Easter Rising and considers the question asked at the time as to whether those Anzacs added 'lustre to the deeds of the heroes who fought and died in Gallipoli for the "Rights of Small Nations"'.[1]

WHO WERE THE ANZACS?

The initials ANZAC stand for the Australian and New Zealand Army Corps, a military formation comprising two divisions of antipodean soldiers that in early 1915 assembled in Egypt before embarking for Gallipoli to fight in the Dardanelles campaign. In time, the initials became the word 'Anzac', which refers to an Australian or New Zealand soldier of the First World War. At the outbreak of the war, a strong bond of friendship existed between the two sister dominions of the South Pacific, which had a shared history. Not only did their soldiers join together in the ANZAC military formation, but, as will become apparent from the stories of some of the soldiers recounted here, many New Zealanders enlisted in the Australian Army, while many Australians enlisted in the New Zealand Army. Their bond of friendship was cemented during the Gallipoli campaign. The two divisions making up the corps were the Australian Division under the command of Major General William Bridges and the New Zealand and Australian Division under the command of Major General Alexander Godley.[2] The latter division comprised two New Zealand brigades and one Australian. After the Anzacs were evacuated from Gallipoli to Egypt in December 1915, reinforcements swelled the ranks, leading to the formation of two corps (I ANZAC and II ANZAC) that transferred to the Western Front in early 1916. There, Australian and New Zealand soldiers continued to fight together until November 1917, when the five Australian divisions were combined into the Australian Corps, while the New Zealand Division transferred to a British corps. So, at the time of the Easter Rising, there existed between Australian and New Zealand soldiers a strong Anzac identity, born of a shared heritage and tempered in battle at Gallipoli.

CONTEMPORARY ACCOUNTS

A number of contemporary accounts document the involvement of dominion troops in suppressing the Easter Rising, particularly the part they played in the defence of Trinity College, where a few had taken refuge after soldiers in uniform had become targets for the rebels. An Australian soldier, the New Zealand-born Private George Davis, recorded that he and his mate Private Bob Grant had a lucky escape in Dame Street when a bullet struck the nearby kerb.[3] A New Zealand Corporal Finlay McLeod wrote to his mother that he and an Australian soldier were fired on,[4] while a New Zealand Sergeant Alexander Don wrote home, 'I was walking past Dublin Castle and everything seemed alright. Then a couple of shots rang out and two "Tommies" who were in front of me fell over … One had a bullet through the head and the other through the neck.'[5] An unnamed New Zealander told the press, 'The rebels deliberately fired on us from their loop-holes above the post office, and a bullet went through the sleeve of a civilian a few feet off.'[6] Perhaps the most dramatic account is that of New Zealand Corporal John Godwin Garland. In a letter to his father, he reported that on Easter Monday at about 2 p.m. he and a friend, Sergeant Frederick Leslie Nevin, were standing in Sackville Street (now O'Connell Street):

> All of a sudden a large motor-car whizzed past. In it was the noted countess, dressed in a green uniform. As she went past she fired two shots at us. One went above our heads; the other caught an elderly man in the arm. It seemed to be a signal to the other Sinn Feiners, for bullets started to whiz all round us.[7]

For reasons that will become apparent, Garland's colourful account needs to be treated with some scepticism.

How many Anzacs were caught up in the Rising in Dublin during Easter Week is impossible to say. Contemporary accounts vary as to their numbers; some clearly exaggerate. A Dublin resident, Lilly Stokes, who was in the provost's house at Trinity College taking tea with the Mahaffys on Easter Monday, wrote in her diary, 'Mr. Alton, the Fellow and an O.T.C. Captain, came in to ask for beer for the 30 Anzacs he had collected to help to defend the College.'[8] Cecil McAdam, an Australian doctor who was serving in the Royal Army Medical Corps, told the Australian press on returning to Melbourne in June that while he was in Dublin's Shelbourne Hotel during the Rising two officers had told him that forty Australian soldiers on furlough had been posted in Trinity College.[9] Yet *The Irish Times*, which published a list of the names of those who served in Trinity College during the Rising, identified only fourteen dominion troops in all: six South Africans, five New Zealanders, two Canadians, and one Australian.[10] In other parts of the city, Anzac soldiers were also involved in the fighting, including Corporal Fred Harvey and Private John Joseph Chapman, who reported at the Royal Barracks (now Collins Barracks), and the aforementioned Australians Davis and Grant, who reported at Portobello Barracks (now Cathal Brugha Barracks).

THE ROLE OF THE ANZACS

No Anzac units were in Ireland during Easter Week nor at any time thereafter.[11] The Anzacs involved in suppressing the Rising were individual members of the Australian Imperial Force (AIF) and the New Zealand Expeditionary Force (NZEF) who had decided to spend their Easter leave in Ireland. Most had been evacuated sick or wounded from Gallipoli. However, two New Zealanders, Sergeant Frederick Leslie Nevin of Christchurch and Corporal John Godwin Garland of Auckland, were on leave from the hospital ship *Marama*, on which they were serving as medical orderlies. One Australian soldier on convalescent leave in Dublin was Private Norman Lindsay Croft. He had lost a leg at Gallipoli. He too was asked to shoulder a rifle until it was realised he was an amputee.[12]

Australians and New Zealanders serving in Irish and British regiments were in Dublin as well when the Rising broke out or were sent there soon after. Some belonged to King Edward's Horse (also known as the King's Overseas Dominions Regiment), which was sent from the Curragh late in the afternoon of Easter Monday to reinforce the Dublin garrison. King Edward's Horse was a cavalry regiment originally formed in 1901 and made up of soldiers from the Empire. When war broke out, the regiment recruited men from the dominions and colonies who were stranded in England and unable to return to their home countries to enlist.[13] Doctors in the Royal Army Medical Corps, such as Cecil McAdam of Melbourne, and antipodean nurses serving in the Voluntary Aid Detachment assisted the wounded as did sundry others who were in Dublin at the time. Edward Oswald Marks, a medical student from Brisbane, treated casualties at Mount Street Bridge.[14]

While, in the overall context of the Rising, the role played by the Anzacs is not significant, they and their dominion comrades made an important contribution to the Crown cause during the first forty-eight hours before reinforcements arrived from England, harassing the rebels and confining them to their initial positions. This was especially so at Trinity College, where six Anzacs had taken refuge, and along the Liffey quays near Kingsbridge Station (now Heuston Station) and at Portobello Barracks near Rathmines.

TRINITY COLLEGE

At Trinity College, the Anzacs teamed up with members of the Dublin University Officer Training Corps (OTC) and other stray soldiers until reinforcements arrived a few days later. They were deployed not only to defend the college should it be attacked but also to keep the rebels pinned down by bringing fire to bear from positions on the roof and upper floors of the main building. Among contemporary accounts that mention the role of Anzac troops in Trinity College is Warre B. Wells and N. Marlowe's *History of the Irish Rebellion of 1916*, published a few months after the Rising: 'Stray soldiers were summoned from the adjacent streets and from the Central Soldiers' Club hard by the College to reinforce the garrison; these included some "Anzac" sharpshooters.'[15] Another is an article in *Blackwood's Magazine* by John Joly, Professor of Geology at Trinity, who wrote of his experiences of the Rising. Using the pseudonym 'One of the Garrison', Joly described how he joined the Anzacs on the roof of the college where they had been posted as snipers: 'They were undoubtedly men fashioned for the enjoyment of danger. And certainly it would be harder to find nicer comrades. Alas for thousands of these fine soldiers who have left their bones on Gallipoli!' Joly claimed, 'There can be no doubt that the accurate fire maintained from the college was an important factor in the salvation of the City.'[16] This was an opinion shared by Robert Tweedy, a member of Trinity OTC, who wrote to his mother,

> A machine gun and a party of sharp-shooters on the roof did good execution down Sackville Street, and TCD may be said to have saved the banks and business premises of the most important thoroughfares of Dublin. Only one shop within range of our rifles was looted ... It is said that TCD saved the city, and I am proud to have been one of the garrison.[17]

Another OTC cadet, Gerard Fitzgibbon, wrote to a friend, '[T]he Anzacs were given all the eligible situations, which it must be allowed they deserved. They were an extraordinary gang. I have never seen their like.'[18] As veterans of Gallipoli, it is little wonder that their service was highly valued. In the first days of the Rising, the garrison at Trinity mostly comprised young officer cadets with no experience of battle.

Despite these contemporary accounts, Irish historiography of Trinity College during the Rising has all but neglected the college's contribution to the defence of the city and the vital part dominion troops played in defending the college. Recently, New Zealand historian Rory Sweetman has challenged this neglect, arguing that Trinity was on the rebels' list of targets and could easily have been captured with potentially disastrous consequences for the college: 'Trinity meant little to soldiers like [Generals] Lowe and Maxwell ... By the end of Easter Week at least some of the university's fine buildings would have resembled the shell-like remnants of the recently refurbished General Post Office.'[19] On Easter Monday night, the rebels occupied buildings overlooking Trinity to provide a covering force for men from the GPO garrison who intended to capture the college. The dominion troops engaged them in a sniping battle, and the next day the rebels withdrew. As it turned out, MacNeill's countermanding order had reduced the number of rebels who turned out on Easter Monday, and faced with armed defenders, the rebels lacked the numbers to seize the college.[20]

One of the rebel leaders, Commandant W.J. Brennan-Whitmore, acknowledged the skills of the Anzacs. In his memoirs of the Rising, Brennan-Whitmore related how the rebels had rigged up a flying fox across Sackville Street in order to convey a tin can carrying messages from the GPO to the rebel position in North Earl Street. After being captured and held in the grounds of the Custom House, Brennan-Whitmore told one of his captors (described as an Australian, but who, in all likelihood, was New Zealander Sergeant Nevin), 'By the way. You British had some pretty good snipers ... We had a cable across Sackville Street and one of your fellows hit the canister from Trinity.'[21]

But it was not only tin cans that fell victim to the Anzac sharpshooters. In his article, Professor Joly related how, early on Tuesday morning, the Anzacs on the roof of the college shot a rebel despatch rider:

> He was one of three who were riding past on bicycles. Four shots were fired. Three found their mark in the head of the unfortunate victim. Another of the riders was wounded and escaped on foot. The third abandoned his bicycle and also escaped. This shooting was done by the uncertain light of the electric lamps, and at a high angle downwards from a lofty building.[22]

The victim of the Anzac marksmanship was Gerald Keogh, a twenty-two-year-old shop assistant from Ranelagh. The youngest of thirteen children fathered by James Keogh in two marriages, Gerald was one of four Keogh boys who joined the rebels. Another brother, John Baptist Keogh, had been killed in 1914 while fighting with the British Army at the Battle of La Bassée. The eldest of the family, Joseph Augustus Keogh, was an actor. He had been working in London when Gerald was killed. He returned to Dublin after receiving news of his brother's death and in August 1916 became general manager and stage director at the Abbey Theatre. Gerald's great-nephew Raymond Keogh poignantly noted in a recent edition of the *Dublin Review of Books*:

> [Gerald] was killed on April 25th, the first anniversary of the landing of the Australian and New Zealand Army Corps ... on the Gallipoli peninsula and the troops who shot him were themselves

Anzacs … More poignantly, Gerald was killed at dawn on that first Anzac Day – the very hour that Australians and New Zealanders cherish to commemorate their own fallen at Gallipoli.[23]

It is not certain who fired the shot that killed Gerald. In a letter to his parents, published in the press, Corporal Finlay McLeod wrote, '[A]t 3.30 a.m. three Sinn Feins, an advance party, came riding towards us, and we dropped them. Only another Australian and New Zealander were with me at the time. We were cheered by the O.T.C., and the officers were pleased with us.'[24]

Corporal J.G. Garland claimed in a letter to his father that he was one of 'four' snipers who brought Keogh down.[25] In his letter, Garland described other incidents in which the Anzacs were involved. He said that on the Wednesday 'we got two more in Sackville Street [who] were armed with double-barrelled fowling pieces'. He also described how on the Friday 'we six Anzacs' shot and killed two rebel snipers who had been firing on them from the spire of nearby St Andrew's church.[26] He further wrote, 'On Saturday morning we killed a woman who was sniping from an hotel window in Dame Street. When the RAMC brought her in we saw she was only a girl about 20, stylishly dressed and not at all bad-looking. She was armed with an automatic revolver and a Winchester repeater.' Garland then described how that afternoon 'the colonials were given the honour of capturing Westland Row station', in which action, he said, they killed five rebels. He went on to claim, 'Altogether we Anzacs were responsible for 27 rebels (twenty-four men and three women).' Corporal McLeod claimed an even higher body count. In a letter to his mother, published in the press, he wrote, 'During [Tuesday] we killed six in one building, 26 in another, and snipers here and there.'[27]

The veracity of these claims is doubtful. In 2015, the Glasnevin Trust published the 1916 Necrology, a list of the names of 485 men, women, and children killed during or as a direct result of the Rising.[28] That list includes the names of sixty-six rebels, not counting the fourteen leaders who were executed. If Garland's claim is true, the Anzacs would have been responsible for more than 40 per cent of rebel fatalities, while McLeod's claim puts the proportion at over 50 per cent, both unlikely propositions given the extent of the fighting throughout the city.

Furthermore, the 1916 Necrology does not include the names of any women rebels. It is possible that the authorities covered up the deaths of women rebels in order to avoid having to admit that the Crown forces had killed women. But it is also unlikely. In the one hundred years since the Rising, much research has been carried out on Easter Week, including the role of women. If the rebel dead included women, surely their names would have been discovered by now.[29] The most likely explanation is that Garland and McLeod either deliberately inflated the death toll or were mistaken due to 'the fog of war'. If neither is the case, then a troubling conclusion is that the Anzacs might have been responsible for the deaths of some of the 260 civilian men and women whose names are listed in the 1916 Necrology.

The Glasnevin Trust also listed the names of 143 members of the Crown forces who lost their lives during the Rising, including Tipperary-born Private Neville Fryday, a member of the 75th Canadian Infantry Battalion from Toronto. Although Fryday was shot near Trinity College on Easter Monday, he was not one of the garrison. Taken to Mercer's Hospital, he died there six days later. He was just sixteen years old, having put up his age to enlist. He was the only member of the dominion forces killed in the Rising.

ROYAL BARRACKS

Dominion troops at the Royal Barracks took part in the fighting along the Liffey quays. There, the rebels had seized buildings on either side of the river to prevent reinforcements from the Curragh Camp in County Kildare, who would be arriving at Kingsbridge Station, from marching into the city. Ballarat-born Private John Joseph Chapman, with the brevity that characterises his diary, wrote, 'Given rifle and ammunition and had to fight enemy in the streets. Nearly got hit several times. Only a few casualties on our side.'[30] Corporal Fred Harvey from Burra in South Australia was more effusive in his descriptions of the fighting. In a letter to his parents, published in the press, he said that he, a Canadian, two South Africans, and two Australians were ordered to guard and patrol Ellis Street and the lanes running into it:

Well here the fun began, bullets were going in all directions … All went well during the day, but as soon as the darkness approached things began to very get [*sic*] exciting but though we all had narrow escapes, I was the only one to get hit, but not with a bullet. As I was walking up one of the lanes somebody kindly knocked my hat off with a bottle, but to my disgust did not see which window it came from so, was unable to retaliate.

The next morning Harvey was included in a raid on the Mendicity Institution, held by the rebels under the command of Seán Heuston. The raid, which Harvey described in detail, was successful, resulting in the rebels surrendering this important position.[31]

PORTOBELLO BARRACKS

Portobello Barracks was home to the 3rd Reserve Battalion Royal Irish Rifles. As elsewhere, it welcomed an influx of sundry British and dominion soldiers, including Privates Davis and Grant. On Easter Monday, after having been fired upon by rebel snipers, they had taken refuge in a furniture store where they fell in with a family who lived in Rathmines. Covering their uniforms with civilian clothes, the two Australians tagged along with members of the family as they walked through the streets to their home. After dinner the Australians reported at Portobello Barracks, where they were informed that there was no transport back to England. Given a rifle and ammunition, they were told to protect themselves and the barracks.

That night, they joined a party of seventy men detailed to escort arms and ammunition to Dublin Castle. They set out on a roundabout route that brought them down near the Liffey. As they passed under a street lamp, a volley of rifle shots rained down on them 'from a dozen rifles across the river from the windows of the upper storeys of the Four Courts Hotel'. The troops scattered, and Davis and Grant made their way to Kingsbridge Station, where they stayed the night and for the next few days were assigned to guard duty. While there, Davis went with a party escorting stores to various parts of the city, including Trinity College, where he records that he 'noticed a digger and several "Enzedders" among the armed guard'.[32]

At Portobello Barracks was another Australian who wrote of his experiences in a letter to Richard Garland, the Dublin-born chairman of the Dunlop Rubber Co. in Australia; this letter was published in the Melbourne *Age*.[33] The soldier described a series of events in which members of the Crown forces committed atrocities against Irish civilians. Although admitting no personal part in killing or wounding innocent civilians, the tone of the letter suggests indifference rather than outrage at the conduct he witnessed. As a result, the letter provoked a strong reaction in Australia, particularly from Catholics of Irish descent already incensed by the British government's methods of suppressing the Rising and the execution of its leaders. Although *The Age* did not identify the officer, who remained nameless during the controversy that followed in the Australian press, he was in fact Richard Garland's eldest son, Charles, who in April 1915 had enlisted as a trooper in the 2nd Regiment of King Edward's Horse and had served on the Western Front before being posted to the Curragh for officer training.[34] When Charles was given leave over Easter Weekend, he visited Dublin and stayed with an uncle. After observing the outbreak of the Rising and finding it impossible to return to the Curragh, Charles reported at Portobello Barracks on Tuesday morning.

Queensland's John Oxley Library holds a typescript of Charles' letter among the papers of Canon David John Garland, Richard's brother and reputed founder of Anzac Day.[35] The typescript version, initially dated Thursday, 27 April, but with postscripts that extend to Thursday, 4 May, is longer than the version printed in *The Age*, and there are differences of wording, some of which are significant. In the letter, Charles described how he participated in a patrol on the Tuesday night to raid a nearby shop suspected of harbouring rebels.[36] The officer leading the patrol was Captain John Bowen-Colthurst. On the way to the shop, the patrol encountered three men in Rathmines Road. According to the letter as published in *The Age*, 'The captain wanted to know their business, and one answered back, so the captain just knocked him insensible with the butt of his rifle. The other two ran, and one shouted something about "down with the military", and the captain just shot him dead.' The published letter then describes the raid and the taking of prisoners who were marched back to the barracks, adding, 'Two were let go. The three others turned out to be head men of the gang and were shot.' The three men shot the next morning on the orders of Bowen-Colthurst were not rebels but the well-known Dublin pacifist and eccentric Francis Sheehy Skeffington and two journalists named Dickson and McIntyre.

After initial reluctance, the military authorities eventually court-martialled Bowen-Colthurst for the murders. On 10 June 1916, he was found guilty, but the court also found him to be insane, with the result that he was detained in Broadmoor asylum for the criminally insane at the king's pleasure.[37] After less than two years, Bowen-Colthurst was released, and in 1921 he emigrated to Canada.[38] In addition to the court martial, a Royal Commission was held under the chairmanship of Sir John Simon from 23 to 31 August 1916, during the course of which Timothy Healy, counsel for Hanna Sheehy Skeffington (Francis' widow), tendered *The Age* article that quoted the Australian officer's letter.[39]

Garland's letter described another patrol in which he and a Canadian soldier raided the home of 'a Russian Countess, who was a keen rebel' – presumably Countess Markievicz, second-in-command of the rebel forces at St Stephen's Green.[40] He wrote, 'In town we didn't see a single civilian – just as well for them, as they would have been shot – and the houses had to be in darkness too. One house had a light in the front window, but one of the officers put half a dozen shots into it, and it soon went out.'

Following publication of the letter in *The Age*, Catholic newspapers published comments from readers highly critical of the Australian officer's account. H.A. Meagher wrote to *The Advocate*, 'This reads like an account of rabbit battues that used to be held in the Western District till common humanity objected to them.'[41] Under the pseudonym 'Innisfail', a correspondent to *The Tribune* wrote, 'As a specimen of cold-blooded atrocity I venture to say that the Hun in his worst alleged excesses has not equalled it ... The letter of this "Australian officer on leave", which is a disgrace to Australian manhood ... stirs up rebel instincts that I thought had perished.'[42] 'Innisfail's' hyperbole illustrates the passion which the letter aroused. It would have been even greater had the editor of *The Age* not sanitised it. According to the typescript, the letter actually said, 'the three others turned out to be head men of the gang <u>and so we shot them</u>', rather than 'and were shot'.[43]

Sydney's *Catholic Press* joined the chorus of outrage, reproducing *The Age*'s article and 'Innisfail's' response, richly sprinkled with sub-headings as if to give editorial endorsement to 'Innisfail's' anger: 'Specimen of Cold-Blooded Atrocity', 'Smashing Brains out of Women and Children', 'Talk of Prussian Militarism', etc.[44] But it was not only Catholic newspapers and their readers who were outraged. A few months after the Rising, the socialist activist D.P. Russell published a 95-page pamphlet entitled *Sinn Fein and the Irish Rebellion*. In the preface, Russell wrote that his pamphlet was 'an attempt to explain the Irish problem from the standpoint of the class struggle'. Russell was a socialist who stood for election to the Australian federal parliament as a candidate for the Labor Party in 1910 and 1913. In 1910, he lost to Prime Minister Alfred Deakin in the seat of Ballarat by only 400 votes out of 20,000 after gaining a 15 per cent swing. He unsuccessfully stood for election to the Victorian parliament in 1911 and 1917. He was one of six delegates from Victoria at the federal conference of the Labor Party in Hobart in 1912.[45] In his pamphlet, Russell reproduced *The Age*'s version of Charles Garland's letter as well as the exaggerated claims of Corporal John Garland (who does not appear to be related). Russell added the comment, 'Did Australia's sons in Dublin add lustre to the deeds of the heroes who fought and died in Gallipoli for the "Rights of Small Nations"?'[46]

Some Australians were not as critical of the letter as the Catholic newspapers or D.P. Russell. A.T. Saunders wrote to Adelaide's *Register* expressing his anger at the 'armed band of cowardly assassins [who] suddenly began a murderous attack on innocent and in most cases unarmed men [and] also killed innocent women and children'. Saunders was referring not to Bowen-Colthurst or the British soldiers who ran amok in North King Street but to the rebel leaders, whom he described with bitter irony as 'gentle dreamers', adding,

> I am glad to say that some Anzacs had the honour of assisting to put down the 'dreamers'. The Anzacs were in Trinity College, and

> *Blackwood's Magazine* gives an excellent account of the defence
> of the college by the Anzacs, the troops, and civilians. One of the
> 'gentle dreamers' was Mr Sheehy Skeffington, and he was one of
> [those] who were rightfully shot.[47]

Neither Bowen-Colthurst's court martial nor the Royal Commission
that later investigated the murders considered Sheehy Skeffington to have
been 'rightfully shot', with both tribunals finding that the killings were
unlawful and the journalists innocent of any involvement in the Rising.[48]

The controversy might have been even greater had it been known at
the time that another Australian was involved in the journalists' murders,
and in a much more direct way. Like Charles Garland, William Dobbin,
a native of Maldon, Victoria, had enlisted in the British Army. He was
commissioned into the 3rd Battalion Royal Irish Rifles in June 1915. On
the morning that Skeffington, Dickson, and McIntyre were shot, Dobbin
was the officer in charge of the guard room. It was to him that Bowen-
Colthurst went demanding that the prisoners be removed from their
cells and shot. Although Dobbin acceded to that demand, he did not
participate in the firing squad. However, on entering the yard where the
men had been shot, he noticed Skeffington's leg moving. He reported this
to Bowen-Colthurst, who ordered that they be shot again, whereupon
Dobbin gave the order to fire.

Questioned at the Royal Commission as to why he had not protected
his prisoners, Dobbin conceded that he did not think that ordering the
men to be shot was the right thing for Bowen-Colthurst to have done.
His evidence, as a whole, indicates that this nineteen-year-old newly
commissioned second lieutenant with no experience of battle had been
overborne by his thirty-five-year-old, battle-experienced senior officer.[49]

ANZACS AND THE EASTER RISING

So, what do we say in response to Russell's question? Certainly, in the
first days of the Rising, the Anzacs made a significant contribution to
the efforts of the Crown forces to contain the rebels, especially at Trinity
College, a position of tactical importance, where the Anzacs played a
crucial role. But Russell's question challenges us to look beyond military

considerations: to ask, how is it that the Anzacs allowed themselves to become involved in the suppression of a nationalist rising? After all, they had enlisted and travelled halfway round the world to fight Germans, not Irishmen. As one New Zealander told the press, 'It was hard lines to have to fight foes in Ireland, while we are putting forth our best efforts in Flanders and France.'[50]

In some cases at least, the dominion troops had a choice. In his letter, Corporal Harvey wrote, 'Next morning we all paraded and volunteers were asked for. I, of course, in common with all Colonial troops, volunteered and again took up arms to defend the King and country.' For some, their participation in the fighting was an adventure. Corporal Finlay McLeod concluded his letter, 'I am back in England, feeling A1, and none the worse for the fun we had.' Others were unhappy about what they had been asked to do. Private Davis recorded in his diary, 'We were in a very unenviable position, for we personally had no quarrel with the rioters … We are making the best of a bad job, but would prefer to be anywhere but in this unenviable city.' Some may have refused to serve. New Zealand researcher Hugh Keane has come across a souvenir card of the Manchester Martyrs on which is written the words, 'Bought by Mr Collins NZ Army in Dublin 1916 (refused to report to barracks and fight rebels)'. Mr Collins' identity and the circumstances of his refusal are yet to be ascertained, but we can infer from his name an Irish heritage that might have influenced his thinking.

In contrast, Private McHugh, a Catholic whose parents had emigrated from Ireland, was on the roof of Trinity College when Gerald Keogh was shot. Unfortunately, McHugh did not leave a diary or letters indicating what he felt about his role in the Rising. In fact, he does not seem to have spoken much about it, if at all. Members of his family were unaware of 'Uncle Mick's' Easter leave in Ireland until I told them about it when I began researching this topic. Along with other defenders of Trinity College, McHugh was given a silver cup. But the family has never seen it.

CONCLUSION

It is easy with the benefit of hindsight to regard the Easter Rising as embodying the aspirations of the Irish people to govern themselves and therefore to conclude that in opposing the rebels the Anzacs were on the wrong side of history. But in the first flush of the Rising, few saw it in those terms. Even Irish nationalists regarded the actions of the rebels as treacherous – a threat to the hard-fought campaign for Home Rule that had all but succeeded with the enactment of the Home Rule Bill, albeit suspended until the end of the war. Moreover, in the first days of the Rising, it was Irish troops who did most of the fighting against the rebels.[51] And the Irish regiments serving on the Western Front received the news of the Rising and its aftermath without any breakdown in discipline or morale.[52]

Although the Anzacs might not have liked doing what they were ordered to do, they would have seen it as their duty as loyal soldiers of the king. On enlistment they had sworn an oath to 'cause His Majesty's peace to be kept and maintained', and in Ireland during Easter Week, a band of the king's subjects were in open revolt and threatened that peace. Today we might cringe at such thoughts, but that was then. Attitudes were different. Ingrained in the Anzacs was a strong sense of duty, something that would keep them going for the four long years of the war.[53]

CHAPTER 2

Women of the Rising in the Australian and New Zealand Press

DIANNE HALL

(*Victoria University, Melbourne*)

D r Nicholas O'Donnell, a Melbourne-based advocate for Irish Home Rule, read the first reports of the Easter Rising at the beginning of May 1916. These articles included descriptions of women who had fought in and supported the Rising and those who had been caught up unwillingly in the fighting.[1] Although women were mentioned in most of the articles about the events in Dublin, usually as unwitting, innocent victims, the participation of most women activists was ignored. When women were mentioned, they were cast as either mad and unwomanly, like Maud Gonne and Constance Markievicz, or tragically misguided, like the beautiful young Gifford sisters. In many press reports the different roles of women as victims or activists were used to emphasise the violence, irrationality, and illegitimacy of the Rising itself. Analysing the coverage in the Australasian press is one way of tracing shifting attitudes to both Irishness and gender among descendants of Irish immigrants in Australia and New Zealand in the years immediately after the 1916 Rising.

Like many Catholics of Irish descent in Australia and New Zealand, O'Donnell was bewildered and angered by the Rising, because it had taken place during the war and just as the treasured goal of Home Rule seemed within reach.[2] In his role as head of the United Irish League in Melbourne, O'Donnell cabled John Redmond, leader of the Irish Parliamentary Party and member of the British parliament, writing, 'The guilt of this horrible bloodshed in Dublin be on the heads of misguided leaders of the outbreak.'[3] His reactions were mirrored in New Zealand, where the annual general meeting in Auckland of the Hibernian Australasian Catholic Benefit Society reacted with shock to the news of the Rising and immediately drafted a cable message of support to Redmond.[4] Redmond, whose political life had been devoted to securing self-determination for Ireland through Home Rule, had on occasions in 1914 called on Home Rule supporters in Ireland to support the British war effort. Many young men of Irish descent in Australia and New Zealand had enthusiastically followed his advice and joined the armed forces and were serving overseas in 1916.[5] Meetings of Catholics were quickly called in many places in Australia and New Zealand to demonstrate support for Home Rule and loyalty to the British Empire and the war effort.

The reaction of men like O'Donnell to the news that Irish women were prominently involved in the Rising can be gauged to some extent by the reception to speeches given by John Redmond's brother and fellow Irish Parliamentary Party MP, William, and his fellow envoy, Mr T.J. Donovan, in July 1912 at the end of their long lecture tour of Australia. At an event organised by the Ladies Shamrock Committee in Melbourne, Donovan and William Redmond both commented approvingly on the enthusiasm and support for Home Rule by Irish-Australian women during their tour. Donovan expressed his disgust at the news recently to hand that a suffragette had thrown a hatchet at British Prime Minister Asquith during his visit to Dublin that had missed its target but had grazed John Redmond's ear: '... but he was pleased to say these women were not of Irish parentage. They were from England, and they adopted tactics towards their Prime Minister such as no Irishwoman would ever have adopted.' These comments were endorsed enthusiastically by the meeting.[6] The view, as expressed by Redmond and Donovan in 1912, that true Irish women could not be violent and unwomanly or engage in direct military action informed reactions in Australia and New Zealand to reports of the Rising, and was commonplace among moderates throughout Ireland and the diaspora.

Newspaper editors in Australia and New Zealand had difficulties accessing accurate and timely reporting of the events in Dublin.[7] The only Catholic newspaper in New Zealand, *The New Zealand Tablet*, commented on 18 May that they were getting news from Ireland only in 'very small driblets'.[8] Wartime government restrictions slowed the flow of news in general. There was also a dearth of reports from Dublin itself. It was not until July, for example, that reports from Irish newspapers were reproduced in *The New Zealand Tablet*.[9] The unionist-focused *Irish Times* was the only Dublin newspaper that was able to continue publication during Easter Week, although its coverage was restricted after the imposition of martial law. Regional Irish newspapers continued to publish; however, they too had difficulty accessing current and accurate information from Dublin.[10] But lack of timely reports did not slow the international press in their widespread coverage. In the first weeks after the Rising, Australian and New Zealand papers received most of their reports from news cables via the English or American papers, such as *The New York Times, Chicago Tribune*, or the London *Times*. The Catholic newspapers in Australia and New Zealand, not surprisingly, covered the Irish situation in the most detail, although the Rising was eventually covered extensively in all the major mainstream newspapers.

Until recently, the women who were involved in the Rising have been neglected by historians and the general public. There are no precise figures, but historians now believe that around three hundred women participated.[11] Many, but not all, were members of either the Irish Citizen Army led by James Connolly, which accepted women, or Cumann na mBan, the women's group supporting the Irish Volunteers.[12] Constance Markievicz was second-in-command at St Stephen's Green and was condemned to death with the other leaders. Her sentence was commuted to life in prison because she was a woman.[13] Many women, such as Dr Kathleen Lynn, Brigid Lyons Thornton, and Linda Kearns, staffed first aid stations and gave essential medical care, while others ran kitchens and organised supplies to be taken by foot or on bicycle to the garrisons. A founding member of Cumann na mBan and daughter of Charles Gavan Duffy, a prominent politician in Victoria in the 1860s and 70s, Louise Gavan Duffy worked in the kitchens at the General Post Office (GPO). Women also took on the work of communications and hand-delivered messages between the different barracks/garrisons because they could move around the occupied city without the British forces suspecting them. It was, however, still very dangerous, and many came under fire.[14] Much of the work of these women has come to light only relatively recently with the renewed interest in the events of 1916 sparked by the centenary.[15] Outside Ireland, their activities were almost unknown to contemporaries as reporting of the Rising concentrated on the men and a few women whose stories either were highly sensational or conformed to the image of a pious and grieving femininity.

Reporting in the mainstream press in Australia and New Zealand was initially hostile to the rebels and used descriptions of women fighting to emphasise the unauthorised nature of the rebellion. One of the main news articles of *The Brisbane Courier* on 1 May 1916 stated, 'Some women carrying bandoliers and ammunition walked alongside rebels. Free fighting occurred in Jacob's biscuit factory between loyalist women and rebel women who were trying to get food into the rebel garrison.'[16] This statement was reprinted in many other newspapers as news was available only through a small number of sources. The idea therefore spread that there was widespread fighting between women from opposing sides. Most of the mainstream papers also picked up on the descriptions of looting via London news cables. In these descriptions, women were mentioned specifically, including details of them using their aprons to carry stolen jewellery and luxury items from upmarket shops on Grafton Street.[17] Later-published accounts continued to emphasise women and looting. In 1919, Katharine Tynan's book *The Years of the Shadow* was reviewed at length in *The Sydney Morning Herald*, which quoted her account of 'Unclean women in shawls [bearing] off freights of costly furs and finery' and 'one old hag literally [dripping] alarm clocks'.[18] Such descriptions fitted with longstanding stereotypes of Irish women as uncivilised and untrustworthy and would not have surprised many Protestant readers of the newspaper.[19]

News reports quickly accused the rebels of mistreating civilians, particularly women. On 16 May, the Melbourne *Argus* included a column titled 'Women in Post-Office Siege. English Girl's Experiences', which reported that a group of women were in the Dublin GPO when it was taken over by the rebel forces, and these women were detained. Some of the women were said to have been subsequently driven mad from shock. It was claimed that two were shot as they were helped to leave the post office.[20] Another article read by O'Donnell and included in his scrapbook was titled 'Cowardly Sinn Feiners'; it reported that the commandant in charge of British forces in Dublin, General Maxwell, when asked to respond to the claim that his troops were firing on civilians, justified this by stating that the 'Sinn Feiners', as the rebels were dubbed, were using women as shields.[21] The twin accusations that the rebels were mistreating women and that they were using women as shields were designed to show how cowardly the rebels were compared with the brave British troops in Dublin and those Irish and British who were fighting in Europe.

'STORMY PETRELS' OF IRELAND: CONSTANCE MARKIEVICZ AND MAUD GONNE

Generalised reports of women fighting and looting, or even as victims, could not be of interest to newspaper readers so far from Ireland for long. Two women whose actions seemed almost designed for breathless newspaper coverage were Constance Markievicz and Maud Gonne – frequently dubbed the 'stormy petrels' of Ireland.[22] Gonne was a controversial figure, whose divorce from John MacBride, well-known as one of the Irish Brigade that fought against the British in the Boer War, had been reported widely in the international press. While she did not play a major role in the Rising, being unable to travel to Dublin from her home in France, she later became prominent in the Irish Women Prisoners' Defence League.[23]

Markievicz, from a distinguished Anglo-Irish family, had bohemian connections as an artist, and descriptions of her larger-than-life gestures when she surrendered were reprinted in many newspapers. O'Donnell collected full-column reports from *The Argus* of 1 May 1916, with a prominent paragraph titled 'The Irish Baronet's Sister': 'A striking figure of the rebellion was an elderly woman, stated to be of high title.' The report then gave her full title, Countess Markievicz, and that of her brother, Sir Josslyn A.R. Gore-Booth.[24] O'Donnell also saved a 3 May clipping entitled 'A Dramatic Moment', describing when Markievicz surrendered: '... clad in green tunic, a hat with green feather, green puttees and green boots ... she kissed her revolver and announced "I am ready"'.[25] Such picturesque elements were repeated in newspaper coverage throughout Australia and New Zealand. The same description of Constance Markievicz as an 'elderly woman' and her green uniform appeared in *The Waimate Advertiser* (Canterbury) on the same day as the Melbourne *Argus* ran the story.[26] In Auckland, *The New Zealand Herald* was typical of many newspapers when it published a long article retracing the same story titled 'Surrender of a Female Rebel Leader'.[27]

In the search for a new angle on Markievicz, *The Argus*, *The Sydney Morning Herald*, and other papers in Australia and New Zealand published an interview with actor Sara Allgood, then appearing in a play in Sydney, who claimed a slight acquaintance with the countess. Allgood said, 'Her [Markievicz's] reputation is that of a lady of pronounced views, constantly tilting at the world's windmills with the idea of righting all wrongs, or championing the oppressed, and, I am afraid I must add, much too fond of a fight!'[28] The *Kalgoorlie Miner* was also typical of many publications when it denounced the Rising as a plot of anarchists and Germans and characterised Countess Markievicz as 'a hysterical woman of aristocratic lineage and associations, and Major McBride [*sic*], a reckless irresponsible adventurer of bad repute and ex-Boer officer'.[29] Other papers painted Markievicz in a more sympathetic light, although they acknowledged that her actions seemed barely comprehensible. On one page of a supplement to the 24 June edition of *The New Zealand Herald*, there were articles on the loyalty of British troops during the fighting in Dublin, a report on the marriage of Grace Gifford and Joseph Plunkett, and a description of Markievicz, subtitled 'A Strange Personality'.[30] The same article on Markievicz was reprinted several months later by *The Waikato Times* under the sub-heading 'The Romantic Countess'.[31]

Several newspapers, looking for a local angle, published accounts from Australians or New Zealanders who had been close to the action in Dublin during Easter Week. In almost every state in June and July, Australian newspapers published an eyewitness account of the Rising by a Melbourne doctor, Cecil McAdam, who had been staying in the Shelbourne Hotel and so had a view over St Stephen's Green where Markievicz was second-in-command. McAdam reported that he had been told by others that she had shot six of her men who had refused to obey orders.[32] Such reports promoted her image as violent and undisciplined.

Undeterred by a paucity of verified information from Dublin, some journalists looked to history to augment their reports. An Otago regional paper, *The Tuapeka Times*, in an editorial on 10 May, was quick to provide its readers with romantic views of war and revolution bolstered by comparisons between Constance Markievicz and the tragic French revolutionary Théroigne de Méricourt, just as news of the executions of the rebel leaders became known. After describing the fate of Mme de Méricourt, driven mad after injuries suffered when she was beaten by an angry mob in 1793, the writer dismissed Markievicz and the other rebels with the comment that 'Such was the prototype of Countess Markiowicz [*sic*] who may have met a similar fate had the mad plot in which she participated proved successful temporally.'[33] She was described, not so much as romantic, but as wilful when, two years later, *The Feilding Star* castigated her for ingratitude following her reprieve from the death sentence.[34] This characterisation of Markievicz as excitable, eccentric, and at the mercy of her emotions continued into the 1920s. In 1922, *The Journal*, an Adelaide newspaper, printed a description of her speech in the Treaty debate in the Dáil. Here, Markievicz was 'trembling with anger and excitement. Her little nervous, darting eyes flashed out on the assembly, her hands beat the table, and her words were rapped out jerkily, irritably with a sort of petulant energy that simulates passion.'[35] The conclusion that Markievicz was mad, unwomanly, and untypical of Irish women continued to be repeated in various versions throughout Australian and New Zealand reports of the Rising and in the years that followed.

TRAGIC WIDOWS

Markievicz and her actions were incomprehensible to many in the diaspora. Much more palatable were the stories of womanly grief and piety that emerged alongside the reports of the executions of the leaders of the Rising. Carried out between 3 and 12 May 1916, these executions were widely credited with shifting public opinion both in Ireland and around the world in favour of the rebels' cause. In Adelaide, *The Southern Cross* was typical of Catholic-Irish opinion in Australia when it reported the executions. While mostly matter-of-fact, the reporting of Joseph Plunkett's execution became more descriptive and 'colourful'. The story of his marriage to Grace Gifford was highly romanticised, and it included details of her tearful purchase of a wedding ring. The article used interviews with Gifford's mother and with the jeweller who sold her the ring from the report printed in *Lloyd's Weekly*, a popular English newspaper.[36] Her mother described Grace as having 'been under the mysterious influence of the Countess Markievicz – the woman who in man's garb led parties of the rioters in Dublin'. In these reports, Grace's father's stroke was said to have been caused by the shock of learning that two of his sons-in-law were executed for treason.[37] Other newspapers in Australia and New Zealand carried similar reports. The Sydney *Sun* also found a local angle on the Gifford sisters, particularly Grace, when it published an interview with Dr Oliver Latham, described as a pathologist from the Sydney University Lunacy Department, whose family knew the Giffords. Dr Latham had met Grace when she was sixteen and described her as a 'bright and witty girl of womanly disposition' with 'no rebel notions'. The only explanation for Grace's behaviour, he said, was the one that her mother had already offered in interviews: that Grace's bohemian lifestyle had meant 'she might easily have come under the spell of the countess and other rebel leaders'.[38] The detail of Latham's professional links with the Lunacy Department underlines the interpretation that Grace was somewhat unbalanced and might have avoided her tragic fate if only she had not fallen into bad company.[39]

Using sources from London, *The Otago Daily Times* reported both on the rebellion itself and on the 'Sinn Fein Romance' of Plunkett and Grace Gifford. The newspaper was pleased it could find a local angle to the story, when it reported that Grace's sister Muriel's husband, the executed leader Thomas MacDonagh, had been to school with Chaplain-Captain P. Dore of the Auckland Rifles, who was then recovering in hospital in London from wounds suffered at Gallipoli.[40] Muriel MacDonagh herself was presented as a pathetic figure in the reports of the widows of the executed leaders. In December 1916, an interview, conducted by the American journalist Eileen Moore of Chicago's *New World*, was reprinted in the Sydney *Catholic Press*.[41] In Moore's report, both Muriel's vulnerability and her youth were emphasised; she had 'a pathetic appearance in her deep mourning, with her three-and-a-half-year-old son, Donagh, clinging to her skirt. She is transparently pale, with copper-coloured hair and blue eyes. Her eyes have an appealing look.'[42] The pathos of Muriel and her very young children was only increased for Australian and New Zealand readers when it became known that she had died in 1917 of a heart attack while swimming, just over a year after the Rising.[43] Concentrating pity and sympathy on the widows and grieving women was a way of expressing support for the Irish cause without necessarily accepting the political aims or actions of the rebel leaders.[44] Many of the women themselves were well aware of this, and many agreed to the publication of photographs of themselves and their children by *The Catholic Bulletin* in Dublin in December 1916. These photographs were then printed as separate postcards and mass cards to raise funds for the organisations supporting the dependants.[45]

IN THE SHADOW OF THE RISING: REPORTS ABOUT THE WOMEN AFTER 1916

Sympathetic newspaper reports highlighting the grief of the widows and female relatives continued in the years after the Rising, with many writers finding more sympathy for the wives, widows, and mothers of the leaders than for the leaders themselves. In Sydney in 1919, *The Freeman's Journal* published a piece by Kathleen M. O'Brennan on a page titled 'Irish Women in the Struggle for Freedom'. In this piece, O'Brennan described the hard work of Sinéad Ní Fhlannagáin, Éamon de Valera's wife, in promoting the Irish language and culture, culminating with her patriotic statement that 'We must never take our eyes off Tara.'[46] In Melbourne in 1919, *The Advocate* published a short article titled 'A Mother of Martyrs' about Margaret Pearse, the mother of executed Patrick and Willie, illustrated by pictures of her two sons. Included in the article was a letter by her, prefaced by the comment, 'How Irish mothers suffer and suffer gladly.'[47] This piece highlighted Margaret Pearse's dual patriotism and grief, providing a model that was easy for women to identify with in post-war Australia and New Zealand, where so many of them were suffering grief at wartime losses.

The Irish-Australian Catholic press shifted the tone of their reporting of Markievicz as they reacted to the executions of the leaders and the change in mood of the people of Ireland. In August 1916, Sydney's *Catholic Press* reprinted a report of her desire to convert to Catholicism after seeing the piety of the young men under her command.[48] From then on, the Catholic media reported Markievicz in relatively positive terms, as when in 1919 her imprisonment was described as 'a violation of justice' and her election to the House of Commons was commended.[49] The latter story was widely covered in the Australian and New Zealand press, as she was the first woman to be elected to Westminster, although most newspapers put their own interpretation on the event. The labour paper *The Australian Worker*, for example, mentioned only her connections with the Irish labour activist James Larkin, while conservative mainstream newspapers, such as *The Argus* (Melbourne) and *The Chronicle* (Adelaide), merely noted that the 'notorious' Countess Markievicz had been elected to parliament.[50] Women's pages in other newspapers went into more detail, but most were similar to the *Barrier Miner* in Broken Hill, which printed a long analysis of her actions, characterising them as 'tragic' and speculating that those who knew her 'can only wonder at the waste and sorrow that has resulted from her wild egotism and the humourless intensity with which she flung herself into one craze after another'.[51]

After the Irish war with the British ended with the disputed Treaty, Australians and New Zealanders sympathetic to the cause of Irish independence struggled to understand the divisions that looked likely to tear Ireland apart just as it had achieved a measure of apparent success.[52] Women's involvement in the civil war was explained to diaspora audiences, in some reports, in terms of their links to the 1916 Rising. On 15 June 1922, *The Freeman's Journal* (Sydney) published an article by Patricia Hoey, a Canadian-Irish woman who had gone to Ireland to fight during 1916. In the article, she explained the split over the Treaty in the republican women's group Cumann na mBan almost wholly in terms of the women's individual experiences in Easter Week. She described how the women who supported the Treaty were those who had seen action in 1916: women such as Mrs Dick Mulcahy (Min Ryan), 'who fought through Easter Week'; Kathleen Browne, 'another Easter week woman and an old gaol bird for Ireland's cause'; Louise Gavan Duffy, 'who fought under [Pearse's] orders'; and Moira Rigney, 'who did 9 months hard labour for helping the Volunteers with guns and ammunition'. In contrast, Hoey argued, 'the women on the anti-Treaty side are mostly those who are relatives of men who have died for Ireland[.] Mrs Pearse, Mrs Clarke, Mrs Ceannt, Mrs O'Callaghan are anti-Treaty leaders', together with Mary MacSwiney, who 'took no part in the fighting in Ireland herself'. Hoey was being deceptively selective in her assessment. While she noted that Dr Kathleen Lynn and Mrs Sheehy Skeffington were also anti-Treaty leaders, she did not mention Lynn's active experience during the Rising and beyond, nor did she mention that Hanna Sheehy Skeffington, who had been widowed during the Rising, was an ardent republican.[53] While Hoey was factually incorrect in some of her history, what is significant is that her account was published and read by many who would not have known the specific details of the women's experiences in the Rising. Her article contributed to the overall view of the Catholic press in Australia and New Zealand that those who had fought at Easter, or who had seen significant action during the war with the British, were supportive of the Treaty, while those without direct military experience, particularly women, were not. This view was broadly in line with other information coming through to the diaspora press. *The Advocate* published a letter from the Very Reverend J.J. O'Reilly, leader of the Australian delegation to the Pan-Irish Conference, which gave his views on the Treaty negotiations. He said, 'It is striking that the most fearless and indomitable of the fighters – men like Collins, Mulcahy, McKeon and O'Duffy – were all Treaty men, while the men who were out of the firing line and the women are against it.'[54] By linking opposition to the Treaty with inaction during 1916, these articles promoted the view that acceptance of the Treaty and the subsequent establishment of the Irish Free State was the logical conclusion of the Rising. Certainly, in Australia and New Zealand, there was little appetite for continued activism to support the republicanism of those opposing the Treaty.[55]

In 1924, two seasoned Irish republican activists visited the Australian states of Victoria, Queensland, and New South Wales on a fundraising tour. Linda Kearns had served as a nurse during the Rising, had transported guns and ammunition during both the war with the British and the civil war, and had been imprisoned for her activities. Kathleen Barry was a veteran activist, fundraiser, and organiser with Cumann na mBan and the Irish Republican Prisoners' Dependants' Fund. Significantly, she was the sister of Kevin Barry, the young Dublin medical student who was executed by the British in 1920 for his role in a republican attack.[56] In their tour of Australia, the two women deliberately styled themselves according to the norms of non-violent Irish femininity. According to these norms, decent Irish women were not like mad, passionate Constance Markievicz; instead, they were the nurses and auxiliaries who bore grief over the deaths of their male relatives with pious grace.[57] Newspaper reports, based on material supplied by the women themselves, usually described them in terms similar to those adopted by *The Bundaberg Mail*: 'Miss Barry is a sister of the late Kevin Barry, the 18 year-old boy, who was executed in Ireland four years ago. Nurse Linda Kearns … was an active worker in the Red Cross during the Easter week-fighting in Ireland.'[58] Kearns and Barry deliberately only spoke of the pressing need for charity to support the republican prisoners, who had by then been released from jail, and their families. That their military activities and active links to 1916 were not mentioned in newspaper reports was orchestrated by Kearns and Barry in order to maximise the success of their fundraising and to obtain support from conservative Catholic clergy and hierarchy. The women actively placed themselves in the roles that had been created by Australian newspaper reports of the Rising post-1916. In taking on these roles, they were adopting the tactics of other Irish republican women who were prepared to assume gender norms in order to achieve practical gaols.[59]

CONCLUSION

Examining the reporting of women's activities during the Rising and in the years that followed is one way of tracing shifting attitudes to Irish republicanism in Australia and New Zealand. Initially, the papers picked up reports in the international press of 'mad' Constance Markievicz, stressing her odd clothes and behaviour that were incompatible with her class and gender. As the executions of the leaders became known, sympathetic descriptions of the tragic young widows and grieving mothers were given a lot of attention in the Irish press; these reports were then carried throughout the English-speaking world, enabling members of the Irish diaspora to channel their sympathy, if not their political support, towards those who had participated in the Rising. As reporting in the diaspora became more sympathetic, coverage of Markievicz's actions also changed: her sufferings in prison and her conversion to Catholicism were emphasised, and these aspects were easier to accommodate within traditional ideas of Irish femininity than her military actions. This change in the way the press in Australia and New Zealand reported Irish women's actions during the Rising and beyond was instrumental in the success of Kearns and Barry's fundraising tour in the immediate aftermath of the Irish civil war: their ability to mould their image to fit the stereotypes developed over the years meant that they could appear as pious, gracious Irish women rather than seasoned activists. After 1925, in Australia and New Zealand, interest in the women of the Rising generation declined as Catholic communities shifted their attention to local concerns, content that the Irish in the homeland had achieved the best outcome available, even if the much-desired full independence of the island of Ireland had not been attained. Although many of the women of the Rising generation continued to be active in Irish local politics and aid organisations, their activities were now only reported locally and were no longer of interest to the Irish diaspora.

CHAPTER 3

'It would really…matter tremendously': New Zealand women and the 1916 Rising

LISA MARR
(*University of Otago*)

News of the Easter Rising reached New Zealand homes one day after the first Anzac anniversary. On 25 April 1916, New Zealand women had commemorated the landing at Gallipoli, attending crowded processions and services and participating in wreath-placing ceremonies. They paid tribute to fallen heroes, those men who, in the language of the time, had heeded the Empire's call and given their lives for the Empire's cause.[1] Anzac Day was a milestone in the dominion's history: for the first time, New Zealanders defended their national liberty, co-operated with the Empire in a just cause, and sacrificed everything they held dear. They believed that this 'great sacrifice' connected them 'more closely' to other people within the British Empire and it added to the Empire's 'strength and glory'. In celebrating Anzac Day, they celebrated that new imperial unity which the war had 'brought into being' and renewed their 'solemn declaration of the steadfast purpose of the Empire' in prosecuting the war.[2] Thus, patriotic and imperial feelings were running high as the first news of the Rising reached New Zealand.

In 1916, most New Zealand women were heartily engaged in the war effort. While hundreds of them were active in Europe and Africa as nurses, ambulance drivers, and Red Cross workers, most were involved domestically, raising funds, providing entertainments and relief, and sending equipment and comfort parcels to the country's soldiers.[3] Some women joined the Women's National Reserve, taking on new and varied work in the absence of men. For decades, New Zealand women had shared in political organisations, such as the National Council of Women and the Women's Christian Temperance Union; with the nation now at war, the focus of some of these organisations had changed, and they fully supported the war effort. Whether in these pre-existing organisations or in new ones like the Anti-German League, many New Zealand women grouped together, pouring their energy into patriotic activities and opposing the Empire's enemies.

While such support for the war effort was expected of New Zealand women, a minority withstood this militarism. Members of the newly formed Women's International League (WIL), for instance, saw 'international sisterhood' as the only means to achieve peace and freedom.[4] Their objects were first 'to ensure that in future National differences shall be settled by some other means than war' and second, 'to demand that women shall have a direct voice in the affairs of the nation'.[5] In May and June 1916, the WIL sponsored Adela Pankhurst's visit to New Zealand. A founder of the Women's Peace Army in Australia, Pankhurst called the war (and conscription) an 'atrocity' run by 'old men who used their votes to benefit class interests', and she advocated replacing 'nationalism and competition with internationalism and co-operation'.[6] Pankhurst's opinions were not always well received: in Wellington, a number of returned servicemen disrupted one meeting she addressed, and later she and two others were charged with obstructing traffic when they stopped to speak to people gathered outside a venue.[7] According to the editor of *The Feilding Star*, Pankhurst was 'a public nuisance', 'a disturber of the peace', and 'a traitor', who must be moved on immediately.[8] Pankhurst was ignored by most women in New Zealand, women whose sons were fighting in the war and who 'probably regarded her activities as unpatriotic or even seditious'.[9] In this hysterical social and political context, dissenting women risked being ignored or considered nuisances at best; at worst, they could be harassed or stigmatised as 'unpatriotic' or even 'traitors'. With these prospective outcomes, some women opted to stay silent.

In these circumstances, how did New Zealand women respond to reports of a rebellion in Ireland? Women were shocked, outraged, or saddened by the reports, interpreting the Rising as disloyal, irresponsible, and ill-timed. Irish New Zealanders attended public meetings in order to show their loyalty and to distance themselves from the rebels, and they redoubled their efforts in patriotic activities, such as fundraising. Few women, however, put pen to paper to comment on the Rising and its aftermath or to explore its causes and Ireland's hopes. The responses of these few women provide the focus of this chapter. They reveal their writers' empathy for the Irish and their desire to understand what had happened, why the Rising occurred, and how the present situation in Ireland could be resolved. As further details of the events in Ireland emerged and the weeks and months passed, the responses changed, and women who were initially pressured into loyal declarations or silence found ways of demonstrating their sympathies and expressing their views.

'Elizabeth' and 'Imogen' were among the first women to respond publicly to news of the Easter Rising; while one writer expressed outrage at the traitorous activities in Ireland, the other impressed upon readers the loyalty of most Irish. 'Elizabeth' conducted the 'Ladies' Pages' in the *Otago Witness*, a weekly paper published in Dunedin. In her summary of 'The Week' on 3 May, she commented briefly on 'the pitiful story from Ireland' before turning her attention to Mesopotamian news. Her outrage became evident as she identified the one person whom 'all right thinking people would like to see removed from the earth as soon as possible': the traitorous Sir Roger Casement, who had been captured on Good Friday as he attempted to land a shipload of German guns on the west coast of Ireland. 'Elizabeth' maliciously desired his 'early and speedy' execution, via some 'unpleasant' method because 'shooting, and even hanging', is 'far too good' for him.[10] In contrast to 'Elizabeth's' vehement condemnation of Casement, 'Imogen' gently reminded readers of the sacrifice Irish soldiers were making. She opened her column in *The Dominion* on 4 May with a paragraph entitled 'In Memory of Irish Soldiers'. It reported the recent celebration of a High Mass at Westminster Cathedral, the Mother Church for Catholics in England and Wales, 'in memory' of Ireland's war dead. It noted the presence of Canadian, Australian, and New Zealand troops alongside a battalion of Irish Guards, suggesting unity of people and purpose in waging a 'righteous' war.[11] While 'Imogen' affirmed Irish loyalty in her 'Woman's World' column, Irish New Zealanders made their own affirmations around the country.[12]

Most Irish-New Zealand women were already involved in fundraising activities and loyally sacrificing their sons and husbands for the Empire's cause. As Angela McCarthy has shown in her research on Irish-New Zealand correspondence, Irish migrants to New Zealand and their children avidly read newspaper reports about Ireland and letters from Irish relatives who informed them about politics and conditions 'at Home', but, in general, these women identified politically, not with nationalist or unionist Ireland, but with New Zealand.[13] Their identification with New Zealand and its political affairs would have determined their response. Thus, when New Zealand entered the war, the allegiance of most Irish New Zealanders was to New Zealand: they enthusiastically 'greeted the outbreak' and seized the opportunity to prove their loyalty.[14] They joined the 'chorus of patriotic harmony', and while Catholics comprised only 14 per cent of the population, *The New Zealand Tablet* claimed that they 'contributed nearly 40 per cent. of the New Zealand fighting force'.[15] Irish-New Zealand women also contributed to the war effort by fundraising. In Wellington, for example, women who belonged to the Hibernian Society energetically raised funds for wounded soldiers, the Red Cross, and others by selling 'green badges painted with the words "It's a long way to Tipperary"'.[16]

As further details of Easter Week appeared, some New Zealand women sympathised with the Rising's innocent victims. Moved by news of the arrests and deportations and especially the executions of rebel leaders, their sympathy grew, and some women empathised with their Irish counterparts. Some women were upset, even outraged, by news of unauthorised killings, in particular the murder of Francis Sheehy Skeffington and his companions, and some would have known – and attended a solemn requiem mass for – the Very Reverend Doctor Watters, the former rector of St Patrick's College in Wellington, who was shot, 'accidentally or otherwise', as he stood in the doorway of his college in Dublin during the Rising.[17]

One New Zealand woman who was moved to sympathise and empathise was Katherine Mansfield (Kathleen Mansfield Beauchamp), who was living in England in 1916. Mansfield was a patriotic colonial. Soon after the war began, she wrote a letter to a close family friend in Wellington which was later published in *The Evening Post*.[18] She describes the activity in London: the way soldiers have filled the city's spaces; the movement of Red Cross trains and troops; the sweep of searchlights in the night sky; and the running and shouting of newspaper boys delivering the 'Latest news of the War'. Having witnessed the arrival of Belgian refugees, she recounts touching details about a dignified old lady and two wide-eyed, dislocated children and the horrors they have survived. While she acknowledges the 'dark and depressing' nature of the times, Mansfield believes they are 'brightened' by the courage and generosity of people. She includes jolly and morale-boosting observations, such as a description of departing trains 'crowded with boys in khaki, cheering and singing on their way to the front', and celebrates the Empire's just cause: 'The fact that England is fighting for something *beyond* mere worldly gain and power seems to have a real moral effect upon the people [my emphasis].'[19] By April 1916, however, Mansfield had seen first-hand the frightful effects of war and experienced the loss of friends and family members, including her younger brother 'Chummie' (Leslie Beauchamp) who was killed in Belgium in 1915.[20]

Only two degrees of separation lay between Mansfield and the rebel leader Patrick Pearse; the intermediary was Beatrice Campbell (née Elvery), later Lady Glenavy, an Irish artist whom Mansfield had met in London. Bici, as Mansfield affectionately called her, had worked with Pearse, illustrating a children's book for him and painting panels for St Enda's, the school Pearse had established in 1908.[21] One of her early paintings, *Éire*, adorned another wall at St Enda's: this romantic nationalist painting was purchased by Maud Gonne who donated it to the school.[22] In the first decade of the twentieth century, Campbell had contributed illustrations to *Sinn Féin* and knew Constance Markievicz from the Arts Club in Dublin.[23] Now living in London, Campbell apparently supported John Redmond's stance and thought the matter of Home Rule could 'rest…till after the war'.[24]

Reading Campbell's letters in the weeks following the rebellion, Mansfield put herself mentally in her friend's shoes and felt her suffering. Writing compassionately to Campbell from Cornwall on 4 May,

Mansfield imagines what Beatrice and her husband, Gordon Campbell, 'must have felt'. Although she wanted to write earlier, she 'felt that Ireland wouldn't permit'. That morning, she had read the 'horrible' news that three rebel leaders had been shot; one of the three was Pearse.[25] In these early days after the Rising, when 'no clear facts' could be discerned, Mansfield found it 'difficult' to locate 'any coherent account' of what had happened in Dublin, although J.L. Garvin's article in *The Observer* 'very nearly' succeeded.[26] Her friend could tell her little more. For days, Campbell was unable to communicate with family or friends in Dublin 'by telephone, telegram or letter'. At this early stage, she 'could only guess what was happening by questions asked in the House of Commons' and reported in the papers, questions about '"Fighting in the streets", "The city burning", [and] "Hundreds killed"'.[27] Mansfield comments on contrasting scenes from the rebellion and how these reflect the incomprehensible and inexplicable character of the Irish situation. Seizing on a detail, possibly from one of Campbell's letters, she says, 'There is no accounting for Ireland – The fact that while one street was under hot fire & people falling in all directions the milkmen with their rattling little vans went on delivering milk seemed as [D.H.] Lawrence would say "pretty nearly an absolute [or perfect] symbol"'.[28]

Ten days later, Mansfield wrote again to Campbell; in the intervening period, further executions had taken place, and Mansfield is 'a little afraid of jarring' her friend by mentioning the affair. Mansfield still relies on Beatrice for details of what has happened in Dublin; she has heard 'no discussion or talk' of the rebellion and knows 'so little', although she has read some articles about it in the newspapers. She is searching for reports so that she can be informed and understand events and how they have affected her friend. After thanking Campbell for her letter and two newspapers, Mansfield says that she must not forget 'Marjory's account *NOR* Gordon's comment upon [Marjorie's] reason for not being a S.F. [Sinn Féiner]'.[29] Without Campbell's letter, the details of 'Marjory's account' and 'Gordon's comment' are uncertain; however, Marjorie, Campbell's younger sister, had attended the Fairyhouse races on Easter Monday and spent four days making her way home across Dublin on foot, much to her parents' consternation.[30] As well as apprising Mansfield of her family's first-hand experiences of the Rising, Campbell likely shared with her friend her concern for Ireland's future and how its people would respond to the executions and martial law; her attention was absorbed by these thoughts and anxieties. Mansfield finds it 'still awfully difficult to credit what has happened and what is happening in Ireland'. She shudders in disbelief at the violence of the British response and wonders if the repressive measures might be counterproductive. She writes, 'One cant [*sic*] get round it – This shooting, Beatrice, this incredible shooting of people! I keep wondering if Ireland really minds – I mean really won't be pacified and cajoled and content with a few fresh martyrs and heroes. I can understand how it must fill your thoughts.' By contemplating how she would feel 'if Ireland were New Zealand and such a thing had happened there', Mansfield is able to put herself in Campbell's shoes and to relate emotionally to her friend's thoughts and fears, saying that 'it would mean the same for me – It would really … Matter Tremendously'.[31]

Mansfield goes on to mention the Grace Gifford–Joseph Plunkett story, which swayed the sympathies of many. Gifford had married Plunkett in his prison cell, hours before he was executed for his part in the rebellion. When selecting her wedding ring in a jeweller's shop in Grafton Street, she broke down and told the proprietor that she was Joseph Plunkett's fiancée and was to marry Plunkett that night. Mansfield believed this latter detail 'spoilt' the story, which otherwise 'was almost an Irish On The Eve'; here, Mansfield draws a literary parallel with Turgenev's novel, in which a young woman's husband 'wears himself out in the cause of his country's political freedom'.[32] She then comments briefly on images of Plunkett and Gifford she has seen on the front page of *The Daily Mirror*.[33] She refers alliteratively to 'Poor Plunket's [*sic*] picture', seeing in the photograph a mix of familiar faces, those of 'Willie Yeats' (W.B. Yeats) and 'Jack [John Collings] Squire', who was the literary editor of the *New Statesman* at the time.[34] In remarking on William Orpen's portrait of Gifford, which occupied almost half the page, Mansfield is more concerned with aesthetics, noting 'a strange passionate cynicism' in the way Orpen paints 'women's hands'.[35]

Two months later, in mid-July, Mansfield visited London and encountered Irish prisoners in transit. She had stayed with the Campbells in St John's Wood for several days and saw the prisoners as she left London for a long weekend at Garsington Manor.[36] In her letter of 15

July, she tells Campbell of how she arrived at Paddington Station to find
it 'crowded with Sinn Feiners' who were being moved 'on the points of
innumerable bayonets' from Wormwood Scrubs to another prison.[37]
The prisoners were likely a batch of detainees who had been brought to
London to be interrogated by Justice Sankey's Enemy Aliens Advisory
Committee.[38] While in London, they were kept in Wormwood Scrubs
or Wandsworth prison, and this group may have been some of the five
hundred or so Irish prisoners who were returned to the Frongoch prison
camp in north Wales – or, perhaps, given their mood, they were among
the 69 per cent of detainees who were released and returned to Ireland on
the next early-morning ferry.[39] Mansfield describes the prisoners in rather
joyous terms, noting their wearing of green and the way she was drawn
to them: 'Heavens!' Mansfield exclaims in her letter, 'What a sight it was
but they all looked very happy and they all wore bunches of green ribbon
or green badges.' She adds, 'I very nearly joined them and I rather wish I
had.'[40] For months, Mansfield has corresponded and conversed with her
friend about the Rising; she has imaginatively and empathetically felt
Campbell's pain and confusion; she has searched for information in order
to understand the facts of the Rising and the horror of the executions.
Now, the very subject of those letters and conversations springs to life
before her. She is captivated and moved by the spectacle and excitedly
shares it with her friend.

By now, many New Zealanders believed that Ireland deserved some
form of self-government;[41] Jessie Mackay supported Home Rule for
Ireland and keenly awaited that reward at the end of the war. Trusting
in the constitutional approach, she thought the Rising 'mad' and
'insane'; her nicest adjective for it is 'frothy', meaning bubbly, exciting,
but insubstantial. Several months after the Rising, she would write, 'It
was madness – stark, criminal unthinkable madness – that threw the few
leaders of the late trouble into the counsels of the Hun.'[42] Mackay was the
daughter of Scottish immigrants, who passed on to her their liberal and
'keen humanitarian views' and their love of justice.[43] From a young age,
she devoured news of people and events in papers and magazines; and by
the age of fourteen, she 'hero-worshipped' Charles Stewart Parnell and
was 'inspired' by him to study Irish history and to support the campaign
for Home Rule for Ireland.[44] Mackay was politically active: as well as

being involved with feminist, suffragette, and temperance groups, she was concerned about the rights of Scots, Irish, Māori, and the working class. She often combined these interests, such as when she drew parallels between Ireland's misgovernment by England and 'the long domination of women by men', the defenceless oppressed by the strong.[45] She was a teacher and one of colonial New Zealand's best-loved poets.[46] Mackay was also a journalist: for thirty years, she wrote a column for the *Otago Witness*, usually on literature, especially poetry.

In May 1916, Mackay chose one of the lesser-known places associated with the Rising and wrote a piece entitled 'Athenry'; she chose this town in County Galway primarily for its symbolic value, allowing her to explore the cyclical nature of Irish history. She opens with a quotation from Thomas Campbell's poem 'O'Connor's Child; or, "The Flower of Love Lies Bleeding"':

> 'And go to Athunree,' I cried;
> 'High lift the banner of your pride.
> But know that where its sheet unrolls
> The weight of blood is on your souls!
> Dead as the green oblivious flood
> That mantles by your walls shall be
> The glory of O'Connor's blood!
> Away, away to Athunree,
> Where, downward when the sun shall fall,
> The raven's wing shall be your pall!'

In these lines, the 'Celtic Cassandra' prophesies the bloody fate that awaits her brothers, the O'Connors, in the battle of Athenry in 1316: the Celtic king would be defeated and killed, and the Irish hope of winning back their freedom would be dented. Now, Mackay writes with a high degree of poetic licence, that ancient battlefield is 'red once more with the blood of Celt and Saxon'; it 'echoes to the peal of gun fire, and points backward through seven centuries of oppression'.[47] Mackay's twentieth-century 'Cassandra' is Francis Sheehy Skeffington, who had tried in vain to warn the authorities of the 'extremely grave' situation in Ireland, hoping that they would restrain the militarists before blood was shed.[48]

Then, during the Rising, he was, in Mackay's words, 'paid ... in lead for a warning of gold, had it been taken'. Arrested as he tried to stop the looting in central Dublin, Sheehy Skeffington and two other men were shot the following day on the orders of a British Army captain, who was later court-martialled for the murders and found guilty but insane. Sheehy Skeffington was not a participant in this 'Made-in-Germany Rebellion': he 'had neither German money in his pocket nor a German gun in his hand' when the authorities captured and unjustly shot him.[49] This atrocity has unforeseen and damaging effects: the murderous shot 'strafes' everyone, and the British are 'stained' with a mark that 'will not whiten easily or soon'. After relating the history of Athenry, Mackay concludes that, in contrast to the fourteenth-century battle of Athenry, Ireland in 1916 has not lost hope; the nation will regain her freedom. Despite 'this frothy rising', every day, she says, 'is great with a nation's *legitimate* hope [my emphasis]'; that is, the Home Rule Britain has justly promised to implement at the end of the war.[50]

In this article, Mackay makes clear her opinion of the rebellion and the events which inexorably led to it; over the coming months, she would reiterate this view and defend it against her critics. Like many of her contemporaries, she depicts the Rising as 'insane', 'criminal', 'wild', and 'mad', and remarks that Ireland could not be raised because 'the nobler policy of English statesmanship' in successive recent governments has 'well nigh righted' the country's 'wrongs'. While she acknowledges that '25 years of placation, of kindness, of development under the once hated rule' have not 'wholly charmed' Irish hearts and healed the deep and terrible injuries inflicted 'through seven centuries of oppression', she eagerly anticipates the imminent application of 'British justice' in implementing Home Rule.[51]

Criticised by F.M. Mackay in August for her views on 'iron Norman–Saxon rule' and its connection to the Rising,[52] Mackay responded in an article entitled 'The Aftermath of Seven Centuries'; in it, she explores the causes of the rebellion and concludes with a moving statement on Ireland's newest martyrs. In replying to her critic's comments, Mackay argues that the time for 'Imperial centralisation' has passed and 'the day of true Imperial unity (including Brito-Irish unity) is arriving'; but in order to achieve 'true' union, Ireland *must* be granted Home

Rule. 'Castle' rule is 'anomalous'; it 'rankles' 'old sores' and wakes 'old memories … in suspicion and rancour'; and it has been found wanting: these, Mackay notes, are the findings of the Royal Commission on the Rising.[53] She presents a series of vignettes contrasting the Irish view of conditions in Ireland in the lead-up to the Rising with the English view: where, for example, the English saw prosperity in the Irish countryside and a revival in manufacturing, the Irish saw women and children starving during the Dublin Lockout and workers being bludgeoned by police 'into submission'. Lastly, while Ireland's 'Orange and Green' sons are united in fighting Britain's battles at the front, yet another betrayal of Celt by Saxon was observed when the prime minister appointed the 'arch-agitator' Sir Edward Carson to the British cabinet; mindful of Carson's leading role in Ulster's resistance to the Home Rule Bill (1912–14), Mackay describes him as 'the embodiment of strife and separation' and points out that he was, in fact, 'the first smuggler of traitorous arms, and the first driller of rebel troops in twentieth-century Ireland'.[54] Despite this long history of misgovernment, oppression, and betrayal, Ireland remained loyal; Mackay observes, 'It was but a handful that joined that insane company of Clan-na-Gael, Larkinites, and ultra-Sinn Feiners last Easter Week. Mad and bad and unutterably sad it all was.'[55] She maintains that those who 'best know' Ireland's history are least likely to condemn that 'handful', this latest group of 'martyrs who were not martyrs', upon whose names 'Silence broods'. In the world of Mackay's present, no one '*dares* to say' that these men 'died for Ireland's right; yet', she concludes, 'no one who knows the deep call of a nation's heart dares to say they did not die for Ireland's wrong'.[56]

Mackay expanded many of the ideas raised in this article in a series of columns entitled 'Two Roads to "Union"'. In this thirteen-part series, she sought to explain 'why a *real* union of friendship and respect was achieved with Scotland, and nothing but a baseless *travesty* of union with Ireland', hence the inverted commas around the misnomer 'Union' in her title.[57] The first part appeared in the *Otago Witness* on 20 September 1916 and the last, on 3 January 1917. Once again, in exploring her ideas, Mackay displays her literary skill and passion, making for colourful reading and memorable images. When examining the failures of the administration which led to the Rising, for example, she compares Ireland's relationship with England under the Union to a working wife's relationship with her husband prior to the Married Woman's Property Act: she makes money for her husband's pocket, 'out of which he has with grumbling and admonishment returned her certain house moneys, loudly commending his own generosity and decrying her slatternly ways'. Worse still, Ireland's role in mothering and guiding her own children has been usurped by 'the wasteful, alien, mediæval Lady of [Dublin] Castle'. This 'Other Woman' continually reminds 'slave-wife' Ireland of 'ancient degradation and present restriction', carelessly and extravagantly spending the 'children's money before her eyes'. Although she was 'discredited before all the world' in Easter Week, the 'Other Woman' remains sitting in 'the housedame's chair', continuing her expensive, 'left-handed, cross-eyed, inept, and archaic' rule.[58] Despite the findings of the Royal Commission, the old regime remained firmly in place, and, without Home Rule, 'real union' could not occur. Mackay earnestly hoped that Britain would see Ireland as one of the 'Little Peoples' or 'small nations' and protect her as she would Poland and settle her rights. If Britain would not see Ireland in this way, the dominions must, for, Mackay says, they 'have won their right to speak on all Imperial questions'.[59] As a result of writing these articles and her activism on Ireland's behalf, Jessie Mackay was later selected as one of the delegates of the Irish Self-Determination League to attend the Gael Race Conference in Paris in January 1922.

The responses of Mansfield and Mackay fell safely within the bounds of what was acceptable in an empire at war, but what about those New Zealand women who disapproved of the heavy-handed way the authorities were dealing with the Irish? Could they translate their sympathies into action and express their opinions? Or would fear of the social consequences paralyse and silence them?

One of the few ways that New Zealand women could demonstrate their sympathy in 1916 was by giving to the Irish Relief Fund. The fund was set up by *The Tablet* in September to relieve the distress in Dublin that had resulted from the insurrection. Responding to an appeal for help from Dublin, *The Tablet* invited Catholic sympathisers to send their subscriptions to its Dunedin office, and the funds would then be 'remitted to the Archbishop of Dublin for distribution to the deserving victims', those innocent families who are destitute because they have been deprived of their breadwinners.[60] Catholics and Hibernians gave generously, raising around £5,000. Looking down the subscription lists, hundreds of women donated to the fund. While most subscribers supplied their names to *The Tablet*, some contributors wished to remain anonymous, including 'Lady Sympathiser' in November.[61] These contributors may have worried about the social consequences for them if friends and neighbours saw their names linked to families of rebels while the war was still raging; they knew what could result from putting their heads above the parapet.

Their response is understandable. Soon after the fund was announced, the editor of *The Press* in Christchurch denied that there was a need for such a fund; he quoted the unionist *Irish Times* on Ireland's prosperity and said that the funds would be used 'for political purposes'.[62] A fierce debate then erupted in *The Press* between the editor and Bishop Brodie, the Catholic bishop of Christchurch, and the controversy was reported in *The Tablet*. In an editorial on the furore which criticised *The Press'* attack, the editor of *The Sun* (another Canterbury newspaper) questioned the timing of the fund, observing, 'No doubt a mistake was made in trying to launch an Irish relief fund at this juncture. Even people who don't know very much about the facts would be inclined to say that if the Irish can afford to buy mausers they can afford to buy bread.'[63] There was little space in New Zealand's newspapers and journals for opinions that could be interpreted as disloyal or 'unpatriotic'; as Rory Sweetman has noted in connection with the argument between Bishop Brodie and *The Press*, New Zealanders refused 'to tolerate any deviation from the narrow definition of loyalty prescribed by an Anglophile establishment'.[64]

With the announcement of the fund, some Irish New Zealanders began to voice their objections to the British response. The Hibernian Society in Wellington unanimously carried resolutions deploring the 'excessive punishment' of the insurgents and abhorring the victimisation of 'hundreds of innocent women and children' under martial law. Stating their alarm at the incarceration of 'hundreds of innocent men … without trial or jury … on the faintest suspicion or whim of the garrison in Ireland', they requested that 'simple justice be granted these men' and demanded the immediate cessation of martial law in Ireland.[65] In 1917, this shift in response became more pronounced, influenced by the opinions of Dr James Kelly, the new editor of *The Tablet*, and guided by attitudinal and political change in Ireland and the swing to Sinn Féin. With the inception of *The Green Ray*, a monthly nationalist review published in Dunedin, women with republican sympathies could have their say.

In May 1917, 'Eiblin ni Connor' (Eileen O'Connor) of Christchurch replied to John Diggins' letter on the 1916 Rising, challenging his criticism of the Irish Volunteers.[66] She rejects his use of the word 'riots' for the Rising. Basing her arguments on 'first-hand information', she describes the Rising as 'a spontaneous and successful effort on the part of a small section of the volunteers to prevent conscription'. She casts Redmond as a 'recruiting sergeant', enlisting young Irish men who pay for parliament's 'unstable promises' of Home Rule with their blood. As the number of fresh recruits diminished and the 'recruiting sergeant' eyed the young men who remained in Ireland, Eoin MacNeill became a protector figure, reminding Redmond of the purpose of the Volunteers and standing between Redmond and the remaining men.[67] O'Connor's account reveals her knowledge of the split that had occurred in the Irish Volunteers between the Redmondite majority and a minority who took MacNeill's line.[68] In a statement signed by Pearse, Plunkett, and others, MacNeill declared that Redmond's policy was 'utterly at variance with the [Volunteers'] published and accepted aims and objects' and that 'Ireland cannot, with honour or safety, take part in foreign quarrels otherwise than through the free action of a National Government of her own'.[69] Under pressure to supply an increasing demand for manpower, Redmond was stuck in this 'recruiting sergeant' role, and his public reputation and that of the Irish Parliamentary Party suffered.[70]

O'Connor argues that Redmond's party was never an Irish national party, displaying her radical politics in advocating for Sinn Féin. She responds to and dismisses Diggins' theory that the Irish Volunteers were 'led, trained, and financed, by Tories for no better object than to break up the Irish party led by John Redmond'.[71] She suggests that Diggins would not have made this error if he knew how the Irish-Irelanders had 'completely reconstructed the Irish National ideal, and altered all Ireland's thoughts and ways'. She observes that there was no 'Irish National' party to break up, characterising the Irish Parliamentary Party as a 'British provincial' party rather than an Irish nationalist one. In contrast, she instructs, Sinn Féin offers Irish people, for the first time ever, a policy that is 'truly National and entirely workable'. She believes that the deaths of a few Sinn Féin representatives in 1916 garnered more support for the movement than all its teachings could in five decades. Abreast of developments in Ireland's 'intellectual life' and politics, O'Connor uses her knowledge to correct Diggins' comments on the Volunteers and to point to the way Irish-Irelanders have influenced recent and present-day circumstances in Ireland.[72]

From March 1918, 'Una' conducted a column for 'modern women' in *The Green Ray*. While the name of the column ('Our Ladies') echoes the English translation of *sinn féin* (ourselves), the pen name 'Una' is both an Old Irish name and a Latin word meaning 'one' or 'only'; together the title and pen name play on the nationalist slogan *Sinn Féin amháin*, 'Ourselves only', which was also the title of the Maoriland Irish Society's anthem.[73] Calling on readers to write to her about 'the great matters disturbing the world', 'Una' encourages them to aid their republican 'sisters' in Ireland and, in doing so, assist themselves, moving with the world and Ireland and being involved with Irish and New Zealand affairs. She concludes her inaugural column by referring to the 'sterling' republican women on the West Coast and exhorting her readers to 'get together and be courageous and sincere' and to write and express their thoughts, 'ambitions, fears, and ideals, without reserve'.[74]

A young West Coast republican immediately answered 'Una's' call, with 'Nora' of Greymouth writing letters published in the April and May numbers.[75] Introduced by 'Una' as 'thinking and teaching in the right direction', 'Nora' congratulates 'Una' on her opening article, assuring her that 'it stirred our enthusiasm' for Ireland and, in the New Zealand context, 'Labour's holy cause'.[76] As 'Una' encouraged writers to do, 'Nora' addresses Irish and New Zealand issues and is keeping pace with changes in the political scene. She praises 'the women and girls of the Irish Rebellion' for playing their 'magnificent' and 'glorious' part in 1916, and she notes how Ireland 'might have been free to-day' if 'Eoin McNeill had not countermanded the order to rise' and the *Aud* had 'landed her cargo [of weapons] safely'. She apprehends that those 'glorious martyrs' of 1916 'have not died in vain, and that others are ready and willing to follow in their footsteps'. She is certain that Ireland soon will be 'a nation free and grand', adding, 'God speed the day.' After commenting on the cruelty and hypocrisy of conscriptionists and providing details of Tom Kiely's case,[77] 'Nora' describes her enjoyment at hearing Father Kimball eulogise Sinn Féiners in his St Patrick's Day sermon: he lamented how they have been 'misrepresented' and their 'lofty' aims ignored, and he admonished 'the congregation to know the history of Ireland, and be able to refute lying statements circulated by the enemies of Ireland'. 'Nora' writes, 'How proud I felt that I was wearing the green, white, and orange.' If some congregants had 'looked askance' at her before the start of the service, their views had been adjusted by the priest's words, and, 'Nora' believes, they now 'understood' her allegiance and the validity of the Sinn Féin movement. Like Kimball's sermon, 'Nora's' letter expresses faith in advanced Irish nationalism and demonstrates an evangelical spirit.

While 'Una' and 'Nora' wrote under pen names, Sis O'Donnell courageously signed her letter with her name. One of the 'sterling' republican women named in 'Una's' first column, O'Donnell was possibly a member of the West Coast branch of the Maoriland Irish Society, and she was a zealous reader of *The Green Ray*. She writes her letter having just received the May issue which commemorated the rebellion. She lauds the leader, 'The Memory of the Dead', written by the editor Thomas Cummins, for its 'cheerful message of hope', as the spirits of the martyrs suffuse Ireland's soul. She praises Casement's last speech and the examples of Connolly's writings that appeared in the number, observing, 'How the memory of the dead appeals to our Irish hearts. Those strong, brave souls, seem to plead Ireland's cause more eloquently than her living heroes, I believe. But, ah, those living, suffering heroes – how we love them.'[78] Her sincere and heartfelt response reflects changes in the way the Rising was perceived in Ireland. Although her view of blood sacrifice is idealistic and romantic, O'Donnell recognises the appeal and potency of martyrdom at a time when 'the conversation of the dead', as Charles Townshend puts it, 'really mattered'.[79] She rounds off her response to the May issue by saying, 'God bless the "Ray," may it live long and prosper.' Sadly for women like O'Donnell, the June 1918 issue of *The Green Ray* was the last: authorities deemed 'The Memory of the Dead' seditious and imprisoned the paper's editor and manager. In the wartime context, dissent was not tolerated, and voices that were intensely Irish nationalist were suppressed.[80]

The way New Zealand women responded to the Rising was determined by social and political conditions. With the Great War raging and New Zealanders fighting loyally for country and Empire, only certain responses were acceptable. Upon hearing news of the Rising, women could be angered, disgusted, or saddened; they could condemn the traitorous rebels or acknowledge the loyalty of most Irish. They could empathise with the Irish or search for explanations and solutions. Most Irish-New Zealand women initially responded by affirming their loyalty to the Empire, and those with dissenting views kept their opinions to themselves or their circle. As the months passed, however, they became more outspoken, objecting to the perpetuation of martial law or glorifying the Rising and its martyrs. Their expressions were not welcome in this outpost of Empire, where unity, loyalty, and sacrifice were paramount.

Play *v.* Play: *The Otago Daily Times* and the Dunedin stage as a regional New Zealand response to the Easter Rising 1916

PETER KUCH
(*University of Otago*)

This chapter will examine accounts of the Rising printed in *The Otago Daily Times* as a context for investigating the rivalry between the staging of patriotic Empire plays featuring Irish roles and the staging of plays that affirmed Irishness – specifically *Cathleen ni Houlihan* and *Peg o' My Heart* – that were performed in Dunedin during the months before and after Easter 1916. It will argue that one of the ways *The Otago Daily Times* distinguished itself from other New Zealand newspapers was the column inches it devoted to interpretations of the Rising provoked by these plays, and the ways theatre and theatre criticism participated in discussions of 'Irishness' elicited by the Rising. It will then briefly investigate the way a national tour of *Peg o' My Heart* contributed to representations of 'Irishness' towards the end of 1916. What was reported and what was staged in Dunedin provide the two major sources for this case study of a regional New Zealand response to the Rising that in one respect was distinctive and yet in other respects proved representative of a general New Zealand response.

Readers might well ask, why focus on *The Otago Daily Times*, on patriotic Irish plays, and on one New Zealand city and its local theatres?

In short, *The Otago Daily Times* was the first daily to be published in New Zealand that was still in circulation in 1916; it was one of the few New Zealand papers to have an office in London; and, while generally considered to be the major source of news and opinion for the South Island, it was also highly regarded as a national newspaper. A major New Zealand city, Dunedin was renowned for its theatres, partly because of the wealth derived from the Otago gold-fields[1] – by 1916 it was well established as an important financial centre for New Zealand – and partly because of its strong shipping links with Melbourne which made it comparatively easy for theatre companies to travel from what was one renowned theatrical city to another.[2] Dunedin boasted nine theatres in 1916, two of which were regularly used by the international touring circuit. The theatres were His Majesty's, Princess', the Octagon, Queen's, the Plaza, the Grand, Everybody's, the Empire, and the Oddfellows' Hall in Stuart Street.[3] According to the 1916 census, Dunedin City had a population of 55,256;[4] His Majesty's Theatre, where the final Irish play considered in this chapter was staged for a season of six nights and one matinee, had a seating capacity of 1,850.[5] Live theatre was still big business in 1916 and was still a significant source of entertainment and public comment, despite the inroads that cinema had begun to make.[6]

Irish plays were widely popular with the local audience – Boucicault played Dunedin to acclaim in 1862;[7] Sara Allgood in 1916[8] – although the Irish, and particularly the Catholic Irish, had not always been welcome in Otago or in its provincial capital, Dunedin. The 1848 'Articles' drawn up by the Lay Association of the Free Presbyterian Church of Scotland emphasised that the new province of Otago was to embrace Free Presbyterians and Evangelicals but, on the Wakefield principle of 'class settlement', to discourage all others.[9] The 1850 census lists only '8 Roman Catholics and 12 Irish (various)' in a Dunedin population of '1149 souls'.[10] Between 1861 and 1864, the peak years of the gold rush, net Irish migration to New Zealand did not exceed 1,600,[11] by which time there were 49,908 people living in the province of Otago.[12] And while Irish migration to the whole country peaked at approximately 20 per cent of net migration for the latter half of the nineteenth century, this percentage had halved by the outbreak of the First World War with the majority of

Irish immigrants being Protestants from the north. According to the 1916 census, approximately 24 per cent of all of New Zealand's Presbyterians and 20 per cent of all New Zealand's Baptists lived in Otago compared with only 10 per cent of all of New Zealand's Roman Catholics.[13] Yet 1916 Dunedin was the only New Zealand city where an Irish republican newspaper, *The Green Ray*, would be published, proscribed, and the editors jailed; where the Maoriland Irish Society would be formed by a small group of advanced nationalists, some of whom claimed to have 'intimate connections' with the 1916 rebels;[14] and where Irish plays that dramatised strong political views would be consistently performed throughout the First World War.[15]

PROBLEMS REPORTING THE RISING

It took some time for detailed, reliable reports of the Rising, which began at midday on Monday, 24 April, and ended with the official surrender at 3.30 p.m. on Saturday, 29 April, to appear in the traditional sources of information for the citizens of Dunedin – the Irish, British, and New Zealand press.[16] Each of these three sources was severely compromised, making it extremely difficult for editors and journalists to provide a clear account of what was actually happening. At first, little could be sourced from Dublin itself. The editorial offices of *The Irish Times* lay between the rebel-held General Post Office and the troops defending Trinity College, making it too dangerous for journalists to venture out. Newsprint from their Abbey Street store was requisitioned to construct barricades.[17] The offices of *The Freeman's Journal* were damaged by shell-fire, while the offices of the *Irish Independent* were occupied by the rebels.[18] The main telephone exchange and the overseas telegraph office near Westland Row remained under government control, effectively cutting off the city from the rest of the world. Although several issues of *The Irish Times* were produced during the week, press censorship was in force by Tuesday. By Wednesday night, the city of Dublin and the county had been placed under martial law.[19]

The first hint of the Rising to be received in Dunedin, half a world away (but eleven hours ahead because of its proximity to the international date line), was signalled by a brief paragraph that appeared on page 5 of the Tuesday, 25 April, issue of *The Otago Daily Times* and in many of the provincial papers circulated in both main islands of New Zealand.[20] Entitled 'Strange Vessel Seized in the West of Ireland', it was dated London, 23 April, with the advice that it had been received in Dunedin on 24 April at 7.10 p.m. from the 'Times and Sydney Sun (Wire) Services' in Australia. It reported that 'A boat containing a large quantity of arms and ammunition was seized on Friday morning by the police at Currabane Strand, County Kerry, Ireland. It was a stranger of unknown nationality, and the crew were arrested. It is not known where the boat came from, nor for whom the arms were intended.'[21] The same day, Tuesday, 25 April, the London *Times* advised its readers that the mystery boat was a tender for 'a German auxiliary and submarine' which had 'made the attempt sometime "between p.m. April 20 and p.m. April 21"' to land arms, ammunition, and five people, one of whom was Sir Roger Casement, who was now in custody.[22] A summary of the information, designated 'Official', duly appeared in *The Otago Daily Times* the following day.[23] Despite having its own office in London, *The Otago Daily Times* took most of its initial information from the wire services, and then from the London *Times* and from that paper's Dublin-based reporter.

But what distinguished initial reports in *The Otago Daily Times* from reports published in other New Zealand newspapers following the imposition of martial law and government censorship was the mix of speculation, ridicule, opinion, and 'fact' that appeared daily between Wednesday, 26 April, and Saturday, 29 April 1916, after which the speculation was reduced and the ridicule stopped. In part, this change was the result of the fragmented information that was transmitted by the wire services, and in part it reflected local prejudice. The people of Dunedin, as Mark Twain crisply observed during a three-day visit in 1895, 'are Scotch. They stopped here on their way from home to heaven – thinking they had arrived.'[24] Unlike other New Zealand cities, Dunedin, with its stone buildings and church steeples and a town plan that mirrored Edinburgh – complete with a 'Waters of the Leith' and an Octagon presided over by a large bronze statue of Robbie Burns – possessed, and still possesses, a rigidly maintained image of what it considers worthy, moral, decent, and respectable. Again, unlike the press in other New Zealand cities, *The*

Otago Daily Times in 1916 was, and still is, one of the few independently owned broadsheets in the region. Speculation and ridicule, revelatory of certain deeply held attitudes by some in the community, filled the gaps in reporting until the beginning of May, when it was learned that the rebels had surrendered.

REPORTING THE RISING: THE FIRST WEEK

The Wednesday, 26 April, issue of *The Otago Daily Times* merely granted the Rising a sub-heading, 'Sir Roger Casement Captured Gun Running to Ireland', and a brief paragraph at the foot of page 5 largely repeating what had been reported the day before. Slightly more space was given to 'The Recruiting Problem', topical because New Zealand was still debating whether or not to introduce conscription. While it was remarked that the 'reopening of Lord Derby's recruiting scheme' was a 'complete victory for the compulsionists [*sic*]', it was noted that 'the measure will not apply to Ireland, for the simple reason that Ireland refuses to have compulsion'. Apart from column-length reports on Anzac Day celebrations, a detailed account of an Empire celebration in London, and local service news, most readers would have agreed with 'Shrapnel', who observed in his 'Notes on the Cables', also on page 5, that there 'is nothing of startling importance from any one of the great centres of war'.[25]

It was in the Thursday, 27 April, issue of the paper that the tension emerged between reporting fact and opinion, engaging in speculation, or simply ridiculing what had apparently happened. There were three items. There was a half column on page 4 under the sub-heading 'Sedition in Ireland' which speculated from 'the few particulars' that were supplied by the morning's cable news about the scale of the conflict, the role of the secretary of state, and whether or not there was a 'direct connection' between 'the Casement raid and the rising in Dublin'. Acknowledging that 'it would be idle to seek to disguise that the incident ... has been of a serious character', the writer nevertheless assured readers that the situation was 'well in hand'.[26] However, the banner headlines of the two-column article on the next page, which announced in large print, 'Riots in Dublin. Outbreak of Sinn Fein. Post Office and Other Places

Seized. Soldiers called to the City. Situation under Control. Numerous Casualties', seemed to contradict the assurance that everything was 'well in hand'. Again, as with the previous day, much of the item was devoted to Sir Roger Casement and to possible links between the Kerry gun-running and the Dublin rebellion.[27] Casement also featured in the adjoining column, 'Notes on the Cables', though 'Shrapnel', feeling sufficient had been said, disparaged the Rising as an 'emeute'.[28] It was not representative of 'the desires and hopes of the Irish people as a whole', he asserted, 'and therefore need not be dealt with at length in this column'.[29]

Like the page 4 column of the previous day, an article entitled 'The Irish Rising' in the Friday issue of *The Otago Daily Times* reassured readers that 'the situation in Ireland is now said to be satisfactory'. It then went on to castigate 'Sinn Fein' for having been 'no less fatuous than treasonable' in a venture that could only be cherished by those who were blinded by 'insensate passion or deluded by unscrupulous leaders'. And like the page 5 article for the previous day, the page 5 article in the Friday issue appeared to contradict the claim that the situation was satisfactory by declaring in banner headlines, 'Rebellion in Ireland. Attracts much Notice. Ulster Volunteers Offered to Government. Martial Law Proclaimed. Street Fighting in Dublin. Buildings Still Held by Rebels. Spreading to the West. Germany's Big Juggle'. Again, Casement and gun-running featured prominently. There was some information about British Army successes and a preliminary report of casualties. Readers were assured that the banks were safe, the provinces were quiet, and that the government had sent additional troops to Ireland. The article concluded with messages of support for the Empire from the United Irish League in Melbourne and the New Zealand Hibernians of Auckland.[30]

By Saturday, *The Otago Daily Times* admitted that the Rising was more serious than it had initially thought. In an article entitled 'The Irish Insurgents', the writer protested that the

> policy of official secrecy, which is being observed respecting the rising in Ireland and which has not unreasonably evoked protests in the British press, renders it impossible to form a judgment as to the actual measure of the outbreak. The statement which Mr

Asquith made in the house of Commons on Thursday, however,
is less reassuring than that of the previous day, when the situation
was presented to be 'well in hand'. We now learn the position is still
serious, and that not only does street fighting continue in Dublin,
but the insurgent movement is spreading in the west.[31]

Yet, the writer of 'Passing Notes', printed on the same page, continued to
disparage what had happened, observing ironically 'that the time chosen
for the redemption of Ireland should be when England is alive with
troops and every mill a munitions factory, and that Sir Roger Casement
landing from his collapsible boat on the Kerry coast should run straight
into the arms of the police is, as an Irish Pleaceman X might say, the
hoight of absurdity'.[32]

However, the tone of *The Otago Daily Times* reports changed markedly
with the 1 May issue of the paper. What was becoming the standard page
4 article advised that 'the cablegrams this morning throw a good deal of
light upon the character of the rising … The evidence furnished from
the various sources tends to accentuate the previous impressions of the
seriousness of the whole affair.'[33] What had taken place was described as
'an amazingly shrewd blow', 'undoubtedly … well organised and carefully
planned'. The banner headlines of the customary page 5 article announced
that the 'Rising' had been 'Planned with Great Cunning and Remarkable
Secrecy' and that the 'Rebel Force [was] estimated at twelve thousand'.
What followed was a digest of cables and news reports from London,
Amsterdam, and Sydney which reinforced the two principal issues of
The Otago Daily Times' previous week's reporting: Casement and the
German plot. 'The whole world is impressed by the dramatic events in
Ireland,' the writer claimed. 'Practically the whole of the allied, American,
Dutch and Spanish press agree that Sir Roger Casement's escapade
and the subsequent rebellion were the outcome of German influence
and money.'[34] The 1 May issue also carried a report of the first protest
meeting organised by the loyal Irish of Dunedin. Although 'attendance
was small', it was said to be 'fully representative of Irish opinion in the
city'. Expressions of 'abhorrence and detestation' were buttressed by
unanimous support for a resolution that 'exceedingly' regretted 'the

criminal and insane action of the Sinn Feiners and their dupes' and called on the 'Home Government [to] stamp out the outbreak as quickly as possible'. 'History' would show, it claimed, that the leaders 'will be found to be men of no standing in their country'; that the 'whole thing' will 'appear but an insignificant though ugly speck' on Irish patriotism; and that to counter the 'disgrace', all fit young Irishman 'who have not yet enrolled' should 'offer their services at once to their country'.[35]

The 2 May issue of the paper differed from previous issues by illustrating the page 4 article with an image of a clock cradled by an open newspaper to suggest that what followed was the editorial. Under the heading 'The Enemy within the Gates', it advised readers that while 'the surrender of rebel leaders is unofficially announced', the Rising was as 'ill-starred as it was sinister' and that it was 'black treachery' 'involving German complicity' which 'cast the vilest stigma possible on the name of Ireland'. Sinn Féiners must be 'stamped out root and branch'. Again, for the first time since the Rising began, the London *Times* was quoted as having published a 'serious warning' of impending rebellion in Ireland, which the government should have heeded. What was now required was increased vigilance and well-publicised severity. The page 5 article, which now occupied five of the eight columns, with some print in bold, was again a digest of cables from London, Dublin, and New York, making it the most comprehensive report to date. It also contained a report of a Dublin Fusilier engagement with German troops at Hulluch, near Loos-en-Gohelle, France, in which one German officer and forty-seven infantry were killed, further proof that the 'soul' of Ireland had not been affected by the Rising. The Dublin Fusiliers were reported saying, 'wish Casement would get a touch of this!'[36]

The next day's issue, 3 May 1916, printed extracts from the proclamation for the first time, mentioned Pearse for the first time, and advised that it was the 'Provisional Republican Government' that had 'ordered' the 'unconditional surrender' under a banner headline that asserted, 'Business of City Ruined. Devastation of Sackville Street'. The issue of 4 May estimated the damage at £2,000,000 and commended General Maxwell for his 'ruthless and severe' handling of the rebellion. Given that he had permitted correspondents' requests to open a press

bureau the day before, the 4 May issue contained a detailed account
of Countess Markievicz's surrender, the fact that 450 rebels had been
transported to England, and a report from the Dublin correspondent
of the London *Times* that Dublin was a 'city of desolation' with 'dead
and dying' lying about the streets, and that the civilian population was
facing starvation. Despite the considerable loss of life and the enormous
amount of damage, the paper nevertheless cited *The Daily Chronicle*'s
'Plea against Vindictiveness' with its advice that the government should
study General Botha's policy on the suppression of the South African
Rising. 'Shrapnel's' 'Notes on the Cables' appeared for the first time since
29 April, and though the column continued to condemn the Rising, it
did so in more measured tones. Perhaps, 'Shrapnel' surmised, the Rising
was a 'blessing in disguise' because it might help 'to bring about in Britain
the enactment of a Compulsion Bill without any compromises', and it
might also 'lead to the installing of a smaller Cabinet' who would pay
'more attention to the war and less to politics'.[37]

By 5 May, *The Otago Daily Times* was proclaiming that 'trouble
in Ireland is practically at an end'. It reported that Pearce [*sic*], Clarke,
and MacDonagh had been shot, that courts martial had been held,
and that Casement had been prosecuted. The Dublin correspondent
of the London *Times* was quoted as saying that 'Ireland has been left
absolutely sound' and that the 'outbreak had segregated and exposed the
elements of disaffection', with the implication that it would be relatively
straightforward to excise such elements from the body politic. That life
was returning to its customary routine was reinforced by the space given
to the first report of a successful recruitment drive in Otago since news
of the Rising broke. 'Otago Quota Largely Exceeded. An Enthusiastic
Farewell', the paper announced, reporting that both the mayor and the
Reverend Clarence Eaton had praised the Irish recruits, convinced that
'some of them would, by their valorous deeds, take the shadow off the
name [of Ireland] and reinstate it in all its greatness.–(Applause.)'[38]
That 'Irishness' was now seen to have two aspects – one of rebellion and
republicanism and the other of loyalty and Empire – would characterise
the way *The Otago Daily Times* reported the Rising for some time.

DUNEDIN RECEIVES A HISTORY LESSON

As with the press in Ireland, Britain, and the rest of New Zealand, *The Otago Daily Times* continued to report the Rising at considerable length as details began to emerge throughout the months of May, June, and July. In general terms, the paper canvassed much the same material and in much the same way, given the complex nature of what had happened. Where it significantly differed was the space it allocated to plays affirming Irishness and patriotic Empire plays featuring Irish roles that were staged in Dunedin in the months before and after the Rising. To associate the Rising with the theatre might seem somewhat unusual, though the connection is one that was made not only by the participants but subsequently by a significant number of cultural historians.[39] Michael Collins' remark that the Rising 'had the air of a Greek tragedy about it' is frequently quoted,[40] as is W.B. Yeats' rhetorical enquiry in 'The Man and the Echo', first published in January 1939, 'did that play of mine send out / certain men the English shot?'[41] There is no doubt that the play *Cathleen ni Houlihan*, which was first staged on 2 April 1902 and advertised to be staged just prior to the Rising, did provide an impetus. But how much and in what context is still debated. P.J. Mathews has recently argued that the original occasion of the play had less to do with the folkloric and mythological associations of the Shan Van Vocht and more to do with Yeats' abhorrence of Royal visits and the recruiting that often followed in their train, such as Queen Victoria's 1900 visit and her mission to recruit for the Boer War.[42] While Mathews rightly draws attention to 'the speed with which cultural and intellectual energies and activities across the networks of activism transformed into military organisation in response to the Home Rule crisis of 1912, and in the context of a militarist zeitgeist sweeping Europe at the outbreak of the First World War',[43] it is also the case that there were other ways in which Yeats and Lady Gregory's play and the Rising were linked.

One such way, which did not have a parallel in the Irish or the British or the New Zealand press, particularly coming as early as it did, is offered in a 1,500-word opinion piece written by 'Constant Reader' and published on page 2 of *The Otago Daily Times* on 6 May 1916, just one week after the surrender had taken place and well before there was any clear idea of what had actually happened.[44] Unfortunately, the identity of 'Constant Reader', who wrote the Literary Column, is not known. It is also not known if they were a member of the Maoriland Irish Society and if they were emigrant Irish or New Zealand-born Irish.

By coincidence, Dorothea Spinney, the well-known English classical actress, had given dramatic readings of *Cathleen ni Houlihan* and Synge's *Riders to the Sea* in the Burns Hall in Dunedin in a season of Irish and Classical theatre three weeks before *Cathleen ni Houlihan* was staged in Dublin as a curtain-raiser to the Rising.[45] Reviewing the Dunedin performance of 4 April 1916, a local theatre critic had remarked that the play contained a 'patriotic theme' that 'might be appropriated to the present times as a slogan'.[46] On 6 May, 'Constant Reader', recalling the three-night season, observed that

> Not one person in the audience which [*sic*] listened to Miss Dorothea Spinney's sympathetic rendering of Mr. W. B. Yeats's dream play *Cathleen ni Hoolihan* [*sic*] had any idea that in the following weeks the meaning and the moral of the play would be sorrowfully and dramatically presented to the whole world. Yet this is what has actually happened.[47]

What is distinctive about the article is the way 'Constant Reader' is able to use the allusions to 1798 in Yeats' play to offer a historically informed defence of the Rising as a military operation and, by implication, a morally defensible bid for freedom, barely a week after it had taken place. Much of the article is devoted to a detailed account of the French forces that were assembled to invade Ireland in the late eighteenth century, first by Wolfe Tone in 1796, when a flotilla of seventeen line-of-battle ships, thirteen frigates, and thirteen sloops brought a force of 14,000 troops who were prevented from landing at Bantry Bay by a storm; and second in 1798 by a force of 11,000 troops under the command of General Humbert, who landed at Killala Bay in the west of Ireland and then proceeded to take a number of significant towns before being obliged to surrender to a superior force near Ballinamuck. While the rebel Irish were slaughtered, the severely reduced French force was given safe passage to Dublin so they could board ship for Calais.

Inserted into this detailed narrative are a number of telling observations that use the historical setting of *Cathleen ni Houlihan* to interpret the 1916 Rising. First, the writer points out that the alleged role played by the Germans in the Rising is not the first time a European nation had come to the aid of the Irish in their quest for independence. Second, they suggest that the support allegedly given by the Germans in 1916 pales into insignificance when compared with the support actually given by the French in 1798. Third, as with the French victory at Castlebar, known ironically as 'the Race of Castlebar', when 4,000 French troops put to rout 20,000 English troops, the week-long stand by several hundred rebels against an imperial army significantly better equipped implies that the Rising should be seen as a heroic engagement rather than an ignominious defeat. Fourth, details of the street fighting provided *The Otago Daily Times* writer with a means of charting the nationalists' appropriation of the city following the success of Sinn Féin in the 1908 Dublin Municipal Council elections, when the council began to rename significant streets, thus stripping them of their imperial connotations. 'Sackville Street', the writer points out, 'which suffered severely, was renamed O'Connell Street when a monument to Daniel O'Connell was unveiled in that magnificent thoroughfare some years ago'.[48] The sub-text here is Catholic Emancipation and the beginnings, via Butt and Parnell, of a long parliamentary campaign for a measure of independence. Fifth, there is the implication that the Irish rebels were as well organised as their imperial enemies and it was only poor planning and inadequate resources provided by a third party, the Germans, which contributed to their lack of success. In what might be characterised as a double-barrelled compliment, the writer declared, 'It is surely a splendid tribute to the vigilance of the British navy that Germany found it impossible to supplement *the carefully organised rising* of last week with an invasion of her troops [my emphasis]'.[49] Finally, the article concludes with a passage from Lionel Johnson's article 'Poetry and Patriotism', published in 1908 by the Yeats sisters' Cuala Press, which contended that it is the celebration of culture rather than the recourse to politics or militarism that will achieve true independence.[50]

A week later, on Empire Day, 13 May 1916, and in defence of militarism and the Empire, the Dunedin branch of the Overseas Club staged *John Bull's Empire Party* with repeat performances on 25 May and 5 June. Advertised as a 'patriotic and spectacular play' involving sixty specially trained young performers, its aim was to represent the unity of the British Empire by having John and Mary Bull entertain their Scottish, Irish, Welsh, Canadian, Indian, Australian, South African, and New Zealand 'progeny'.[51] Representing the dominions as offspring provoked 'Anglo-Celt' to write a letter to the editor to protest that representing Scotland, Ireland, and Wales as 'the progeny of England is so crudely absurd as to make one rub one's eyes in bewilderment'. It 'would have in no way', he went on to point out, 'detracted from the spectacular effect' to have John Bull appear with 'his brothers Sandy, Pat, and Taffy'.[52] Being depicted as descendants rather than family, it seems, was more of an issue for 'Anglo-Celt' than considering whether or not the 'progeny' should be so openly committed to a war in which so many lives were being lost.

The glories of defending the Empire were again celebrated on 26 July 1916 with a Dunedin season of the Irish-American Allen Doone's overtly patriotic *O'Leary V.C.*,[53] a five-act melodrama based on the exploits of No. 3556 Lance-Corporal Michael O'Leary, 1st Battalion, Irish Guards, who shot six of the enemy and took four prisoners when he ran ahead of his company as they were attacking a German machine-gun post.[54] O'Leary soon became a celebrity. Songs and poems were written in his honour, posters and cigarette cards featured his portrait, and a fund to support Irish widows and orphans was set up in his name.[55] The army was quick to capitalise. Newsreel footage of 11 July 1915 shows him arriving for a recruiting rally at Hyde Park, London, where over 60,000 people turned out to see him.[56] In October 1915, he was sent on a recruitment drive to Dublin and to the west of Ireland.[57] Doone's dramatic tribute did not receive the same accolades in Australasia as his exploits had received in the United Kingdom. A Wellington critic, for instance, dismissed the play as replete with 'sickly sentiment … feeble humour … melodramatic situations and unreality'.[58] Doone's two other patriotic plays, *The Bold Soger Boy* and *A Bit of Irish*, fared little better in Dunedin, although they were said to have proved popular with the overtly patriotic in the audience.[59]

INTERPRETING EVENTS, CONFRONTING STEREOTYPES

By October 1916, when the internationally renowned Irish play *Peg o' My Heart* opened for a six-night season in Dunedin, *The Otago Daily Times'* regular reporting of the Rising and its aftermath had come to frame 'Ireland' as a loyal majority demonstrably committed to defending the Empire, whose lives were periodically disrupted by a rebellious, republican minority hell bent on self-determination, with the Home Rule movement, led by John Redmond, caught uneasily between the two. The dilemma for the British government, as *The Otago Daily Times* explained in a brief article in its 7 August issue, was crisply illustrated by the following – '*The New York World* says: "Now that the Dublin rebels have been shot and Casement has been hanged, the conciliation of Ireland is further away than ever." *The New York Tribune* says: "Casement's guilt is such that no Government could pardon him without destroying the whole fabric of national duty."' But, as 1916 progressed, it became increasingly difficult for the British, and for that matter the New Zealand government, to issue calls to 'national duty', given the huge loss of life and the blatant military incompetence evidenced by Gallipoli, Verdun, and the Somme and increasingly, as reported by *The Otago Daily Times*, its treatment of Ireland before, during, and after the Rising.

The editorial policy of *The Otago Daily Times* in reporting these complex and competing issues was to juxtapose brief stories of commendable 'Irishness' with nuanced accounts of the plight of Ireland. So, when the rebel signatory to the 1916 Proclamation Thomas MacDonagh's *Thomas Campion and the Art of English Poetry* was published posthumously, it received the same attention in the newspaper as the literary work of Thomas Kettle, a barrister and former MP for East Tyrone, who was killed in action on the Western Front. Readers were told that Kettle's 'wife was the sister of Mr Skeffington who was shot during the Dublin riots'.[60] And when *The Otago Daily Times* reported Redmond's attempt to get a bill passed in the House of Commons attributing blame for the Rising to British government mismanagement, it also printed Asquith's admission that 'some stupidities had been repeated in Ireland at the beginning of the war, and many things had been done that offended the national sensibilities'.[61]

Using the production of an Irish play, or a play featuring Irish roles, in a Dunedin theatre as a means of interpreting Irish events – whether to reinforce or combat stereotypical images of 'Irishness' – has a distinguished history, reaching back at least to the Boucicault season of 1862 with its sell-out performances throughout New Zealand of *The Shaughraun* and *The Colleen Bawn*.[62] In the event, the most influential counter to 1916 Empire Day pageants and Allen Doone's patriotic vaudeville was offered by the hugely popular comedy of manners *Peg o' My Heart*. Written by Hartley Manners in 1912 when his leading lady, Laurette Taylor, bemoaned the lack of good parts for Irish women, it became an immediate hit, running for 604 nights in the Cort theatre in New York and for over two years at one of London's main theatres.[63] The play was brought to Australia and New Zealand after the Tait brothers saw Sara Allgood receive critical acclaim for her performance in the title role in New York.[64]

Eagerly anticipated, *Peg o' My Heart* opened at His Majesty's Theatre in Dunedin on 16 November 1916 for six nights and a matinee. Audiences were told to expect a light-hearted comedy of manners about 'a bright Irish girl from the wilds of the Western States of America', who must learn to be an 'English lady' by living with the upper-class Chichesters, haughty distant relatives who, unbeknown to her, had recently fallen on hard times.[65] Success, although she is not aware of it, will entitle her to inherit her father's fortune. Although 'Peg' is ignored, disparaged, and sometimes ridiculed, she 'eventually conquers everyone with her charm'.[66]

To what extent Dunedin audiences would have seen a November 1916 performance of the play as symbolic of British mismanagement of the Rising is open to speculation, although competing interpretations of the Rising were still very much in the news. In addition to items such as the rebuilding of Dublin, the resumption of Irish munitions production, the role of Germany, and the debates about conscription for Ireland, there was a first-hand account given to *The Otago Daily Times* by Lieutenant J.D. Campbell, who arrived in Dunedin on the *Willochra* at the end of September 1916. Campbell had been convalescing in Galway when the Rising broke out and had immediately gone to Dublin, 'where he took part in the fighting, and was twice wounded during the attack on the Four Corners [*sic*]'.[67] German attempts to use Irish-America to influence American parties prior to the Presidential election generated considerable comment in the newspaper,[68] as did a speech Redmond gave in Waterford, where he declared that

> Never again would he enter into negotiations on the Irish question. Any proposal for settlement must be submitted to a convention of representatives of all Ireland. The rebellion was an act of insanity, and had altered the whole political conditions. Ireland's magnificent response to the war had earned the gratitude of the whole Empire, and just at that moment the Dublin rising took place. The real responsibility rested with the British Government, which had been marked by colossal ineptitude and stupidity in its attitude to Ireland since the war commenced.[69]

What merits emphasis are the ways in which a Dunedin and subsequently a New Zealand audience – both the 1916 and 1918 national tours of *Peg o' My Heart* sold out – were invited to identify with an Irishness that was not cowed by English class consciousness or the British establishment. 'Peg' is lauded for being justifiably irritated by upper-class pretension, and for deploying a highly desirable strategy for coping with the power structures of colonial life. As one critic presciently remarked of the 1916 New Zealand season, 'The author has hit on an ingenious theme when he makes the members of one of the "real old families" the butt of an attractive but unpolished Irish girl's witticisms. All the English-speaking world dully resents the airs and affectations of a certain silly section of the upper classes.'[70]

W.B. Yeats was fond of quoting Victor Hugo's dictum that in the theatre the mob becomes a people.[71] It does so because the powerfully imagined world of the stage offers alternatives to what audiences encounter in everyday life. What the ideological rivalry of Irish play versus Empire play offered Dunedin, and for that matter New Zealand, immediately before and after the Rising, were contrasting images of Irishness: the one stereotypically subservient to Empire, the other a poised self-sufficiency that could marshal elegant strategies for reframing contested images of identity.

CHAPTER 5

Harry Holland, *The Maoriland Worker*, and the Easter Rising

JIM McALOON

(*Victoria University of Wellington*)

T he New Zealand Labour Party was established two and a half months after the Easter Rising. Most accounts of the party's early years have noted its support for Irish self-determination. New Zealand liberals and labour movement leaders had long supported Home Rule – internal self-government by an Irish parliament, subordinate to Westminster. The Labour Party conference in 1919, however, resolved in favour of 'self-determination for Ireland, Egypt, India, and all subject peoples, self-determination meaning the right of the people to determine by the vote of the adult population their own form of government'.[1] This support was based as much on anti-imperialist principle as on the electoral advantage that party leaders perceived in courting Catholic voters, most of whom at that time were of Irish birth or descent, and many of whom were working class or lower middle class. Most accounts have also noted the attention that the radical labour newspaper *The Maoriland Worker*, and its editor Harry Holland, paid to Irish self-determination.

The Maoriland Worker was established as the Shearers' Union newspaper in 1910, and in 1911 it was taken over by the radical Federation of Labour. The Red Federation, as it was popularly known, was based on miners, watersiders, labourers, and other 'unskilled' unions, and espoused a generally syndicalist approach to industrial organisation. In political terms, the federation and its newspaper were characterised by a preference for propaganda and suspicion of parliamentary politics and incremental reform. In 1913, many in the federation leadership modified their suspicion of parliamentary politics and supported a unity programme which created a new United Federation of Labour and a new Social Democratic Party (SDP). In July 1916, the SDP merged with some other labour organisations and formed the New Zealand Labour Party. The masthead of *The Maoriland Worker* described the paper as the party's official newspaper.

Harry Holland became editor in April 1913 and, except for a break between April and August 1914 when he was imprisoned for sedition, remained editor until he was elected to parliament in 1918. Holland had only been in New Zealand since May 1912; in his native Australia, he had trained as a printer and worked mainly as a journalist and editor for socialist newspapers. From 1919 until his death in 1933, he was the Labour Party's parliamentary leader. He was formidably well read in the way that many self-educated labour activists of the day were. The only full-length biography of Holland was published in 1964; the author, Patrick O'Farrell, criticised Holland for a dogmatic and unrealistic Marxism, which, when combined with an austere public image, made him an electoral liability.[2]

This view of Holland can be debated.[3] Certainly, Holland was committed to socialism and anti-imperialism; he included Ireland among the victims of imperialism.[4] Like O'Farrell, Barry Gustafson emphasised the political benefit of what was undoubtedly a principled position; Labour's identification with Irish nationalism appealed to Catholic voters of Irish descent.[5] Richard Davis made similar suggestions, although he also implied that Catholic workers of Irish birth or (more usually) descent were coming to support Labour because they were workers.[6] The Labour Party's position on Irish self-determination emerged over many months, in the context of the rise of Sinn Féin and the developing War of Independence. In the months after the Rising and its suppression, however, Ireland's future was, to say the least, unclear. New Zealand supporters of Irish independence, including Holland, could not foretell the future. This chapter explores Holland's efforts in the year after Easter 1916 to make sense of the Rising, for himself as much as for readers of *The Maoriland Worker*.

THE MAORILAND WORKER AND IRELAND: DUBLIN LOCKOUT TO EASTER RISING, 1913–16

Prior to the Easter Rising, Ireland featured only occasionally, and usually briefly, in *The Worker*'s columns, although the major industrial conflict in Dublin in 1913–14 was discussed at some length. In the months before the Rising though, *The Worker*'s attention was on more local concerns, in particular the threat that the New Zealand government would impose conscription for overseas service, the proper attitude of labour to conscription, and the efforts to unify Labour's political forces.[7]

Relatively little information was available in the days following the Rising. *The Worker*, like other New Zealand newspapers, was at a disadvantage not only because of prevailing censorship but also because of its distance from events.[8] *The Worker*'s early reporting placed considerable emphasis on Connolly's execution and hardly mentioned the others, including Patrick Pearse, who had been the president of the provisional government. Connolly had been badly wounded in the fighting and, notoriously, was tied to a chair to be shot when already mortally ill. *The Worker* quoted *The Manchester Guardian* on the pointlessness of shooting Connolly and referred to 'horror in the world of Labour, and the almost universal protest that has arisen in working class ranks at the shooting of the Irish leaders, [which] will be intensified a thousandfold by the killing of James Connolly'.[9] Only in July did the paper print Pearse's last letter to his mother. The others whose deaths were discussed at length were the socialist and pacifist Francis Sheehy Skeffington, who had not taken part in the Rising and was murdered by British troops while trying to prevent looting, and Roger Casement, who had organised German arms for the rebels and was hanged for treason in August.[10]

Earlier, *The Worker* had discussed the 1913–14 Dublin Lockout in terms that problematised nationalism. One workers' meeting had been banned as seditious; the Irish Transport and General Workers' Union leader Jim Larkin publicly burnt the notice of proscription, and troops charged the gathering. *The Worker* described Ireland as the latest 'scene of British ruling class wickedness'. The paper expected that the repression to which the workers and their supporters were subjected

will go far in the direction of bringing the Irish people to a
knowledge of the fact that Irish troubles are economic more than
national, and that their enemies are not so much national enemies as
class enemies. Ireland's working-class tears of blood will bedew the
industrial and political soil, and the result will be a great working-
class solidarity that will rise triumphant and invincible, with 'Ireland
for the workers' written on its every banner.[11]

Holland thought Home Rule was inevitable but would only be a stage
in emancipation.

Hitherto Ireland's battle has been conducted along national lines –
Ireland's foe was erroneously supposed to be a national foe. Today
the great working-class mind is seeing what Emmet in the shadow
of the scaffold saw dimly: what Michael Davitt – grandest and best
of all Ireland's modern fighters for her freedom – saw more clearly
than any other Irishman of his day. They are recognising that their
war is a class war, with an economic foundation.[12]

In 1913, Holland dwelt on the iniquity of Edward Carson, the
prominent unionist politician, and the Ulster Volunteers being allowed
to get away with 'preaching rebellion … and entering into a multiplicity
of conspiracies for the purpose of conducting an armed revolt against
a constitutional change that would give to the people of Ireland a
Parliament of their own, and the Government in no way intervened'. The
Ulster Volunteers had been established in 1912 to prevent Home Rule
and had smuggled in thousands of weapons from Germany, without
legal consequences. Contrasting this with the treatment of the Dublin
workers, Holland observed that no 'more direct proof than this of the
class war' was needed. But, although Home Rule was, as he thought,
inevitable, when it was won, the mystifications of nationalism would
disappear: '… the Irish master class will – as a class – demonstrate
by its law-making and its administration, as well as by its industrial
tyranny, that its interests and its methods are identical with … [those]
of the English master class'.[13] Nationalism was again problematised in
a brief notice of James Connolly's 1915 pamphlet, *The Reconquest of*

Ireland (which readers were invited to purchase for ninepence from the Auckland Social Democratic Party). A short passage was quoted to the effect that as Labour became more powerful in Ireland, so would follow 'the enthronement of the Irish nation as the supreme ruler and owner of itself and all things necessary to its people – supreme alike against the foreigner and the native usurping ownership, and the power dangerous to freedom that goes with ownership'.[14] Nationalist victory, then, would intensify the class struggle.

The Worker's early reactions to the Rising – apart from its 'horror' at Connolly's execution – were ambivalent. The paper's first substantial piece on the Rising appeared on 3 May and was written, not by Holland, but by the Wellington lawyer and radical Liberal Patrick O'Regan. Born on the South Island's West Coast from Clonakilty ancestors, O'Regan had long supported Home Rule and regretted that Ireland's 'soil is once more stained with bloodshed'. Drawing on the English radical J.A. Hobson, O'Regan thought it 'a grievous disappointment to us to learn that in this age of ordered and constitutional progress, recourse should have been had to armed rebellion'. But he was in no doubt where the blame lay: in a combination of 'German intrigue' and the near-treasonous undertakings of Carson and the Ulster Volunteers. O'Regan thought that Carson, with the active support of the Conservative Party leadership and the connivance of the Asquith Liberal government, had dashed the 'hopeful anticipation' that had prevailed following the 1906 election and, in turn, incited 'younger and more daring men' on the nationalist side while diminishing Redmond's influence. The Ulster Volunteers had been the first to threaten armed force against the state; in the Curragh 'Mutiny' of March 1914, some sixty British Army officers had resigned rather than accept orders to implement Home Rule.[15] Strictly speaking, this was not a mutiny, as the officers had not received any orders to act against the Volunteers and implement Home Rule, but the episode quickly became part of nationalist mythology.

A fortnight later, Holland wrote a longer article entitled 'Ireland's Darkest Hour'. He was surprisingly tentative, agreeing with *The Australian Worker*'s observation that 'We are sorry for the Sinn Feiners. We do not loathe them. We pity them.' Part of the problem was that the general situation of 'war, with its vitiated moral atmosphere ... the savage psychology that war-time developes [*sic*]', created the climate in which the rebels staged the Rising.[16] Holland's article, which owed a good deal to the views expressed in *The Australian Worker*, repeated the line that Carson and his colleagues had made the decisive shift to physical force and, more, had conspired with Germany to procure arms in 1914. That 'the Government quietly looked on and allowed Carson to proceed with his work of treason must have had its effect on the Home Rulers, the Sinn Feiners, and the workingmen'. Holland extensively dwelt on this argument: 'arch-conspirator Carson walks abroad insolent and free, apparently protected by powerful class interests, while the other rebels are courtmartialled [*sic*] and shot'. Had Carson and his associates been dealt with firmly before the war, 'Dublin would not be a shattered city, and the soil of Erin would not have been drenched with the blood of her bravest sons, nor yet with the blood of the women and children who were shot down in the battle'. Indeed, while Holland emphasised his opposition to the death penalty, he averred that if it was going to be imposed, 'Carson should have been the first man placed in front of a firing squad'.[17]

Holland then went on to observe that Connolly's involvement meant the Rising 'had a deep working class significance', because Connolly was 'a clear-thinking Socialist of the Marxian school, with a long, loyal and brilliant record in the Irish working-class movement'. Holland was confident that whatever the nature of the 'Sinn Fein' connection with Germany, 'James Connolly would never have been a party to any arrangement that would end in exchanging the British for the Prussian yoke. His ideal was ever the World's Socialist Republic, which is the ideal of every thinker in the Labour movement.' Holland repeated Connolly's line that 'the Home Rule the Irish workers want' would not bring utopia, but, while intensifying class conflict without the mystifications of nationalism, Home Rule 'would give the Irish people the right and power to develop according to their own genius'. While revolution 'may be madness [or] futility', rebellion, Holland repeated, was an inevitable consequence of colonial subjection.[18]

'HISTORIC FOUNDATIONS OF THE IRISH REBELLION': A SERIES, 1916–17

It was in this frame of mind, then, that Holland began his long series on the 'Historic Foundations of the Irish Rebellion'. Why did Holland devote so much time and space to explaining the 'Historic Foundations'? The series extended over forty-eight instalments in the weekly newspaper. In an important study of Holland's attitude to New Zealand's colonial rule in Samoa, Nicholas Hoare has shown that Holland's anti-imperialism, although sometimes sentimentally idealising subject peoples, nevertheless was fundamental to his politics. And the Irish were demonstrably, in Holland's view, a subject people.[19]

Richard Davis was, I think, right to suggest that Connolly's participation legitimised the Rising for Holland and those of like mind. Was part of the reason for Holland devoting so much space to the project that he wanted to explain (to himself, as well as to his readers) why Connolly, a renowned Marxist thinker, had thrown in his lot with a nationalist struggle, led, as Marxists might say, by bourgeois nationalists? Did Holland perhaps hope that the Irish struggle might reverberate beyond Ireland? Lenin had written in July 1916 – in a text that Holland would not, of course, have seen – that a 'blow delivered against the power of the English imperialist bourgeoisie by a rebellion in Ireland is a hundred times more significant politically than a blow of equal force delivered in Asia or in Africa.'[20]

The similarities between Connolly and Holland also bear noting. They were almost exactly the same age (Connolly was five days older); both had left school young; both had lived lives of considerable hardship; and both were self-educated to an extraordinary degree. Both, of course, were propagandists of some skill. Therefore, as well as suggesting that Connolly's participation legitimised the Rising for Holland, perhaps we could see Holland's lengthy discussion of Irish history less as an attempt to facilitate a labour alliance with New Zealand's supporters of Irish nationalism and more as an engagement with – perhaps a homage to – James Connolly and his analysis of Irish history.

Holland's series drew explicitly on Connolly's writing, especially on *Labour in Irish History*, and on a much larger, established canon of nationalist historical writing. Holland often quoted lengthy passages from his sources, sometimes clearly acknowledged, sometimes not.[21] Much of this material, as Kevin Molloy has observed, would have been familiar to some New Zealand readers, as it was often recycled by publications like Dunedin's Catholic newspaper *The New Zealand Tablet*. In the mid-1880s, the canon included histories of Ireland by D'Arcy McGee, A.M. Sullivan, Justin McCarthy, and Charles Gavan Duffy, among others.[22] Holland drew on Sullivan, McCarthy, and Duffy as well as later works by T.P. O'Connor (*The Parnell Movement*) and J.M. Davidson (*The Book of Erin*).

Holland also drew extensively, especially for earlier instalments, on the historical writing of Alice Stopford Green (1847–1929). Green was the daughter of a Church of Ireland rector from Meath, and the widow of John Green, an English cleric and historian who emphasised the history of the common people. When her husband died in 1883, leaving her very well off, she became increasingly interested in Irish history and associated with progressive anti-imperialists and nationalists. She was a friend of Casement and Eoin MacNeill, the Gaelic scholar and chief of staff of the Irish Volunteers. Green was a Home Ruler, a constitutional nationalist. She was, however, an active supporter of the Irish Volunteers and contributed a considerable sum of money (some say the royalties from her husband's *A Short History of the English People*) towards the purchase of the rifles landed at Howth in July 1914. Yet she supported the call by the Irish Parliamentary Party leader John Redmond to back the war effort and did not support the Easter Rising.[23]

Green published nationalist histories in 1908 and 1911: *The Making of Ireland and Her Undoing* and *Irish Nationality*, respectively. James Connolly regarded the former as 'the only contribution to Irish history we know of which conforms to the methods of modern historical science'.[24] The nationalist historiography of Green and Connolly can be easily faulted, of course, for its simplistic dichotomies and its romanticisation of ancient Irish society.[25] This essay is concerned with how Holland understood Irish history, and there is neither need nor space to engage in a detailed critique of his views in the light of modern historical scholarship.

Holland began his series on 24 May, a month after the Rising. Its tone was romanticised, sometimes histrionic. Ireland was a martyred nation: '... through long centuries the bloody sweat of Ireland's national crucifixion has rained from her collective brow'. The first five instalments largely distilled or reproduced Alice Green's *Irish Nationality*. In this account, the lost utopia, immune to both Roman and barbarian invasions, was a decentralised tribal society; in Green's words, 'a true democracy' with 'a literary language of great richness and of the utmost musical beauty' where teachers and poets were honoured and learning thrived (even with, as both Green and Holland admitted, a certain propensity to feuding and border raiding).[26] The Irish took learning and literacy to Britain and to continental Europe and, in Green's words, '[p]robably in the seventh and eighth centuries no one in western Europe spoke Greek who was not Irish or taught by an Irishman'. The Irish were even able to maintain this decentralised society against the Vikings, who, while conquering most of England, were only able to establish enclaves in Ireland and were in time absorbed.[27]

The Normans, likewise, although seeking to conquer, were absorbed into Gaelic Ireland. As Holland put it, the incomers 'found that the English theory of Irish barbarism had no foundation in fact' and anyway 'the new settlers could not live without coming to terms with the "conquered" people'. Green went into considerable detail about a fourteenth-century golden age, Holland quoting her on 'the rich national civilisation which the Irish genius had built up, strong in its courageous democracy, in its broad sympathies, in its widespread culture, in its freedom, and in its humanities'.[28] Henry VIII destroyed this utopia, and by the 1620s, in Green's words, 'all the great leaders, Anglo-Irish and Irish, had disappeared, the people had been half exterminated, alien and hostile planters set in their place, tribal tenure obliterated, every trace of Irish law swept clean from the Irish statute-book, and an English form of state government effectively established'.[29]

Matters only got worse in the seventeenth century. As Holland quoted Green,

> every vestige of their tradition was doomed – their religion was
> forbidden ... their schools were scattered, their learned men hunted

down, their books burned; native industries were abolished; the
inauguration chairs of their chiefs were broken in pieces, and the
law of the race torn up, codes of inheritance, of land tenure.

The Irish people, however, said Holland, 'clung to their language, their
poetry, their history and their law', encouraged by 'bards' trained in
clandestine schools in the forests.[30]

At this point, in the fifth instalment, James Connolly's *Labour in Irish
History* reinforces Green. (It bears emphasising that Connolly himself
shared Green's interpretation of the pre-Tudor utopia.)[31] Connolly dated
the end of the clan system to Cromwell's invasion in 1649, at which
point 'the social aspect of the Irish struggle then sank out of sight, and
its place was usurped by the mere political expressions of the fight for
freedom'.[32] These are Connolly's unacknowledged words; he maintained
that 'capitalist-landlordism' would inevitably have replaced communal
ownership, but because it was imposed from outside, 'Irish patriotic
movements fell entirely into the hands of the middle class', which
was able to subsume class conflict into nationalism and to obscure the
truth that middle-class nationalism had little to offer the Irish working
class.[33] Holland also quoted from a Socialist Party of Ireland pamphlet
by Thomas Brady, *The Historical Basis of Socialism in Ireland* (1905),
to point out that after 1689 there was increasingly a conflict between
the 'exploiting British middle class and the would-be exploiting Irish
middle class'.[34] The war of 1688–91 was a war between rival factions of
the propertied, and neither the army of William of Orange nor that of
James II, as Connolly noted, 'had the slightest claim to be considered
as a patriot army combating for the freedom of the Irish race'.[35] Holland
summarised Connolly's argument that 'once the question of political
supremacy had been settled by the Williamite Conquest, a relentless
economic slavery developed, and under its yoke both Catholics and
Protestants suffered a common oppression, and the subject class – the
Irish tenantry – endured inconceivably greater miseries even than those
inflicted by the Penal Law'.[36] Here, Holland summarised the view of J.R.
Green, Alice Green's late husband, in his *A Short History of the English
People*: English policy prevented Ireland from exporting anything but
raw wool. Only with food shortages after 1740 did England open the

door to Irish food exports, but that had the consequence of small tenants being displaced in favour of cattle ranching.[37]

In the mid-eighteenth century, agrarian unrest prompted the emergence of secret societies like the Whiteboys; in discussing this, Holland largely relied on Connolly, concluding that 'Protestant and Catholic proprietors united to protect their common interests'.[38] For Connolly too, Grattan's parliament – the significant degree of autonomy enjoyed by the Irish parliament between 1782 and 1800 – was simply a Protestant bourgeois tool. Holland was ambivalent on this point, for he referred extensively to Alice Stopford Green, who, of course, thoroughly approved of it, arguing that an Irish parliament, however elite, would have to take notice of the condition of Ireland.[39] In the end though, Holland followed Connolly's depiction of the parliament as consisting entirely of landlords and of Henry Grattan himself, who had been a leading figure in the agitation for autonomy, as one of a long line of elite nationalists who betrayed the common people. At the opening of parliament in April 1782, the Irish Volunteer militias turned out in force to demand autonomy. London made significant concessions, including free trade, which was to the advantage of established Irish farmers and manufacturers. Holland quoted Connolly's observation that

> at that moment an Irish Republic could have been won as surely as Free Trade. But when the rank and file of the Volunteers proceeded to outline their demands for the removal of their remaining political grievances – to demand popular representation in Parliament – all their leaders deserted. They had elected aristocrats, glib-tongued lawyers and professional patriots to be their officers, and all higher ranks betrayed them in their hour of need.

When a convention met to discuss 'popular representation', Grattan himself dismissed them as a 'rabble'.[40] Connolly and Holland drew the lesson that the workers could not rely on bourgeois reformers. Holland quoted Connolly's summary: '[t]he working men fought, the capitalists sold out, and the lawyers bluffed.' For Holland, the 'Irish Volunteers passed out – the revolutionary working men in the ranks betrayed by the more class-conscious capitalist elements functioning as officers and leaders'.[41] Conversely, proletarian virtue was to the fore in Robert Emmet's intended insurrection; that those involved were mostly workers, as Holland quoted Connolly, was one reason why there were no traitors in the ranks. (Someone, however, must have told the authorities where they could find the fugitive Emmet after the rebellion collapsed.)[42]

Holland dealt with the rebellion of 1798 and the 1801 Act of Union in relatively short order. For the 1798 Rebellion, he mostly relied on *An Outline of Irish History* (1883) by Justin McCarthy Jr, the Irish Parliamentary Party MP, but Holland included Alice Stopford Green's observation that 'suppression of the rebellion burned into the Irish heart the belief that the English government was their implacable enemy, that the law was their oppressor, and Englishmen the haters of their race'.[43] Quickly handling the Act of Union, Holland quoted Green's description of it as a disgrace: 'the most corrupt parliament ever created by a government: it was said that only seven of the majority were unbribed'; and the terse description of the English historian J.A. Froude: 'dirty work'.[44]

Holland's discussion of hardship and famine after the Union drew extensively on *An Impeached Nation* (1909) by Henry Cleary, the Roman Catholic bishop of Auckland. Cleary espoused Home Rule rather than independence; where Cleary hoped for Irish prosperity within the United Kingdom, Holland argued for independence and socialism.[45] Holland described the Owenite experiments at Ralahine, County Clare, in the early 1830s, as a complete success in Connolly's utopian terms and as demonstrating the viability of socialism;

> In the most crime-ridden county in Ireland this partial experiment in Socialism abolished crime; where the fiercest fight for religious domination had been fought it brought the mildest tolerance; where drunkenness had fed fuel to the darkest passions it established sobriety and gentleness; where poverty and destitution had engendered brutality, midnight marauding, and a contempt for all social bonds, it enthroned security, peace and reverence for justice, and it did this solely by virtue of the influence of the new social conception attendant upon the institution of common property bringing a common interest to all.[46]

Catholic Emancipation in 1829 allowed Roman Catholic men who met the property qualification to sit in parliament and opened many other public offices to them. As Holland put it, emancipation benefited the 'Catholic middle, professional and landed class, [who] … had the way opened to them for all the snug berths in the disposal of the Government'. This, again, was Connolly's analysis, and Holland also relied on Connolly for the observation that, while Daniel O'Connell won his parliamentary seat on the votes of forty-shilling tenants, with emancipation the bar was raised to ten pounds, which excluded thousands of marginal tenants, Catholic and Protestant alike, from the franchise. Worse, as these tenants now had no vote, so Connolly said, landlords lost the ability to direct the votes of those tenants, and consequently 'began the wholesale eviction of their tenantry and the conversion of the arable lands into grazing farms'. Sold out, again, by the middle class, the agrarian poor resorted to futile expressions of resistance – destroying crops, filling in ditches, assaulting and killing landlords and their agents.[47]

Holland's account of the Young Ireland cultural revival and the Famine years drew on several works besides Connolly and Green. He relied on *Four Years of Irish History* (1883) by Charles Gavan Duffy, the Irish land reformer and Victorian premier, and *The Book of Erin* (1888) by J. Morrison Davidson, an Aberdeenshire-born radical lawyer and journalist, ethical socialist, and exponent of 'home rule all round' – that is, not only for Ireland but for Scotland and Wales.[48] For much of the official material he quoted, Holland relied on *The Parnell Movement* (1886) by Thomas Power O'Connor, a journalist and Irish Party MP for Galway and then, from 1885, for a Liverpool seat.[49] Holland's account emphasised the plentiful food that was available but that was exported. Quoting Connolly, he observed that 'had Socialist principles been applied to Ireland in those days not one person need have died of hunger, and not one cent of charity need have been subscribed to leave a smirch upon the Irish name'.[50]

Unsurprisingly, famine was accompanied by agrarian protest. Here, Holland tended to elide Young Ireland, which emphasised cultural revival from the early 1840s, the more radical Irish Confederation, and unstructured agrarian protest. His account drew on John Mitchel's *The*

Last Conquest of Ireland – Perhaps as well as Michael Davitt's *Fall of Feudalism in Ireland*, alongside Connolly and A.M. Sullivan. Holland repeated Connolly's argument that, again, bourgeois nationalists sold out the movement and 'strove by every means in their power to disassociate the cause of Ireland from the cause of democracy'. Holland emphasised Connolly's view that workers and peasants were 'clamouring' for leadership, of which they got none, for 'everything had to be done in a "respectable" manner ... no mere proletarian insurrection, and no interference with the rights of property'.[51]

Fenianism, in turn, Holland wrote, 'was the inevitable revolutionary climax of the economic and political oppression of that day. Given similar conditions in any community, similar results would be produced. In whatever country the constitutional right to change an intolerable environment has been denied the people, physical force methods have been employed.' Holland drew on O'Connor's *The Parnell Movement* for the general narrative of Fenianism and the Manchester Martyrs of 1867.[52] Holland described one Fenian, Michael Davitt, as the 'greatest Irishman of the Nineteenth Century – the man who above all others understood the economic foundation of Ireland's woes, the underlying causes of her class antagonisms and class struggles'. In this, he departed from Connolly, for Connolly, in reviewing Sheehy Skeffington's biography of Davitt, complained that Davitt, in order to stay onside with the Catholic clergy, sold out Charles Stewart Parnell when the latter's career was destroyed by the O'Shea divorce case.[53]

Holland treated his readers over five issues to a long description of Davitt's life, including, with little detail spared, an account of his lengthy imprisonment, drawn largely from Francis Sheehy Skeffington's 1907 biography. Interestingly, Holland did not discuss Davitt's tour of New Zealand in 1895, in which Davitt had emphasised that the Home Rule Ireland sought was no more than the self-governing prosperity which New Zealand enjoyed.[54] On the Land League of the 1870s and early 1880s, Holland relied on O'Connor and argued that the league was a proletarian movement and was – inevitably – sold out by the landed gentleman Parnell. In 1881, the league issued a No Rent manifesto, calling on tenants to refuse to pay rent until 'constitutional rights' were restored. Parnell and Davitt were among the leaders of the league who signed the manifesto from prison. Parnell subsequently negotiated with the government and secured a commitment to land reform. Radicals excoriated him. Sheehy Skeffington expressed it more bluntly than Holland, although Holland would have agreed:

> Parnell virtually abandoned the whole of the advantages gained by the Land League at the very moment when Gladstone was casting about for a scheme of pacifying Ireland by the concession of some form of self-government. Davitt and the movement Davitt had created had put all the cards into his hands; and Parnell had failed to play them.[55]

At that point – it was now February 1917 – Holland drew the 'historical' discussion to a close by reciting a long list of failures and refusals by the British parliament, over the nineteenth century, to grant Ireland justice. The list was largely taken from Davitt's *Fall of Feudalism in Ireland*, with some material from Bishop Cleary.[56] The lesson Holland drew from 'the terrible story of Ireland's 700 centuries [*sic*] of servitude' was

> that back of all of Ireland's desperate woes – back of the bloodstains that lie on every page of her history, back of her ruined and shattered homes, her millions of famine-stricken graves, her stricken sons and daughters in exile in many distant lands – is the question of the ownership and control of the land, the primary source of wealth production.[57]

That Holland emphasised radical land reform, following Davitt, was slightly curious. Here, Holland placed less emphasis on the concerns of urban workers in the industrial northeast and in Dublin. In the final passages of his 1915 pamphlet *The Reconquest of Ireland*, Connolly had looked to unity between rural and urban workers as the key to radical political and social change.

In the final instalments, Holland discussed poverty and child mortality, low wages, and bad working conditions. This more current material drew on Connolly's *Reconquest* and on Arnold Wright's discussion of the 1913 Dublin Lockout, *Disturbed Dublin*.[58] Coming to the Rising itself, Holland repeated his earlier line that Carson and his Tory colleague, the attorney general F.E. Smith, were 'held by nearly every writer', of whatever position, to have 'carried a heavy responsibility for the immediate outburst of the 1916 rebellion'. Holland had already obtained a published account, Mary Louisa Hamilton Norway's *The Sinn Fein Rebellion as I Saw It*.[59] She was no fan of the Rising; indeed, her husband was the manager of the GPO (their younger son would become the novelist Nevil Shute). Yet Holland quoted her, with some relish, on the Asquith government 'pandering to Sir Edward Carson's fanaticism ... In Ulster the wind was sown, and, my God! we have reaped the whirlwind.'[60] Holland devoted another three instalments to a narrative of the Rising and to the executions and terms of imprisonment handed down.[61]

Holland's account is notable for what it omitted. He said nothing about Eoin MacNeill's opposition to the Rising. He minimised the overwhelming support within the Irish Volunteers in 1914 for Redmond's commitment to the war effort and the subsequent enlistment of many thousands of Irishmen. Holland asserted that 'by the early part of 1916 the Irish Volunteers [that is, the small anti-war minority] are said to have formed the only live organisation in the country'.[62] Far more significant, for Holland, was the responsibility of Carson and the Ulster Volunteers for reintroducing armed revolt into the equation and, as he implied, the unwillingness of the Liberal government to challenge the Conservative Party. Thus was 'the promise of Home Rule shattered, rebels and traitors allowed to flaunt their treason'.[63]

HOLLAND AND THE LESSONS OF HISTORY

What lessons, then, did Holland draw from his long historical exposition? They were, of course, much influenced by Connolly:

> Home Rule will not solve Ireland's problems. Capitalism must develop there as elsewhere; the period of the class struggle must be passed through there as in all other countries. But Home Rule – if it

is Home Rule based on universal adult suffrage, and not a caricature – will make it possible for the Irish people to develop according to their own genius and peacefully work out their own economic salvation.[64]

As Holland had argued a year earlier, the Rising was the inevitable consequence of blocking constitutional approaches. Whether the Home Rule legislation of 1914 – which, problematically for nationalists, excluded all Ulster – could have proceeded after the war cannot be known. For Holland, though, the Rising

> was the inevitable product of an accumulation of wrongs born of long centuries of economic exploitation and political and economic oppression and repression. It was just one more exemplification of the fact that if the people are denied the right to advance by intellectual methods along political highways, they will still seek to advance and the methods they employ will be whatever are to hand.[65]

This was no glorification of blood sacrifice. Whatever the views of those who fought in the Rising, Pearse had at times written of national purification by blood, and these observations and the fate of the Rising's leaders were easily absorbed into a popular Catholic piety which emphasised martyrdom. Holland also eschewed the demonisation of the English, *as English*, in which Pearse and some other nationalists sometimes indulged. For Holland, as for Connolly, the real enemy was the class enemy.[66] The Irish Republic, proclaimed at Easter, Holland wrote,

> went out in a fury of fire and blood, even as the Paris Commune went out in [18]71 … Over and above everything it was a working-class revolt – side by side with Ireland's educationists, her thinkers and poets, stood the greatest, the truest and best of her Labor men.[67]

This was, again, to imply that Connolly and his Citizen Army had legitimised the Rising for socialists in seeking to lead the nationalist movement in order to influence its direction.[68]

Holland could not bring himself to see that the workers' republic for which Connolly hoped was not foreordained. Human progress was inevitable; he wrote,

> and when the blood mists have lifted from Europe, and the Star of Peace once more illumines the world, Ireland is destined by all the laws that govern the Universe to rise rejuvenated from the ashes of her agony and take her place among the self-governing nations in a United States of Europe, the forerunner of the World's Socialist Republic, which, writing War and Militarism out of its constitution, shall bring to earth that era of Peace and Goodwill that sages have foretold, poets have dreamed of, and that is at once the hope and the salvation of the Race.[69]

This was Holland at his most utopian; it bears remembering that he had once been an adherent of the Salvation Army.

This chapter has examined Holland's account of Irish history in some detail. Rather than projecting forward to the Labour Party's engagement with the Irish-Catholic population of New Zealand – an engagement that developed from 1918, as conscription, the rise of Sinn Féin, and the general election which resulted in the First Dáil all changed the contours of Irish politics – it has examined Holland's writing in the context of 1916–17. Holland had no more foresight than anyone else about the future course of Irish history – hopes, yes, but these were misplaced.

At this stage, Holland, it seems, was not particularly concerned about deploying Irish issues in the service of the Labour Party's electoral fortunes; that was not an evident agenda in his year-long series. His evident intention was to analyse the course of Irish history in the context of imperialism and capitalism and the possibilities for future development. Certainly, he dwelt extensively on the oppression that the Irish had suffered. Undoubtedly, the account could be faulted along with the nationalist historiography on which it drew; that nationalist historiography could be criticised for its over-simplifications, its romanticisation of a lost past, and a cultural essentialism, sometimes explicit, sometimes implicit. And Holland's anti-imperialism is very much on display. But there was, for Holland, an inevitability about the lost utopia and the replacement of decentralised clan society by capitalist landlords. This narrative fused Connolly's orthodox Marxist schema with contemporary nationalist accounts of ancient Irish society. Reflecting his absorption in Marxism, Holland emphasised the working class as the essential agents of social change.

The thread in the narrative from 1600 is that gentry and bourgeois nationalists were not to be trusted. They would betray the workers and peasants every time. It followed, therefore, that national independence for Ireland depended on the working class and that, once independence was won, the class struggle in Ireland would only intensify. Holland continued to take that line as the 1921 Treaty was being signed.[70]

What is also evident is that Holland was not particularly enthusiastic about redemptive notions of blood sacrifice. He remained ambivalent about the Rising and, I think, regarded Connolly's death, in particular, as a tragedy. Rather than seeing Holland's exposition of Irish history as concerned with domestic political advantage, this chapter contends that the forty-eight instalments comprising the 'Historic Foundations of the Irish Rebellion' were in essence an extended homage to James Connolly.

CHAPTER 6

Bishop Henry Cleary and the North King Street Murders

RORY SWEETMAN

(Associate of the Centre for Irish and Scottish Studies, University of Otago)

enry William Cleary, Catholic bishop of Auckland, New Zealand (1910–29), spent the worst winter of the First World War serving as a military chaplain in the Flanders trenches. On a visit to his native Ireland in February 1917, Cleary interviewed several witnesses to the British troops' nefarious activities during the dying stages of the rebellion in Dublin some nine months earlier. Fifteen innocent civilians in North King Street were murdered in or near their homes, the culpability of the Crown forces being exposed by their hasty attempts to conceal the bodies of their victims.[1] What Cleary did with the explosive information he discovered throws light on the dilemma posed by the 1916 Rising – and the subsequent War of Independence (1919–21) – for Catholic leaders in Australia and New Zealand. Drawing on Cleary's unpublished diaries and correspondence, this chapter explores the reluctance with which some Irish constitutional nationalists abandoned the comfortable assumptions of 'a war to unite us all' for the wilder shores of republican separatism.[2]

THE NORTH KING STREET MURDERS

The North King Street murders would have become even more notorious but for the execution of fourteen insurgent leaders in the immediate

89

aftermath of the rebellion. However, as news of the killings spread over the following weeks and months, it helped to change the public perception of the events of Easter Week.[3] This process was aided by the rather farcical military court of inquiry subsequently held, which found the South Staffordshire troops responsible to be 'a quiet and very respectable set of men'.[4] The harrowing details of the killings, as related to the coroner's court by surviving relatives and eye-witnesses, were well ventilated in the Dublin press.[5] Despite these gruesome events, the North King Street episode has only recently been given the attention it deserves by historians.[6]

The small area around North King Street and Church Street witnessed some of the most brutal and sustained fighting of Easter Week. Here were fired among the first and almost certainly the last shots of the Rising. According to Charles Townshend, the stronghold of the 1st Battalion (Dublin Brigade) was the most strategically vital of all rebel positions, and Ned Daly was perhaps the shrewdest of the rebel commandants.[7] Drawing on his extensive interviews with participants, Max Caulfield wrote a vivid account of the battle on Friday and Saturday (28–9 April), in which British forces took over thirty hours to cover some 120 yards, with steadily mounting casualties.[8] The North King Street area rapidly became a popular site for post-Rising tourists in Dublin, notably the writer Katharine Tynan, whose guide may have been the same Capuchin priest who showed Bishop Cleary around several months later.[9]

In his official report, General Sir John Maxwell, Ireland's military governor, dismissed these civilian deaths as 'the inevitable consequence of a rebellion of this kind', adding that 'the number of such incidents is less than I expected considering the magnitude of the task'.[10] However, as the awful details became public, he was forced to offer further excuses: 'No doubt in districts where the fighting was the fiercest, parties of men under the greatest provocation of being shot at from front and rear, seeing their comrades fall from the fire of snipers, burst into suspected houses and killed such male members as were found.'[11] Although few historians follow Charles Townshend in swallowing Maxwell's apologetics, it is clear that both sides deserve blame for the high civilian death toll.[12] Dubliners had to cope with *two* largely irresponsible military bodies. The rebel force chose the battlefield and adopted tactics that put innocent lives directly at risk. Both sides took possession of private houses and businesses as it suited them, sniped indiscriminately, tunnelled through the interior walls of terraced houses, and moved stealthily from roof to roof. Civilians were thus placed directly in the firing line, despite desultory efforts to protect them. Maxwell's belated advice to residents to leave areas 'now surrounded by His Majesty's troops' led some locals to take refuge in what they considered to be 'safe' houses. For those who gathered in 172 North King Street and nearby residences, this proved to be a tragic mistake.

The rebel outposts were often small-scale victuallers, provision stores, or business premises – Reilly's pub (which became 'Reilly's Fort'), Moore's Coach Works, Monk's Bakery (where Kevin Barry was captured four years later) – and so were most of the houses where the murders took place. The killings were largely a consequence of the collision of rival forces: the 1st Battalion's outer defensive line and the northern boundary of the British cordon around the Four Courts. The terrain, a network of narrow streets, could almost have been designed for urban warfare, in which the advantage lay with the defensive side. The Crown troops were largely young recruits, fresh out of basic training. Few would have fired their gun in combat, let alone in such a furious battle, much of it fought in gloom and darkness.[13] They did not know who was a rebel or from which house the gunfire was coming. Infuriated as they were by their slow progress and increasing losses, their inexperience was reflected in ill-chosen tactics and a correspondingly high death toll. Most of the South Staffordshire troops would have witnessed the earlier slaughter of their comrades at Mount Street Bridge.[14] The Crown forces alternated between attempting to storm rebel strongholds and attempting to bypass them. 'They would rush an armoured car to a point in the street,' recalled Volunteer Patrick Kelly. 'A party would jump off and batter their way into the nearest house. Their advance was slow and costly, as our men contested every inch of the street.'[15] Behind the armoured car came the infantry – according to Caulfield, 'pouring fierce and indiscriminate fire into all the houses before entering and occupying them'.[16]

There was considerable confusion over how the Crown forces were to deal with suspected rebels. The issue was complicated by Brigadier-General Lowe's order that 'every man found in a house from which fire has been opened, whether bearing arms or not, may be considered as a rebel'.[17] Maxwell later claimed that rebels deliberately mixed with civilians in order to ambush the troops.[18] His advice to leave the area clearly led some soldiers to assume that *innocent* civilians would have fled and that those remaining were somehow implicated in the rebellion. Once troops entered a house, they had to identify who was there legitimately and decide what to do with those who failed this test. The Sheehy Skeffington case revealed that some British officers believed that the declaration of martial law gave them the authority to shoot civilians without trial.[19] Prime Minister Asquith's legal advisor later noted – with an appalling frankness – that 'the soldiers did not accurately distinguish between refusing to make prisoners and shooting immediately prisoners they had made'.[20]

BISHOP CLEARY AND IRISH NATIONALISM

Henry William Cleary was the leader and chief spokesman of New Zealand's Catholic community for the first three decades of the twentieth century.[21] His equivalent in Australia was Daniel Mannix, archbishop of Melbourne (1917–63); yet, while numerous books have been written about Mannix, there is not a single biography of Cleary.[22] Paradoxically, I would suggest that Cleary's successful avoidance of the sectarian firestorm that consumed Australia (and particularly Mannix's Victoria) has ensured his continued obscurity. That and what Patrick O'Farrell long ago identified as a failing of antipodean historians, most of whom 'take an English view of appearances, accept English priorities, reflect Protestant value-judgements. The sub-world of Irish Catholics had no real existence for historians who wrote from and about the walled gardens of the establishment.'[23]

Cleary was born in County Wexford in 1859, trained at St Patrick's College, Maynooth, St Sulpice in Paris, and the Lateran in Rome, and was ordained in 1885. He went to Australia for his health's sake in 1888 and served for nine years in rural Victorian parishes. An enthusiastic controversialist, his celebrated study of Orangeism (*The Orange Society*) ran through eleven editions following its first publication in 1897. It earned its author an invitation to come to Dunedin to edit *The New Zealand Tablet*. During his twelve years as editor of the sole Catholic organ in the country, Cleary was well placed to further the policies of quiet integration adopted by his mentor, Cardinal Moran of Sydney.[24] He believed that Catholic interests would best be advanced by educating public opinion through moderate exposition and defence of Catholic beliefs and social attitudes. His editorial career was devoted to disentangling the various strands of misunderstanding, ignorance, and prejudice that he saw as threatening the position of his church.

As most Catholic clergy in New Zealand supported Irish nationalism, Cleary needed to display delicacy in explaining these views to his colonial audience. He carefully managed the centenary commemoration of the 1798 Irish rebellion, encouraging the participation of several Protestant Irish clergymen, and exercised a discreet censorship over any controversial Irish material submitted to *The New Zealand Tablet*.[25] As he explained to the Irish parliamentarian John Dillon in 1898, 'I have not permitted the insertion of any letters, news or correspondence that could create divisions here on the question of Irish politics.'[26] Cleary wished to see a similar unity in nationalist ranks at home, promising to support with leading articles and funding appeals any movement to 'put an end to a disunion which has been the despair of our people in these colonies for many years past'.[27]

Cleary was as good as his word after the reunified Irish Party resumed its fundraising tours of the British dominions. He orchestrated the visits of successive Irish Home Rule delegations in 1906–7, 1911, and 1914, who were not disappointed in the generosity of their New Zealand sympathisers.[28] *The New Zealand Tablet*'s columns regularly featured appeals for various Irish causes. In 1909, Cleary published a compilation of articles he had written in defence of his native land under the title *An Impeached Nation*.[29] It was somehow appropriate that he was en route to Ireland when news came of his appointment as bishop of Auckland; he was consecrated in his native Wexford on 21 August 1910.

CLEARY AND THE NORTH KING STREET MURDERS

Cleary's determination to present the loyal face of New Zealand Catholicism was best seen during the First World War, when he chose to spend three months doing chaplaincy work in the Flanders trenches. It was a deliberate and practical demonstration of Catholic commitment to the war effort. Despite his almost three score years, Cleary displayed a bravery bordering on foolhardiness in the front lines, all the while ensuring that his exploits were well advertised in the New Zealand press. He was staying with relatives in Wexford and recuperating from his gruelling military experiences when he paid his visit to North King Street. On Saturday, 3 February 1917, guided by a local priest from the Franciscan (Capuchin) order, he interviewed what he described as 'a large number of eye-witnesses' from the houses where the murders took place, including the widows of at least two victims.[30] Cleary's diary (more accurately, aide-memoire) contains the awful details of the killings, most of which he outlined in a long letter to *The New Zealand Tablet* of 3 May 1917.[31]

That newspaper was now being edited by Dr James Kelly, Cleary's fellow-priest and Wexfordman, an enthusiastic (not to say rabid) Sinn Féiner, resident in New Zealand only since 1913 – the year that Daniel Mannix arrived in Australia – and very much of the same political mind as Mannix on the legitimacy of the radical Irish nationalist cause.[32] Kelly brought to his new post an uncompromising attitude towards the perceived enemies of his faith and fatherland.[33] Despite an unfavourable climate in the war-weary country, where his co-religionists numbered only one in seven, Kelly presented Catholic economic and social grievances in New Zealand with no uncertain voice. His sense of outrage at the continued denial of Irish self-determination also led him to turn *The New Zealand Tablet* into a vigorous apologist for advanced Irish nationalism. For Kelly and the numerous Irish-born clergy in New Zealand, the struggle in Ireland was as much religious as it was political; the suppression of Irish freedom was regarded as a form of religious persecution.

Drawing on his network of correspondents in Ireland, many of whom were closely associated with the nascent Sinn Féin movement, Kelly challenged what he saw as the anti-Irish bias of New Zealand's press and attempted to educate his readers on the failings of British policy in Ireland.[34] He dismissed Irish constitutionalism as 'a sham and a fraud', denounced the name of England as 'a synonym for oppression and tyranny', and raged against what he termed 'the heresy of conciliation'.[35] For Kelly, Irish history was 'one long arraignment' of England, a country that Irishmen had 'every reason to curse'.[36] He was to refight all of nationalist Ireland's lost battles in his editorial columns: the Treaty of Limerick, the 1798 Rebellion, the Famine, Fenianism, and the Land War were his constant points of reference.[37]

Kelly had initially dismissed the Easter Rising as 'mad, bad and sad', although adding that 'Maxwellian monstrosities made heroes of those who were only fools'.[38] However, the second *Tablet* issue under his editorship endorsed a sacrificial interpretation of the Rising: 'The Sinn Feiners died like men', he declared, 'bearing the punishment for the faults of all.'[39] The rebel leaders 'kept aloft the torch of freedom', while the rebellion had 'saved the soul of Irish nationality'.[40] There was nothing of this flavour in Cleary's letter to *The New Zealand Tablet*, written immediately following his North King Street visit. It focused instead on the victims of military brutality and listed four points on which Cleary's informants were unanimous: that on Friday, 28 April, 'the day preceding the killing of these civilians, the last remaining Sinn Feiners had abandoned or been driven out of North King Street'; that on Saturday, 29 April 'there was in North King Street no insurgent, firearm or offensive weapon of any sort; and that no shot was fired from that street against the soldiers, or any other form of attack made on them'; that all those killed were innocent, not insurgents, none were armed, and all were murdered; and, finally, that the guilty parties could be easily identified.[41]

Cleary did not name the twenty-seven alleged victims (around twice the now-accepted number) or mention the looting of money and jewellery by British troops, of which he was told by his interviewees. More to the point, the rebels were certainly not gone from the vicinity by Friday; far from being safe on 29 April, North King Street was still a killing field, as confirmed by the witness statements of Volunteers Patrick Kelly, Frank Shouldice, and Charles Skelly.[42] Shouldice later recorded how a bayonet charge at dawn on Saturday was repulsed by the seven rebel riflemen stationed in Reilly's Fort – 'a terrible slaughter ensued', he recalled.[43] Ellen Walsh testified that when the troops broke into her house ('like infuriated wild beasts or like things possessed'), 'there was a terrible firing going on outside in the street and an armoured car was near the door' – the troops were clearly under rebel fire.[44] Father Aloysius Travers OFM, who was probably Cleary's Capuchin guide, confirmed that 'the firing was intense all through Friday night and without cessation until 3 to 4 o'clock on Saturday afternoon'.[45]

Cleary referred to his priest guide as 'a locally well-known and prominent anti-Sinn Feiner', but all of the Capuchin clergy were strongly sympathetic to the rebels, however much they may have regretted the actual rebellion. Prior to the Rising, they permitted Father Mathew Park to be used for Volunteer drill and shooting practice, and during the fighting Father Mathew Hall at the northern end of Church Street became a temporary headquarters for the 1st Battalion. Described by Katharine Tynan as 'a meeting and recreation place for the people', it was part first aid station and part ammunition dump during Easter Week.[46] The Capuchin priests acted as de facto chaplains to the rebels before and after the surrender, which they also helped to facilitate.[47]

Cleary's letter dealt exclusively with the North King Street affair and made no mention of the unlawful killing of Father Felix Watters SM, the president of the Catholic University School in Leeson Street. Watters was well known to most New Zealand Catholics as one of the founding fathers of St Patrick's College, Wellington. (Cleary privately informed his fellow bishop Matthew Brodie that Watters was 'murdered by a sentry' when leaving a central city presbytery.)[48] Cleary's real message lay in the letter's sub-text, where he consistently minimised the significance of the Rising and the degree of support it had evoked among the general population. He stressed that his witnesses were all 'wholly out of sympathy with the foolish physical force movement'.[49] He placed the blame for Ireland's ills on (among others) Asquith, who had broken a promise to publish the results of the North King Street inquiry; Edward Carson, the original Irish rebel; and those unionist employers who refused to re-engage employees wrongly deported as suspected insurgents.[50] According to Cleary, it was *their* actions rather than those of the rebels that had disturbed the peace and 'greatly intensified the horror with which the people of Ireland view the unspeakably stupid methods adopted to suppress a little physical force movement that was strongly antagonised [*sic*] by 99½% of the population of the country'. Carson and Maxwell were, he concluded, 'Sinn Fein organisers such as the Sinn Fein had never, even in their wildest dreams, hoped for'.[51]

This was a period of considerable flux in Irish politics with the Irish Parliamentary Party coming under an increasingly strong challenge from a reinvented 'Sinn Féin' party, an amalgam of advanced nationalist bodies that won a series of by-elections in 1917 and was to sweep to power following the national poll in December 1918.[52] In this context, Cleary's letter reads like a calculated effort to 'spin' the Rising and the current troubled state of Irish politics for his colonial readers. Over the previous six months, he had written home several times, ostensibly for his clergy's edification, but all his letters soon found a wider audience. He described life at the front as a great adventure, highlighting the self-sacrifice of those fighting what he saw as a just war, the noble service of Catholic clergy as military chaplains, and the general beastliness of the Hun – the Protestant Prussian Hun, that was, rather than the good Catholic Bavarian Hun. Around the time of his visit to North King Street, Cleary was busily turning this correspondence into a pamphlet entitled *Prussian Militarism at Work*. It was published later in 1917 under the auspices of the British Department of Information.[53] His letter to *The New Zealand Tablet* is a similar exercise in propaganda. While Cleary did not allow the paper's editor to identify him as its author, Kelly effectively gave the game away with strong hints as to the distinguished correspondent's identity and by predicting the appearance of another damningly revealing pamphlet from his temporarily anonymous source, entitled *The Shame of Britain*.[54]

Kelly could not have been more wrong. On returning to New Zealand in October 1917, Cleary was shocked by the ferocity of local sectarian conflict, much of it fuelled by the deteriorating political situation in Ireland. He soon became a relentless opponent of *The New Zealand Tablet*'s aggressive Irish policy, going so far as to found a rival periodical – *The Month* – in order to protect his church from the contagion of what was perceived in Britain's white dominions as Irish disloyalty. In its columns, Cleary attempted to reconcile the advocacy of Irish national rights with professions of loyalty to Empire. During the subsequent War of Independence (1919–21), he defended a degree of violence as a necessary response to outrageous British provocation, but much preferred his clergy and people to pray for Ireland rather than campaign for Sinn Féin.[55]

Cleary was responding to the hysterically patriotic atmosphere in wartime New Zealand, the farthest-flung of Britain's dominions, teetering on the very edge of Empire. Unlike Australia, the dominion had imposed conscription on its citizens and sent over 100,000 of them overseas.[56] (Around 12,000 did not return, a huge casualty rate by any measure.) The war also encouraged the rise of an aggressive anti-Catholic organisation in New Zealand – the Protestant Political Association – which furiously peddled the theory that the conflict was a papal-inspired conspiracy against the Protestant faith and the British Empire, using Ireland as a prime example.[57] When Cleary's coadjutor bishop, James Liston, made a rash speech in the Auckland Town Hall on St Patrick's Day in 1922 referring to the Irish rebellion as 'that glorious Easter' and describing its victims as having been 'murdered by foreign troops', a nationwide howl of protest culminated in his being prosecuted (unsuccessfully) for sedition.[58]

More closely attuned to the prejudices of his community than Kelly, Cleary had earlier banned the use of provocative Sinn Féin emblems, flags, and mottoes in his diocese. He never reconciled himself to the failure of Irish constitutional nationalism, and his diary reveals his closeness to the Redmondites – indeed, his personal friendship with John and Willie Redmond, his fellow-countrymen, and with John Dillon and Joe Devlin. He dined with them in London, attended 'Irish' debates in the House of Commons, and shared their hope that some form of Home Rule could be resurrected from the post-Rising wreckage. Cleary embraced the Redmondite belief that Irish nationalism could be reconciled with British imperialism. It was this faith that led him to the front-line trenches, not far from those occupied by Willie Redmond MP (both men were in their late fifties) and along with a couple of hundred thousand other Irishmen.[59] He convinced himself that Irish political unity was being created by shared sacrifice in the mud and blood of France and Flanders, forging bonds between Orange and Green that would hopefully transcend their historic differences.[60]

CONCLUSION

Redmond and Cleary exemplify what Terence Denman has termed an 'imperial nationalism', which held that the so-called 'British' Empire belonged as much to Irish nationalists as to English Tories, Irish blood and sweat having built up much of it.[61] Their dream was that a generous measure of self-government would cement Ireland firmly within the Commonwealth of Nations that was emerging from the former British Empire. The Easter Rising meant death to this fond dream, to be sure, and there was no William Butler Yeats to write it out in verse – but its dreamers do not deserve to be dismissed as 'collaborationists'.[62] Dr James Kelly was keen to ensure that Cleary – like the Irish nationalist parliamentarian Tom Kettle – would go down in history as 'a bloody British officer'.[63] In mid-1919, *The New Zealand Tablet* published a photograph of its chief episcopal critic resplendent in his military chaplain's uniform in an issue full of criticisms of British policies in Ireland.[64] By refusing to allow the advocacy of Sinn Féin in his diocese and by attempting to curb Kelly's uncritical commitment to Irish politics, Cleary defended the vital interests of his church at the price of his reputation as a patriotic Irishman.

CHAPTER 7

Rebel Hearts: New Zealand's fenian families and the Easter Rising

SEÁN BROSNAHAN

(*Toitū Otago Settlers Museum*)

This chapter will examine the response of New Zealand Irish families to the Easter Rising by examining resistance to military service for the British Empire in the aftermath of the Rising. This was strongest among families with a tradition of 'fenianism' (small 'f'), which in New Zealand was much less about formal membership of bodies like the Irish Republican Brotherhood and more about a general sense of antipathy to British rule in Ireland.[1] Such an amorphous anti-English, anti-Crown, anti-Empire disposition had lacked focus in New Zealand before 1916 but, nonetheless, represented a deep-seated attitude among some New Zealand Irish families. They were mostly those immigrants who came to the colony with recent experiences of eviction or carried historic resentments whose memory was passed on through the generations and could be easily revived.

A MATTER OF TIMING

Early twentieth-century political developments in Ireland – the infiltration of the Gaelic Revival by a new generation of Irish Republican Brotherhood physical force advocates with revolutionary political ambitions – made relatively little impact in New Zealand. One reason

was the relatively short timescale of substantial Irish migration to New
Zealand. This was concentrated from about 1860 to 1880, a period
when 'Fenianism' was in something of a decline in Ireland. Then, once
large-scale assisted immigration programmes came to an end, the Irish
proportion of subsequent New Zealand migration shrank to a mere
trickle.[2] A minor surge in migration just prior to the First World War,
however, included a small number of republican agitators and others
exposed to the Gaelic Revival and possibly entangled in IRB subversion.
They were to play a key role in wartime acts of Irish resistance in New
Zealand.

Irish 'Home Rule' as a political position, on the other hand, was
meeting with increasing acceptance in New Zealand on a broad front in
the pre-war years. Unity within the Empire on the Australasian model
was its template for Ireland's future. The outbreak of war offered a
superb platform to demonstrate this. Catholic soldiers giving their lives
on New Zealand's behalf paid the price for common citizenship within
the Empire. Fenianism, in contrast, seemed a relic of another time and
place and irrelevant to the new colonial society emerging with increasing
Irish integration in New Zealand. Fenianism was still there, as an
attitude and a folk memory rather than a formal organisation, waiting
to be re-energised by propitious circumstances, as wartime events would
demonstrate.

The situation was broadly similar in Australia in 1914;[3] however,
the wartime trajectories of the two countries would be quite different.
The Australian government's inability to impose conscription, a failure
popularly attributed to opposition to conscription referenda in 1916 and
1917 by Irish Catholics, meant that no Irish Australian of a nationalist
disposition would be compelled to war service. In comparison, military
service evaders from New Zealand were able to use their larger neighbour
as a refuge from the punitive regime that emerged after conscription was
imposed in their own country in 1916, although there is little evidence
of co-ordinated activity between Irish nationalist organisations across
the Tasman Sea.[4] These contrasting recruiting regulations made for
substantively different wartime contexts for Irish radicals in Australia
and New Zealand.

THE RISING AND NEW ZEALAND'S WAR

The Easter Rising (24–30 April 1916) corresponds with the redeployment of New Zealand troops to the Western Front after the failed Gallipoli campaign. The New Zealand Division arrived in Marseilles in mid-April 1916, just before the Rising in Dublin. The fighting in the Dardanelles through 1915 had eviscerated the original New Zealand Expeditionary Force (NZEF), the 8,500-strong contingent that set off for war in October 1914. Some 2,800 New Zealanders were killed at Gallipoli and about 6,000 more became casualties. While worse slaughter lay ahead for New Zealand's war effort on the Somme and in Flanders, enough had already happened by April 1916 to prick New Zealand's pre-war bubble of hyper-imperialism.

A three-fold expansion of the Expeditionary Force also increased pressure on New Zealand's manpower commitments. With over 5,000 new recruits needed every two months, the pool of willing volunteers began to dry up. By early 1916, it was clear that some form of compulsion would be required to keep up the flow of reinforcements. It would be November 1916 before the necessary legislation and administrative machinery was in place for conscription to begin. By that time, events in Ireland were beginning to cast a significant shadow over Catholic New Zealand's enthusiasm for what some now saw as 'England's war'. Support for the war effort remained the majority Catholic position, but there was now room for an alternative view, and alternative responses.

SUPPORTING SINN FÉIN: JOINING THE STRUGGLE IN IRELAND

Active participation in armed struggle in Ireland was not really an option, except for a tiny number of New Zealand servicemen who deserted while on leave in Ireland and joined armed republican bands. New Zealand military police records document two such cases. A report from the New Zealand Provost Corps in March 1918 stated that 'the majority of our deserters are hiding in Ireland, where special inducements are offered them by the Sinn Fein element. At least one of our deserters, J. Griffen [*sic*], is known to be drilling Sinn Feiners in County Kerry.'[5] Jeremiah

Griffin, a recent immigrant from County Kerry, had been working as a gold miner near Nelson, when he was called up in early 1917. Griffin objected to military service and was given a temporary deferral by the military service board so that he could sell his sluicing claim. Once he had done so, he entered camp and went overseas with the 27th Reinforcements. While still in training in Britain, however, he deserted the NZEF and made his way home to Kerry.[6]

Recapturing New Zealand deserters in Ireland had become problematic by 1918. Sinn Féin activity made the country an ideal refuge for deserters and absentees. Ireland was accordingly placed out-of-bounds for New Zealand soldiers for a fortnight in early 1918, and the Irish police instructed to arrest every man they found in New Zealand uniform. Just one 'absentee' was arrested, however, although many more were known to be in the country. The case of Frederick James McKenna, who deserted in mid-1918, illustrates the difficulties that Ireland posed for the New Zealand military authorities. Even though it was known that McKenna was in Miltown Malbay, County Clare, it was no simple matter to go and pick him up, given the strength of Sinn Féin in that county.

McKenna was New Zealand-born, from Patea in Taranaki, and volunteered for military service the day after his twentieth birthday in May 1917. He went overseas with the Wellington Infantry Regiment in February 1918 and served for a time at the front line in France before falling ill. Recuperating in hospital in England, however, he absented himself and headed to his father's people in County Clare.[7] There he remained for the next year, becoming involved alongside his relations in Sinn Féin activity with the newly formed Irish Republican Army. Eventually, the New Zealand military arranged for Irish police assistance to apprehend McKenna. When they swooped, in July 1919, 'owing to the hostile attitude of the Sinn Feiners in Co. Clare, the escort and prisoner had to be conveyed in an armoured car from Ennis to Limerick'.[8]

SUPPORTING SINN FÉIN: THE NEW ZEALAND OPTIONS

For the Irish ethnic group in wartime New Zealand, practical ways of supporting the republican cause were limited to undertaking propaganda on behalf of Sinn Féin and/or withdrawing support for the imperial war effort. For men of military age, the latter meant avoiding military service or evading military service, often with consequences for those who had supported those men who had actively withdrawn support. The New Zealand War Regulations made either option difficult. Seditious speech was defined as any expression of opposition to the war. Leading members of the newly formed Labour Party discovered this to their cost when they spoke out against the conscription regime. Public comments by Paddy Webb, Bob Semple, future prime minister Peter Fraser, and others put them in breach of the 'seditious utterances' regulations and they quickly found themselves in prison. Drunken Irishmen mouthing off about the war in a hotel bar were equally liable to find themselves before the court. John O'Neill and Thomas Finucane were jailed for eleven months for expressing such sentiments in a hotel at Morrinsville in August 1917.[9]

Nonetheless, there were those prepared to test the boundaries of resistance. A small group of Irish Sinn Féin supporters came together in Dunedin in late 1916 to form the first branch of what would become the Maoriland Irish Society. Ostensibly an Irish social organisation, a number of the new organisation's key players were relatively recent immigrants who claimed Irish Republican Brotherhood pedigrees.[10] Alongside their dances and musical evenings, these radical members of the new society organised a publication to promote their republican and socialist views. The first issue of *The Green Ray* appeared in December 1916, just a month after the conscription ballots had begun. Declaring itself 'the only truly Irish newspaper South of the Line, and the only Republican journal in Australasia', *The Green Ray* was unequivocal in its support for Sinn Féin and its opposition to conscription.[11]

It reported positively the efforts of conscientious objectors to evade the New Zealand military authorities and lauded the West Coast Irish in particular for providing a haven for evaders. Over the next eighteen months, the Dunedin journal pushed these editorial lines without fear or favour until finally coming to the attention of the authorities. Its May 1918 edition, a memorial issue to the Easter Rising martyrs headed 'The Memory of the Dead', finally prompted *The Green Ray*'s suppression. Dunedin police raided the magazine's office and arrested its editor, Thomas Cummins, and manager, Albert Ryan, for sedition. In their subsequent trial, the presiding judge declared that it 'seemed to him that on every page [of *The Green Ray*] there was a seditious utterance' and sentenced the pair to eleven months' hard labour.

Thomas Cummins, from County Kildare, was the son of a sergeant in the Royal Irish Constabulary and a founding member of the Gaelic League at Portarlington.[12] League founder Douglas Hyde had been a visitor to the Cummins home, while Thomas also had dealings with Patrick Pearse and Thomas MacDonagh through the league. In Dunedin, Cummins claimed for himself an exciting (but probably bogus) pre-New Zealand background as a journalist, teacher, and soldier in the United States, Mexico, Argentina, and Uruguay. In fact, he had followed his father into the Irish police force, serving from 1905 to 1912 before emigrating to New Zealand with his new wife, Kathleen MacOwen. He then joined the New Zealand Police, only to become enmeshed in agitation over police conditions. He left the force in 1913. Cummins came to Dunedin as correspondent for *The Truth* newspaper.

Married and with three young children, Cummins was not liable for military service. This left him free to be the public face of *The Green Ray* as well as its chief writer. Albert Ryan, the business manager, was born in Waitahuna. He had a family history of dispossession in Ireland, his father coming to Otago via the United States and Victoria reputedly with something of an 'attitude' towards authority. The youngest in a family of ten, Albert *aka* Bert had lost his mother when young and grew up in his father's care. He was also strongly influenced by a local priest, Monsignor O'Leary, who was unique among the Otago Catholic clergy for his fervent fenian sympathies. Ryan was working as a commercial traveller in Dunedin when he became embroiled in the radical Irish politics that would see him jailed in 1918.[13]

Two other key players behind the scenes at *The Green Ray* were post-1900 arrivals from Ulster with apparently strong republican pedigrees. James *aka* Jim Bradley, a carpenter from Magherafelt, County Derry, is credited with the idea of establishing the magazine though his name never appears in it. Family tradition suggests that he had been active in the militant republican movement prior to coming to New Zealand around the turn of the century. He was even reputed to have been a representative on the Supreme Council of the Irish Republican Brotherhood for a time.[14] Bradley was called up in a conscription ballot in mid-1917 while farming near Mataura. After failing to appear for his army medical, he was automatically deemed a deserter and went 'underground' in Dunedin. He was sheltered for a time by prominent Dunedin socialist Arthur McCarthy, who was writing a column for *The Green Ray*. When McCarthy's son, Arthur Gregory McCarthy, was also called up, he joined Bradley on the run. The pair then took shelter in Sawyers Bay with the Gordon family, Church of Ireland Protestants from County Antrim.[15]

Bradley was fortunate not to be picked up in the police raid on *The Green Ray* office. He managed to evade the authorities successfully until stowing away to Australia. Arthur McCarthy was not so lucky. He was captured in Christchurch in 1920 and sentenced to a year in prison for desertion. Both men returned to Dunedin after the war and married the two Gordon daughters. *The Green Ray's* resident Gaelic language expert, Sean Tohill, was another key figure to escape capture in the raid. Tohill was a member of a large Ulster Catholic family who had immigrated to New Zealand in 1909 and settled in Napier. Also from Magherafelt, Sean had been a close friend of Jim Bradley's in Ireland, where the Tohills are remembered as 'notorious Fenians' and where Sean is believed by descendants to have been an IRB member. In one of his *Green Ray* columns, he describes himself as being a founding member of the Dungannon Clubs, a front organisation for IRB recruitment in pre-war Ulster, and claims to have personally known Pearse, Plunkett, MacDonagh, MacBride, and Clarke – the ringleaders of the Easter Rising.[16]

The Tohills were key personalities in the Napier branch of the Maoriland Irish Society, and three of the boys, including Seán, became military evaders once their names were drawn in conscription ballots. Sean had headed south to Dunedin in early 1918, and after his *Green Ray* colleagues were taken into custody, he hid out at Gimmerburn in Central Otago. He went under the alias 'Ferguson', passing himself off as Scottish. He stayed with the Dougherty family from County Cork and began a relationship with the daughter of the house, Sarah. The couple married in 1920 and moved to Wellington after an amnesty was declared at the end of that year for all military defaulters still at large. Family members recall that on his deathbed, Sarah called Sean 'Fergie', recalling the name by which she had first known him in the dark days of the First World War.

If there was an oath-bound IRB circle in Dunedin in 1916–18, these four were almost certainly in it.[17] The Maoriland Irish Society offered a classic 'front' for their promotion of Irish republicanism, with *The Green Ray* their most important propaganda tool. Oath-bound or not, it is notable that the branches of the Maoriland Irish Society that were established around New Zealand – at Dunedin, Wellington, Gisborne, Napier, Hastings, Riversdale, Auckland, Invercargill, and the West Coast – co-relate closely with the geography of Irish resistance to military service. These include the centres most associated with conscription evaders and their support networks.[18]

OPTION TWO: EVADING MILITARY SERVICE

Refusing military service was the second option available to New Zealand fenians. This was probably the primary expression of Irish resistance to British imperialism in New Zealand after 1916. Easy enough while enlistment was purely voluntary, resistance became more challenging once conscription made service compulsory for men selected in the ballots. As well as public opprobrium, resisters faced imprisonment. There was little allowance for conscientious objection under the regulations, with exemption limited to a very narrow definition of religious opposition to war. Pacifism, socialism, or opposition on wider religious grounds were deemed insufficient for principled objection. Irish objections did not even merit consideration. Men with these views claiming exemption were lumped together into a single category – 'shirkers'.

Delineating the motivations of evaders is difficult. The records of those who were caught do not usually report the grounds of their objection. There is even less trace in the historical record of the much larger number who evaded successfully. Just because an evader was ethnically Irish, it does not necessarily mean their objections to service had an Irish basis. There was also significant overlap between categories of objectors: many Irish objectors were also socialists, while others were pacifists or members of religious sects. Apart from a very limited review in 1919 by a 'Religious Objectors Advisory Board', there was scant interest from the authorities as to what motivated the evaders.

Working out how men avoided arrest while on the run is also a challenge. About half of the 240,000 New Zealand men of military age served in the First World War. The other 120,000 men, for whatever reason, remained at home. This meant that there were always a lot of men around New Zealand who looked as if they should be in the army but had legitimate grounds not to be. They provided excellent cover for those actively avoiding service. There were also large parts of the country that were difficult to access and had transient populations of male workers in hard-to-monitor frontier-style camps. Official records of the hunt for evaders refer to the difficulty posed by such 'backblocks' areas all over the country, often acknowledging the limited capacity of police to provide surveillance and identify military defaulters in these locations.[19]

Efforts to trace military defaulters took up a considerable amount of police time. Denis Mangan, for example, was a Kerryman who had been in New Zealand since 1905. When he 'disappeared' after failing to appear for medical examination after call-up in March 1917, the police chased him for six months, from Taumarunui to Auckland to Balclutha. His file records that he was finally captured in Invercargill, where he had assumed the name 'Denis O'Sullivan'. Remaining defiant, he refused to submit to military authority and was sentenced to two years' hard labour in November 1917.[20] An even more extensive file documents police efforts to track down Patrick Fitzpatrick, a self-employed cartage contractor from South Dunedin. First arrested in April 1917 after ignoring his call-up, Fitzpatrick 'deserted' from Trentham Military Camp the following December and destroyed his army uniform. He was captured at his aunt's house in Ponsonby (Auckland) in March 1918 and sent to the Wanganui Detention Centre. He escaped from there and was hunted all over the country before being recaptured in Ponsonby in April 1919 and sentenced to eighteen months' hard labour.[21]

Yet much of the police effort to track down defaulters proved fruitless, even though police could claim a £1 reward for every deserter they captured. From the beginning of 1917 until the end of 1918, for example, there were 3,019 arrest warrants listed in the *Police Gazette* that remained unexecuted.[22] The vast majority of these, 2,474, or 82 per cent of them, were for military-service-related offences. In April 1918, police undertook a major operation to check the status of every man attending a race meeting at Trentham. Over two days the papers of 890 men were looked at, but only six of them proved in any way questionable. A similar exercise at the Awapuni and Palmerston North races found not a single 'shirker'.[23] This suggests that those in hiding were aware of the risks and avoided such locations.

EVASION STRATEGIES IN PRACTICE

Evaders could 'hide in plain sight', usually by adopting an assumed name and moving to a location far from their home district. Or they could 'go bush', taking refuge in isolated or remote areas. Finally, they could head overseas, mainly to Australia but also as far afield as South America. All three evasion strategies required varying degrees of community support from networks of family or sympathisers, possibly giving an advantage to Irish Catholics who already formed a sub-culture within New Zealand society. Nonetheless, sheltering evaders was risky for all concerned and required highly secretive behaviour, which obscures such incidents in extant historical sources. There are fortunately a few documented cases of each of these evasion strategies, which can stand in for the stories of many more men whose difficult years in hiding cannot be described in such detail.

Jack and Bill Doyle described themselves as of 'anti-British' Irish stock. The brothers were born in New Zealand to parents from Ennis in County Clare who had settled in Napier. Before the war they were members of the New Zealand Freedom League, an organisation founded to oppose compulsory military training. Called up in March 1917, the brothers went into Trentham Military Camp but soon escaped and headed to the South Island's West Coast. Jack took an engine-driving job under the name 'Neil McCarthy' on the railway line near Otira, while Bill worked for the Post and Telegraph Department in Otira as 'J H Morton'. Bill was arrested at Otira in October 1917, and Jack was picked up soon after in Greymouth but managed to escape. He was recaptured at Otira and taken to the Buckle Street Barracks in Wellington where Bill was already being held. Further escape attempts were foiled, and the brothers each received a sentence of four months' hard labour in November 1917.[24]

Interviewed in 1970 about his experiences during the First World War, Jack Doyle described the support offered to other evaders who elected to 'go bush' by the Donnellan family of Nelson Creek. The Donnellans were a prominent Catholic mining family whose patriarch, Patrick, also hailed from County Clare.

> The Donnellan family of Nelson Creek set up a refuge for those seeking to avoid conscription. This consisted of a bush hut near the Donnellans: at one time there were 13 men living there and some of them lived there for up to two years. They were fed by the Donnellans and spent their time fossicking for gold in the area. It became known by word of mouth among radical and Irish circles that the West Coast was the place to go to evade conscription, and many with an Irish background gravitated to the West Coast and to the Donnellans.[25]

Doyle also recalled that when he was captured, the Donnellans had apparently considered mounting a rescue attempt to break him out but the police guard proved too formidable to risk the attempt.

Another group who took refuge in the West Coast bush were exposed after an accident befell one of their number, Vince Carroll, who was killed by a falling tree branch. He was one of seven sons born to parents from County Cork who farmed near Palmerston North and were prominent rugby players in Manawatu. With cousins involved in the struggle back in Ireland, the Carrolls grew up with a strong sense of Irishness. Vince, Frank, and William were subject to some of the earliest arrest warrants for military defaulters when they failed to respond to their call-ups in early 1917. All went into hiding. Frank was subsequently caught in South Canterbury, as 'Frank Brennan', and sentenced to two years' hard labour. William was never caught but was penalised as a defaulter in 1919. Vince, meanwhile, had hidden out successfully with Tom Kiely and Pat Skinner in their bush camp on the West Coast, twelve miles from

Ikamatua, from April until his fatal accident in November 1917. His two mates were arrested when they brought his body out to the road and reported his death in Reefton. Thomas Shanahan was subsequently prosecuted (unsuccessfully) for employing the three men as bush fellers and supplying them with food.[26]

Other locations are also remembered as sheltering evaders. There are anecdotal accounts of large numbers of Irish evaders finding shelter on the East Coast north of Napier. Many were helped by the proprietor of the Royal Hotel in Gisborne, Joe Martin.[27] One Irish evader from the Royal Hotel who successfully reached Australia was Dan Butler. A letter intercepted by the authorities in 1919 described his experience:

> I was in Brisbane at Easter and there I met Dannie Butler. You know him, big James Butler's son of Dongonnell. He escaped from New Zealand during the conscription campaign, come to Sydney and from there to Brisbane, he is working 50 miles up in the Bush … I think he had a rough time before he left New Zealand evading the Military authorities.[28]

In mid-1918, *The Wairarapa Age* reported public fears about large numbers of armed evaders hiding out in remote areas near the military camps in that district.[29] This may have been prompted by the case of Robert and John Larkin. Captured stowing away on a ship to Australia in November 1917, the two brothers from Kawakawa were in custody at Trentham Military Camp when they overpowered their guards and escaped in January 1918. They were recaptured five months later in scrub-cutting camps at a sheep station near Martinborough with false papers and having assumed false names. In lieu of further detention, the brothers agreed to go overseas with the 40th Reinforcements, but Robert deserted in South Africa as soon as their troop ship reached Cape Town. John did his time in uniform in military camps in England, returning to New Zealand in 1919 without ever firing a shot in anger.[30]

Heading overseas is another indicator of the support networks that existed for military evaders. Information on this escape route is found in police records too. In March 1917, for example, *The Green Ray* manager Bert Ryan was reported to the police after being overheard in a Dunedin hotel offering to get someone away to Australia. He boasted of having already succeeded in getting five or six men away through marine firemen smuggling them onto ships for a £10 fee. A couple of months later, police reports acknowledged that deserters were stowing away on ships with assistance from seamen, and the military authorities sought greater assistance from customs officers with ship searches.[31] Bernard Bradley (Jim Bradley's brother) was part of a group of five Irish stowaways on the *Manuka* to Australia in August 1918. A police tip-off led to the ship being searched in Sydney, and the five evaders were discovered. They were returned to New Zealand to face charges varying from leaving New Zealand without a permit to desertion. The most interesting detail, however, is that the men were found to have a large sum of money with them, evidence perhaps of financial support from sympathisers in New Zealand.[32]

OPTION THREE: DEFYING CONSCRIPTION

Once captured, military service evaders came under great duress to serve as soldiers. For those who continued their defiance, the stakes could become very high. The most famous group to pay severely for their resistance are the fourteen conscientious objectors who were shipped overseas on a troop ship in July 1917. Their story has become well known thanks to the memoir written by Archibald Baxter. *We Will Not Cease*, first published in 1939, tells in horrifying detail of the systematic abuse meted out to these men, most of whom ultimately agreed to serve as stretcher bearers or infantrymen. The 'Fourteen' included a general mix of pacifists, socialists, and Irish objectors, though, unfortunately, none apart from Baxter have left any detailed account of their motivations.

Two, however, were identified at the time as having Irish objections. Daniel Maguire was a Catholic labourer from Foxton who had been born in England to parents from County Derry. Only in New Zealand since 1915, his next-of-kin was listed as his father in Derry, so he was probably close to contemporary developments in Ireland. Maguire first spurned military service in April 1917 and endured repeated terms of detention.

He remained resolute through the ill-treatment meted out to the men aboard the troop ship and through the increasing pressure to submit once they reached England. He continued to resist until they were sent on to France where they were subjected to further brutal treatment and threatened with being shot. Maguire finally agreed to serve as a soldier and joined the 2nd Wellington Infantry Battalion in the field on 8 December 1917. He returned to New Zealand after the war and died in Auckland from tuberculosis in 1932.[33]

Gradually, all fourteen of the group succumbed to illness, were broken in health, or were forced to submit to some form of military service. As their numbers dwindled, the last few were subjected to a form of punishment that Baxter's memoir has immortalised: Field Punishment No. 1. This standard military punishment involved the men being tied by their hands to a sloping post for a set number of hours per day for however many days of a sentence. The last to hold out on the poles was Lawrence Kirwan, a plumber from Hokitika who was the second 'Irish' objector among the Fourteen. Kirwan did *two* 28-day stints of Field Punishment No. 1, double the time that any other man in the group endured. Faced with the potential for an indefinite number of further stints on the pole, he finally agreed to serve as a stretcher bearer on 28 March 1918.[34]

There is no statement of the beliefs that underlay Kirwan's incredible defiance. He never wanted to talk about it after the war, and when Archie Baxter passed through Hokitika in later years, Kirwan spurned a meeting.[35] Family tradition, however, is that he refused to wear the king's uniform because of what the British had done to the Irish. This suggests a 'fenian' family background, since, like the Codys,[36] the Carrolls, the Doyles, the Larkins, and numerous other 'Irish' objectors in the First World War, Lawrence Kirwan was actually born in New Zealand, to Irish parents.[37] In his case, his father's place of origin was Clogherhead, County Louth, where the family still had close connections in the early 1900s. It is also pertinent that Lawrence had served as a Territorial soldier before the war, which suggests that his opposition to the war was quite specifically against that war, not against military service in general.

THE WANGANUI NINE'S 'DETERMINED IRISHMEN'

In early 1918, revelations emerged that military objectors were being mistreated back in New Zealand as well at a special military detention centre in Wanganui. Its commandant, Lieutenant Crampton, had taken upon himself the challenge of 'breaking' his prisoners with brutal beatings until they agreed to serve. When some prisoners managed to smuggle out a letter detailing the treatment they had received, there was a significant outcry, led by family members and publicised by Labour Party leader Harry Holland. An official investigation followed, which detailed the involvement of three men described as 'Irishmen' among a group that came to be called the 'Wanganui Nine'. One was the same Patrick Fitzpatrick from South Dunedin, referred to above, who had escaped from Wanganui and was thus not available to give evidence to the enquiry. The treatment of his fellow inmates Thomas Moynihan and William Donovan, however, was central to the magisterial review.

Both men were New Zealand-born Irish. Moynihan was a gold-miner from Kumara on the West Coast with Irish parents, while Donovan was a flax-cutter from Wellington whose parents had been born in England. Yet both were described at the enquiry as 'determined Irishmen' set on defying the military authorities. They also both had reputations as hard men:

> Donovan is said to have been a man who, in resisting capture, had fought with two policemen, and Moynihan is described as something of a pugilist. I am satisfied that it would take something more than moral suasion to reduce Moynihan to subjection if he had made up his mind to resist. Yet he and Donovan, in less than an hour, were transformed from determined and defiant objectors to obedient and well-conducted prisoners.[38]

Evidence was presented of exactly how Moynihan's resistance had been broken at Wanganui:

> They brought him a uniform one Sunday morning and ordered him to dress in it. Of course, Tom was having none, so three or four

hopped into him, and after handing out punches and kicks, one of which landed over the heart, and which he still feels the effects of, they put the uniform on him and ordered him two hours' pack drill. He refused to carry a rifle and also refused to march, so they tied the gun to his side, and then started him off round the yard, by turns pushing, punching, kicking, and dragging him by the hair of his head. Whenever they pushed him off his feet, as they did on several occasions, they put the boot into him until he got up again.[39]

Photographic evidence exists of Moynihan undergoing the treatment described.[40] When they gave in and agreed to serve, neither Donovan nor Moynihan (nor Fitzpatrick once he was recaptured) was sent overseas to fight. Submission to the state was all that was required, after which home service posts were found for many such 'defiant objectors'.

SINN FEINERS

Few of the men who evaded or defied conscription have a voice in the historic record. Press reports of court cases usually omitted any personal statements of their motivations. When Thomas Spillane went before the military service board in Napier in May 1917, however, his Irish protestations against service were widely reported. Spillane denied being a British subject and refused to swear an oath of allegiance to the British Crown. He had only been in New Zealand for four years and was still supporting family back in Ireland. There were terse exchanges in the court with Spillane citing Irish misgovernment by the British, but his 'voluminous protestations' were cut short by the chairman of the board who dismissed his case. *The Green Ray* noted in its report that Spillane had been supported by members of the Napier Maoriland Irish Society, who presented him with a gold watch in appreciation of his stand.[41]

An even more explicit statement of Irish conscientious objection was published in *The Green Ray* in October 1917 when Tim O'Sullivan wrote to the magazine from his prison cell. Under the header 'Sinn Feiner in Detention in Wellington', O'Sullivan recounted his arrest in Hawkes Bay in August and refusal to either take the oath of allegiance or wear a uniform. He reported that he was being held with 120 other objectors in the Wellington Barracks, with more coming in all the time. More importantly, he stated his principles as a Sinn Féin supporter: 'A soldier I shall never be: I'm a Sinn Feiner. There are a good few of them here so when I have served my 28 days solitary I will probably get 11 months or be put aboard a transport. I am going to stand by my convictions, and am prepared to suffer for doing so.'[42]

Another defiant Irishman whose stand was reported by *The Green Ray* was Tim Brosnan, a recent immigrant from County Kerry. He was described by the magazine as 'an Irishman of the sturdy Republican order' when he became the first *Green Ray* subscriber to renew his annual subscription from his prison cell. Called up in January 1917, Brosnan had left his home at Owhango, near Taumarunui, and headed south. Keeping ahead of the law for six months, he was finally caught at Winton in Southland in August 1917. After stints in detention in Dunedin and Wellington, he went on trial at Trentham and had a chance to proclaim his beliefs: 'I said I was an Irishman, a Sinn Feiner and refused to fight for a country that had prosecuted and murdered my country and my people for hundreds of years.'[43] Time in jail did nothing to cool Brosnan's republican ardour. Supported by his wife, 'also a Sinn Feiner', his letters to family members in Queensland from prison were subsequently intercepted by military censors in Australia who were shocked by their contents:

> Dear sister Maggie … you know how long ago I was sentenced to two years hard labor in a New Zealand prison, because I would not shame my good parents [*sic*] name or become a traitor to my country, by donning a uniform and taking an oath of allegiance to fight and die for my greatest enemy and oppressor and tyrant of my native land.[44]

HOW MANY?

Paul Baker, in his classic study of conscription, *King and Country Call*, suggested that the number of men who evaded military service in New

Zealand, or who failed to even register for it in the first place, could be anywhere between 3,900 and 8,500. He further estimated that between 2,800 and 6,400 were never found by the authorities. The minister of defence released a press statement in October 1918 that acknowledged the scale of the department's challenge tracking 'shirkers':

> The general public has but a faint conception of the mass of work that has fallen upon the Defence Department (or at least the particular Branch responsible) in connection with absentees, deserters, shirkers and military defaulters of all colours, creeds and nationalities, who from various causes – some accidental but more often deliberately and wilfully engineered – have failed to concentrate [*sic*] at appointed times and places.[45]

It said that 10,460 men had failed to appear for call-up, though departmental action had subsequently tracked down 8,352 of them. Warrants for the arrest of the remainder had been issued with most still unexecuted at war's end. Thousands more had kept their names out of the data pool by not registering their details in 1915.

Additional penalties were imposed on the 2,155 men that the government could positively identify as military defaulters at war's end: men who had failed to appear for medical inspection, attend camp, or had deserted after attestation. About a quarter of them bear surnames that suggest an Irish heritage. This is a much higher proportion than the estimated 10 per cent of Irish-motivated objectors among the 286 men who ended up in prison.[46] It is tempting to see this as evidence of successful evasion and a tribute perhaps to the Irish networks that supported men on the run. However you cut the figures, there were a lot of men – thousands – who defied the conscription regulations in New Zealand during the First World War and sought to avoid military service.[47] As the individual stories above attest, Irish men (both Irish-born and Irish ethnics) were notable among them.

CHAPTER 8

Challenging Times: The Irish-Catholic press in Dunedin and Adelaide, 1916–19

STEPHANIE JAMES
(*Flinders University*)

T his chapter investigates some of the challenges the Irish-Catholic press faced in Australasia in the period from 1916 to 1919.[1] It focuses on two periodicals: *The New Zealand Tablet*, published in Dunedin, New Zealand, and *The Southern Cross*, published in Adelaide, South Australia, and examines ways in which these journals took cognisance of one another between the 1916 Easter Rising and the inauguration of an Irish Republic, marked by the first meeting of Dáil Éireann, in January 1919. Having strongly supported John Redmond and the Irish Parliamentary Party (IPP) for many decades, both periodicals found themselves suddenly obliged to take account of the radical intervention and growing influence of Sinn Féin.

After investigating the similarities and differences between *The Tablet* and *The Southern Cross*, the chapter then looks at the contexts in which their respective editors were working, before briefly examining the external and domestic factors impacting on both periodicals. The chapter then assesses the significance of a range of *Tablet* 'exchanges', selected by the editor of *The Southern Cross*, Frederick Martin Koerner, between mid-1916 and early 1919, as a way of understanding how these 'exchanges' plus the known role of significant individuals in Adelaide might have influenced what was published in *The Southern Cross*. The conclusion suggests how and why the Catholic press of Dunedin and Adelaide need to be understood in relation to one another in their reporting of Irish events.

The 'exchange' process utilised by both newspapers, and many other diaspora publications, provides a crucial underpinning to the argument. Editors typically communicated with their fellows, sending copies of their own papers and receiving others in return. In these papers, editors occasionally referred to the 'exchange table', conjuring up images of an office fixture specifically devoted to presenting an array of incoming newsprint from a range of countries.[2] Exchange items were usually attributed, so readers were clearly informed about their precise origin. Across the diaspora, such an interconnected information network was often able to counteract the bias of the secular press.[3]

SIMILARITIES AND DIFFERENCES BETWEEN *THE TABLET* AND *THE SOUTHERN CROSS*

The Tablet, established by Bishop Patrick Moran of Dunedin in 1873, and *The Southern Cross*, set up by Adelaide's Archbishop Christopher Reynolds and advisors in 1889, operated as public companies involving directors and shareholders.[4] But they were also enmeshed within the structures of the Catholic Church, with the local bishop exercising significant control. By 1916, John Askew Scott was the fourth editor in Dunedin and the second layman, whereas in Adelaide, Frederick Martin Koerner followed two earlier laymen and was only the third editor. The consistent appearance of small, often personal items about *Tablet* editors in the weekly 'Purely Personal' column in *The Southern Cross* is evidence of connections across the Irish-Catholic newspaper network.[5] When *The Southern Cross* achieved its twenty-fifth year of publication in mid-1914, Scott's editorial noted his appreciation for the Australian publication, undoubtedly because of a felt kinship.

> Our excellent contemporary, the Adelaide 'Southern Cross', has just celebrated its silver jubilee, and we extend our most cordial felicitations on the occasion. Speaking as an absolutely disinterested

outsider, we can truthfully say that, for its size, the 'Southern Cross' is one of the brightest, most readable and best edited papers that comes to our exchange table. We do not know whether South Australians fully realise how exceedingly well they are served in the matter of their Catholic paper.[6]

The pre-1916 attitudes of both papers reflected 'devotion to the Irish Party' and its longstanding endorsement of Home Rule,[7] but the Rising announced an Ireland that was, in the words of the poet, 'all changed, changed utterly'. The more the British reacted, the less the IPP's constitutional solutions seemed feasible, and the more Sinn Féin, which was established by Arthur Griffith and Bulmer Hobson and wrongly but widely attributed with responsibility for the revolutionary events of 1916, was viewed as offering a way forward.[8] In fact, neither Griffith, who opposed the use of force, nor Sinn Féin was involved in the Rising. Nevertheless, due to widespread but inaccurate beliefs in its achievements, the organisation's potency, in terms of a 'condition of possibility' for Ireland, was not recognised at first, either within the country itself or by observers across the diaspora.[9] The fluidity of post-Rising Ireland was testing in every way. For editors across the diaspora, the long-distance recipients of details, the weekly task of conceptualising and explaining this radically new 'condition of possibility' proved particularly challenging. Some seemed better equipped, by experience, conviction, and/or personality, both to shift their newspaper's perspective and to fulfil their readers' urgent need for information and clarity. In New Zealand from 1917, as will become evident, *Tablet* readers were privy to a much clearer position on post-Rising Ireland than were their fellow diaspora readers in South Australia.[10]

A TRINITY OF EDITORS: F.M. KOERNER, J.A. SCOTT, AND J.J. KELLY

In Dunedin, Scott, an English-born convert from Presbyterianism, had followed Irishman Father Henry William Cleary as editor of *The Tablet* when the latter became bishop of Auckland in 1910.[11] Just before news of the Rising reached Australia, *The Southern Cross* reported that Scott's poor health had precipitated a lengthy restorative trip to Australia.[12] And by November, readers learned of his resignation on health grounds and his willingness to remain in the role of editor until the position had been advertised and filled.[13]

In March 1917, there was good news from Koerner that Dr James Joseph Kelly, an Irish priest already in New Zealand for his health, had accepted the editorship. Kelly's potted biography mentioned revolutionary and ecclesiastical credentials. He was 'born on the ... slopes of Vinegar Hill, County Wexford' and was a 'nephew' of Sydney's Archbishop Kelly. Educated in Rome, he had been 'four years already in the Archdiocese of Wellington'.[14] Researcher Heather McNamara describes 'a rapid shift in the tone' of *The Tablet* after Kelly's appointment.[15] Elsewhere she writes, 'More than the editors who preceded him, Kelly used the immediacy of his connections in Ireland to garner information with which to inculcate Irish-Catholic readers ... with his particular version of Irish nationalism.'[16] Kelly was subsequently dismissive of his 'convert' predecessor as having 'imperialistic views and general indifference to Irish questions', arguing that *The Tablet* 'was hardly read at all even by the subscribers'.[17] However, as McNamara's archival material shows, Kelly's repositioning of *The Tablet* in relation to Ireland was of concern to the directors and to some of the hierarchy. Diaries kept by Catholic layman Thomas J. Hussey, who was 'in charge of the account books' when Kelly became editor early in 1917, provide glimpses into the nature of Kelly's relationships.[18] In particular, Hussey 'repeatedly' highlighted directors' meetings and 'private conversations' where the 'fired up' editor was engaged in lively discussions about the 'Irish policy of the paper'.[19]

By November 1917, according to Hussey's diary, Dr Cleary was 'on [the] warpath'. McNamara categorises this as 'a personal campaign against Kelly's extreme Irish policy'.[20] In his assessment of this period, Seán Brosnahan has argued for the church achieving some success against what many viewed as Kelly's extremism. Mentioning the episcopal onslaught Kelly survived in late 1917, he states, 'a week later the directors of the *New Zealand Tablet* responded directly. They struck down the proud assertion carried on the paper's masthead for some years: "Sole Organ of Catholic Opinion".'[21] For her part, McNamara refers to a number of directors' meetings in 1919 when they attempted to 'steer Kelly towards a more moderate tone'.[22] The context of *The Tablet* editor's well-documented radical perspective from March 1917 assumed greater importance when *The Southern Cross'* use of its exchanges began to increase from that point; although, in Adelaide, the nature of the relationship between editor and directors seems to have been very different.

Koerner was *The Southern Cross* editor from May 1903. He was also treasurer of the local United Irish League (UIL), the voice of Irish nationalism and promoter of Home Rule in Australia since 1900. In both roles, Koerner, Australian-born of Irish and German descent, played a pivotal part in supporting the visits of IPP delegates in 1906 and 1911–12. Given these dual, interconnecting roles, it seems likely that Koerner faced acute personal pressure as editor following the Rising, which suggests why the newspaper's dramatic move from constitutionalism to Sinn Féin was so difficult. As editor, Koerner, without Dr Kelly's close links to Ireland, was nevertheless supported by six directors, three of whom were senior priests and three of whom were prominent, newspaper-experienced laymen. Beyond this group was Cork-born Robert William Spence, Adelaide's archbishop from 1915 to 1934. (Given that *The Southern Cross* was under his aegis, he could exercise control.) Throughout the war years, the clerical directors were Irish-born but resident in South Australia since the 1880s, while their lay colleagues were second-generation Irish Australians.[23] Two lay directors were former editors, and both served their country during the war.[24] While no record of monthly directors' meetings has survived, W.J. Denny, the second editor and a lay director, wrote of the absence of friction in the relationship between editor and directors.[25] Following the defeat of the first Australian conscription plebiscite in October 1916 and decisive opposition from *The Southern Cross* in three consecutive editorials, Koerner revealed that the decision to use the paper to oppose conscription had been made by the directors.[26] And in April 1917, just prior to the May federal election, Koerner's editorial was followed by the statement that it was '[w]ritten [by him] after consultation to express the views of the *Southern Cross*'.[27] Unlike Dr Kelly's first years with *The Tablet*, surviving evidence points to a consultative and productive relationship between Koerner and the directors.

EXTERNAL FACTORS

Given the evolution of Sinn Féin, the rapid and, for the most part, unpredictable movement of British policy on Ireland after the events of 1916 – aside from continuing support for Home Rule and opposition to a republic – caused major problems for editors, newspaper staff, and their readers.[28] The immediate declaration of martial law in Dublin represented the first period of British response. Having acknowledged that government machinery had disintegrated, Lloyd George was then tasked by Prime Minister Asquith with renegotiating a settlement of the Irish question. His duplicitous negotiations, promising Home Rulers the unattainable in terms of temporary partition, resulted in IPP withdrawal and the reinstatement of Castle rule. Lloyd George, by then prime minister, announced the Irish Convention in May 1917, promising to accept its proposals if agreement was reached. Remaining a broad church that accommodated adherents of physical force, former Home Rule supporters, and those opposed to political violence, the emergent Sinn Féin refused to participate. Its refusal, coupled with its by-election victories of January, May, July, and August 1917, meant that its non-participation became a live fuse. In April 1918, the joint bills for Irish conscription and Home Rule further united Irish opposition, and the subsequent publication of the convention report appeared to end any official possibility of Ireland determining its own future. Britain then abandoned the process of broad discussion about Home Rule for all Ireland, postponed conscription, and, after uncovering an alleged (but timely) German plot, arrested and deported many in Sinn Féin. Martial law was imposed; public gatherings were banned. After the Armistice, at the United Kingdom's general election of 14 December 1918, the IPP won only six seats while seventy-three Sinn Féin members were elected. Home Rule, it became evident, had been decisively destroyed. The Ireland of 1918, it seemed, bore little if any relationship to the Ireland of 1914.[29]

While optimism about Ireland's future dominated 1919, the atmosphere soon changed. In that year, euphoria surrounded the January declaration of the Dáil, President Woodrow Wilson's promise of 'self-determination', and the widely held belief that, as a 'small nation', Ireland's independence would be peacefully achieved at the post-war 'peace' conference. In the wake of British intransigence, reinforced by Wilson's strong disinterest in Irish pleas and the failure of Sinn Féin delegates to receive any hearing at Versailles, violence in Ireland increased, and the Dáil was banned. By the end of 1920, British decisions – such as the introduction of the Black and Tans to augment the Royal Irish Constabulary and negotiations towards the December passage of the Government of Ireland Act, which effectively partitioned the country – facilitated hard-line control of Sinn Féin.

Thus, for the editors of both weekly newspapers there were ongoing difficulties arising from sourcing up-to-date, reliable information about an increasingly volatile Ireland. Inevitably, many of their readers accessed other sources, such as international, national, local, and provincial newspapers.[30] But readers of both *The Tablet* and *The Southern Cross* expected that the Irish-Catholic press would provide explanations, especially when so many other newspapers condemned the Rising as treachery. As McNamara argues, 'the dailies constantly and perniciously misrepresented Irish affairs and "Catholic opinion"'.[31]

The Irish-Catholic press was severely disadvantaged in its attempts to source a variety of Irish and English secular and Catholic newspapers because it took six weeks for all newspapers to be shipped to Australia. And then, in 1914, further attempts to source a range of opinions were frustrated by the introduction of wartime censorship. Irish news had always been filtered in London, but it became more so after the Rising. In August 1916, Koerner referred to the initial 'silence from Ireland', even while acknowledging that there had been earlier interpretations where balance was missing.[32] Later, he questioned the extent to which 'scanty' cable messages about Ireland 'and the prospects of Home Rule ... [were] due to [British] censorship'.[33] By March 1917, the irregular arrival of the latest 'Irish exchanges' led to publication difficulties; Koerner's solution was to present news of Home Rule developments that came from parliamentary debates in London.[34] In mid-1917, he explained that, in future, only 'important items by cable or mail' would be published; there would be no more of what had existed throughout the paper's history: the regular Irish summary.[35]

Although Koerner had voiced doubts about IPP policy from as early as mid-1916 – he described Redmond's acceptance of the proposed exclusion of Ulster counties from Home Rule as 'compromise carried to the verge of capitulation' – his views did not equate with jettisoning a relationship that had developed over four decades.[36] His editorial hesitation in abandoning the IPP was reinforced by the repeated Sinn Féin by-election victories in 1917. Although it might seem a windlestraw, the admission by the president of Adelaide's United Irish League (UIL) in October 1917 that 'the outlook [in Ireland] did not look too bright' represented a significant shift from optimism to doubt.[37] Despite some local optimism about the convention, the death of Thomas Ashe, a Sinn Féin hunger-striker, in November 1917 was described as an 'atrocity' in Koerner's editorial titled 'British Barbarity in Ireland';[38] the comment from former editor J.V. O'Loghlin, that the 'official murder' would assist 'Sinn Feinism [more] than all the harangues … [of party leaders]',[39] evidenced further recognition of changing realities. When IPP leader John Redmond died in March 1918, his commitment to Ireland was noted in *The Southern Cross*; however, there was no eulogising editorial from Koerner and no hesitation in enumerating Redmond's mistakes.[40] The enormity of the IPP defeat and Sinn Féin's parliamentary victory of December 1918 went without any editorial comment in *The Southern Cross* until 17 and 24 January 1919. While Koerner argued that the UIL should continue to exist locally because it was still needed, he wrote, 'There can be no doubt of this – the Sinn Fein Party and the Sinn Fein policy swept … [Ireland]. The old Nationalist Home Rule Party has been virtually annihilated.'[41]

By early 1918, under pressure from two radical Irishmen – Father M.V. Prendergast and Dr J.A. Hanrahan[42] – about increasing coverage of Sinn Féin by using specific Sinn Féin newspapers, Koerner affirmed the Catholicism of *The Southern Cross* as primary, with its 'Irish character [as] secondary, and it is not the organ of any Irish party'. Justifying contemporary adherence to the IPP, he was clear that this could change if the Irish electors voted differently. Having outlined the history of the paper's twenty-five years of exchange policy – comprising the nationalist press, *The Leader* (edited in Dublin by D.P. Moran), and some American papers – he described the wartime reduction of exchanges, which resulted in greater reliance on *The Weekly Freeman*, *Irish Catholic*, and *Liverpool Catholic Times*. He further clarified his role and that of others in any newspaper policy change: 'I could not allow a discussion as to the policy of the paper in suppressing the Irish Nationalist party until constitutionally replaced by another. That policy was laid down long before I was editor and can only be altered by the Directors and Shareholders.'[43]

The Dunedin response differed. According to McNamara, Kelly initially retained the press links he had inherited, but as Ireland descended further into overt friction during 1918, 'he turned to other sources of information'.[44] *The Tablet*'s 'free list' reveals connections across the diaspora, *The Southern Cross* being one of seven Australian newspapers exchanging copies with Kelly.[45] Like Koerner, Kelly publicised the number of Irish, especially nationalist, newspapers that had been closed by the British authorities.[46]

DOMESTIC ISSUES IN NEW ZEALAND AND AUSTRALIA

Governments in both Australia and New Zealand introduced censorship soon after the war broke out in August 1914. Extensive control of the population was also speedily established: Australia's War Precautions Act (WPA) and New Zealand's War Regulations were both operational before the end of the year. In response to new threats and changing circumstances, these controls could be broadened in both locations. Mail censorship was conducted in Australian post offices in order to intercept material and, from August 1917, to identify networks of correspondents who could be subjected to additional surveillance. In an editorial of May 1918 that responded to an alleged Sinn Féin–German plot, Koerner emphasised that 'censorship prevents us from dealing with Irish material as fully and frankly as we would wish to'.[47] However, his caution protected *The Southern Cross* from experiencing the same heavy scrutiny as Melbourne's Irish-Catholic papers, *The Advocate* and *The Tribune*, both of which were required under WPA 28A to submit all war-related material to the censor in November 1917.[48] According to Seán Brosnahan, by June 1918 the Wellington government's reluctance to be seen to be victimising the major Catholic newspaper was overcome when *The New Zealand Tablet* 'was added to the [minister of justice's] surveillance list'.[49] From July 1918, New Zealand's chief censor was also empowered to require editors to present their complete copy before printing.

Australia's surveillance system emerged in late 1915.[50] With close links to MI5, according to historian Frank Cain, the Special Intelligence Bureau (SIB) 'grew in size and status' between the conscription plebiscites of 1916 and 1917 with its 'official role in surveillance recognised'.[51] From August 1917, the SIB established a national framework which facilitated monitoring Irish Australians.[52] 'It will be well to watch closely all persons known to be connected to ... [Sinn Féin],' cautioned the SIB when British intelligence alerted local authorities that the organisation existed in Australia.[53] The second defeat of conscription proposals in 1917 intensified questions about Irish-Australian loyalty; those associated with Irish organisations and newspapers became obvious targets for surveillance.[54]

The New Zealand government worked to ban the entrance of what were judged disloyal items. From January 1917, for example, *The Gaelic American* newspaper could no longer enter the country. McNamara links such prohibition to the attorney general's warning that *The Tablet* was becoming increasingly 'offensive to a section of the community', arguing that such events 'created an atmosphere in which accusations of sedition and threats to suppress newspapers had real potency'.[55] Richard Davis has shown that some New Zealand papers, previously supportive of Home Rule, 'regularly featured anti-Irish Propaganda' after the events of 1916.[56] And, in 1919, Kelly declared that there was 'a conspiracy against Ireland' in the country.[57]

TABLET EXCHANGES IN *THE SOUTHERN CROSS*, APRIL 1916 TO FEBRUARY 1919

Between June and December 1916, Koerner cited *The Tablet* on four occasions. The first was a 'Topic', one of the weekly semi-editorial items, a small piece that immediately followed the main editorial. Coming while Scott was at least nominally the editor, the piece was entitled 'Syndicalism and Socialism'. It suggested that the plans of 'Pearse and Connolly, and the rest to work up the [April] rebellion and to inflame the minds of their followers ... [were developed] along Socialistic as well as along the more familiar patriotic lines'. Its tone was critical of 'imported Socialist propagandists' and dismissive of syndicalism as 'not a legitimate constitutional working man's movement' and 'little better than anarchism'. The Topic claimed, '[Syndicalism's] one gospel is the gospel of irreconcilable class warfare.'[58] In November, the next reference came from a letter written by a 'well-known New Zealander, now in Ireland'. Headed 'The Situation in Ireland', it listed 'numerous blunders about recruiting', the Dublin executions, the arrest of the innocent, and their immediate deportation as 'chang[ing] Irish feeling towards English officialism'. Displaying a negative attitude towards the 'wretched little insurrection', the writer laid blame for the growth of Sinn Féin on both English policy and panic.[59] By 8 December (after Scott's official resignation), as part of a discussion on the need for relief in Dublin (following contrary assertions by some Irish papers, assertions that were then reproduced in Australia), two young Irish women were interviewed for *The Tablet*. Having witnessed the insurrection, they attested to the 'appalling' misery and need and the unemployment levels, stating simply that '[e]very shilling you send home will be most welcome and needful'. Their 'eyewitness' status was used to reinforce the local need for the 'Irish Distress' fund.[60] Closely aligned with the recent Australian rejection of conscription,[61] the final *Southern Cross* item about 1916 was headed 'Attempt to Conscript Priests in New Zealand'.[62] In 1917, this theme recurred often; it was certainly topical when Australians faced a second conscription plebiscite in December 1917.

In that year, Koerner's use of *Tablet* material increased dramatically. At least fifteen articles were based on or referred to his Dunedin colleague's material, though not all items related to Ireland.[63] But Kelly's items provided some clear perspectives on his homeland, these being articulated in several ways. In his 'Prayers for Ireland' exchange of mid-April, for example, he wrote of the 'gloomy' Irish outlook due to England's determination to crush Ireland 'and maintain ... her historical reputation for tyranny and bigotry'. Writing about prayer across the diaspora, he described more than 5,000 Irish children as committed to saying 'one Hail Mary [daily] for the welfare of Ireland'.[64] Using an interesting comparison between the 'Maori and the Kelt [*sic*]', he drew on

Ireland as a means of explaining Britain's imperial focus on controlling everything.[65] But his far more explicit recognition of Irish reality focused on his understanding of Sinn Féin and what it offered; thus in August his 'The Sinn Fein Viewpoint' emphasised the Sinn Féin contention, in line with the war's early rationale, that Ireland's rights must be settled along with those of other small nations[66] – the Wilsonian emphasis on 'self-determination' neatly abutted this perspective. By December, his tone was more emphatic, particularly in response to readers who thought of the term 'Sinn Feiners as a sort of reproach'. Arguing that to be a Sinn Féiner was something for which Irishmen should be proud, he insisted,

> A Sinn Feiner means … a man who is convinced … that only by self-reliance and by working together can Ireland receive her rights … Sinn Fein means a faith in the old Celtic standards of culture and civilisation, a devotion to Christian principles and a pride in the immemorial traditions of … [the] race.[67]

The number of *Tablet* exchanges utilised in *The Southern Cross* slightly increased in 1918. However, while many items examined aspects of the war or sectarian issues in New Zealand, Koerner's use of specifically Sinn Féin-oriented material did not dominate the year. In the opening exchange, 'The Catholic Spirit and Sinn Fein', Kelly made his editorial stance clear. He wrote, 'The Irish Sinn Feiners have ideals for which they count it a small thing to die, and, because they can die for their ideals, they are now the most powerful party in the world in proportion to their numbers. We [Catholics] have largely the same ideals.'[68] By March, in 'Sinn Fein Everywhere', he advanced the claim that 'the Sinn Fein movement has captured the country'; it was their espousal of an ideal nationality that had attracted wide support. 'For years,' he argued, 'the patient teachers of the language were preparing the soil for the present revival.' He judged those executed in May 1916 as having 'watered the seed' for the present, inspiring 'harvest'. Kelly anticipated that England 'cannot refuse to allow the majority of the Irish people to govern themselves'. As part of the same *Tablet* exchange, *Southern Cross* readers also benefited from an item from *The Dublin Leader* headed 'Sinn Fein and the Irish Language'. At a time when speaking or advertising in Irish was discouraged, '[o]ne of the surest and most lasting things that the new political movement [Sinn Féin] can do is to give a big push to the Irish language cause', because the 'Irish [language] was an essential aspect of Irish nationality'.[69]

Two years after the Rising, Kelly's response to an Irish correspondent encapsulated his attitude to and criticism of England. While England had gone to the defence of 'little Belgium', it had callously disregarded Ireland's right to self-determination; had England practised 'what she preaches' and given 'Ireland Colonial Home Rule three years ago the Irish would' have fought with England rather than against it.[70] In a cynically argued exchange from May 1918, Kelly identified certain 'Imperial Pontiffs' or leaders (like Prime Minister Hughes) whose 'rightness' on Irish issues and guidance for Catholics allowed them to sit in 'judgement over bishops and archbishops': Archbishop Mannix; Archbishop Redwood (of Wellington), 'a sterling Home Ruler who appreciates what Sinn Fein is'; and 'over in Ireland men like Archbishop Walsh ... Bishop Fogarty, and the new Bishop of Limerick; not to mention the vast majority of the ... clergy'. Despite the clamour from such imperial pontiffs, Kelly argued, 'For the present we are entirely satisfied to go on, taking our Irish views from Irishmen whose ability and judgement we appreciate very highly, and our Catholic guidance from the poor bishops whom the Imperial Pontiffs would depose in their own favour.'[71]

In the first two months of 1919, Koerner's reliance on *Tablet* material was more evident; although of the seventeen published exchanges, only six related directly to Ireland. Among the most pertinent were two in mid-February. The first, from someone unnamed but nominated as 'among the senior [Irish] clergy', covered the factors involved in Sinn Féin's electoral victory of 14 December 1918. This item demonstrated the time factors involved in receiving Irish mail in Dunedin and it then being forwarded via *The Tablet* 'exchange' to Adelaide. The writer, one of Sinn Féin's 'prominent leaders', described the effect of the Easter Rising. Kelly's introductory comment about this letter was telling: 'we are struck by the quiet confidence in the power of a united Irish people to assert their rights against the rule of brute force'.

We have prevented the attempted revalidation of the fraud of the unnatural union between Ireland and England; at the cost of a little blood we snatched our generation from being inoculated with West Britainism, and delayed, at least, a national apostasy. Were it not for the men of Easter week, Ireland would be conscripted and partitioned.

Kelly acknowledged Sinn Féin's opposition to the Rising but also pointed to the regeneration of the Irish race – something that had been fully activated by British 'brutality … and criminal treachery'. He was clear that these factors had 'turned the scale in favour of Sinn Fein, made its policy possible, and gave it a stupendous victory'.[72]

While Koerner utilised many *Tablet* items in these years, none were accompanied by comments that explained his choice, nor was there any indication about how these 'exchanges' impacted on his thinking. The general content of the 1916 exchanges probably reinforced his struggle to accept that the 'wretched little insurrection' was anything but a disaster for Ireland.[73] In 1917, however, the emphases of the 'exchanges' changed: not only was Britain blamed for Irish 'gloom' and need for control,[74] but Sinn Féin was eulogised with explicit connections to many positives in Ireland's past. In that year, Sinn Féin's astonishing by-election successes likely impressed Koerner, possibly challenging his opinions about Ireland. And Kelly's direct, personal alignment of Sinn Féin with Catholicism, although not totally consistent with the Irish hierarchy view, was doubtless influential.[75] The powerful ongoing endorsement of Sinn Féin, revisiting the 'small nations' issue and identifying the Catholic archbishops as leading the Irish, especially in the atmosphere of early 1918, seems to have made an impact on Koerner.[76] After the United Kingdom's December election, Kelly's explicit conclusion in the first months of 1919 about Sinn Féin's victory meshes fully with Koerner's communication in May 1919 with Irish editors of Sinn Féin newspapers.[77] In his request to the editors of *Nationality* and *The Catholic Bulletin* in Dublin – correspondence fortuitously captured via SIB surveillance – Koerner documented his mother's Irish birth to establish his credentials. His communication demonstrated not only the extent of *The Southern Cross'* policy shift but also his significant adaptation to Ireland's altered circumstances.[78]

> Dear Sir, I am forwarding you by mail copies of the *Southern Cross*, the only Catholic and Irish paper in the State of South Australia, with a view to exchange. Hitherto we have only exchanged with organs of the Irish nationalist Party. Now that a new party is supported by the majority of the Irish people and the censorship is being lifted, we are desirous of exchanging with a Sinn Fein paper.[79]

Koerner, as previously explained, was supported by six directors and Archbishop Spence. Two of the wartime directors, J.V. O'Loghlin and Father Michael Hourigan, attracted SIB attention in relation to their attitude towards Ireland. Founder of *The Southern Cross* and a second-generation Irish Australian, O'Loghlin was an early Irish nationalist. The intensity of his commitment, as well as the depth of his knowledge about Ireland, was revealed in many lengthy letters to the editor in the 1880s as rebuttals of inaccurate or unbalanced discussions about Ireland.[80] O'Loghlin represented the colony of South Australia at the 1883 Irish Convention in Melbourne (called by John Redmond), and his subsequent involvement at the executive level in all local Irish nationalist organisations reflected the strength of his nationalist pedigree. But he was also, as indicated by his wartime service, an imperial patriot.[81] However, events in March 1917 demonstrate that he was reading the signs in Ireland. Asked to respond to the toast of 'Ireland a Nation' at the UIL St Patrick's Day dinner, O'Loghlin focused on Sinn Féin's increasing strength and the IPP's decline since the beginning of the war. When he spoke of the wisdom of dealing with the Dublin rebels 'in a more magnanimous and generous spirit', he was greeted with 'Cheers.' Similarly, when he posed a rhetorical question about why there were now ten Sinn Féiners to every one previously, his listeners applauded.[82] In May 1918, O'Loghlin chaired the meeting that founded Adelaide's more radical Irish National Association (INA), something noted by the security authorities;[83] he also presided over the August launch of that organisation.[84] In 1921, he became president of Adelaide's INA and the de Valera-backed Irish Self Determination League (ISDL). Like many Irish Australians in these years, O'Loghlin changed his position from IPP support to acknowledgement of Sinn Féin, as he adapted to post-1918 Irish reality. His influence on policy towards Ireland in *The Southern*

Cross can only be implied; however, as managing director from 1896 until his death in December 1925, O'Loghlin was well placed to influence new policy directions for the paper.

Irish-born Father Hourigan was one of the clerical directors of *The Southern Cross* between 1914 and 1926. By 1916, he was a valued senior cleric located at Goodwood, a city parish near where F.M. Koerner and his family were long-term residents. In Koerner's obituary in 1943, Hourigan was described as 'his life-long friend'.[85] The cleric's prominence in local Irish affairs was clearly demonstrated over decades. He donated to all Irish causes, supported visits from IPP delegates (in 1889, 1906, and 1911–12), and in 1916 headed the clerical committee, composed largely of Irish-born members, responding to 'Irish Distress'.[86] In May 1918, Father Hourigan attended the meeting at which the establishment of the INA was proposed.[87]

By mid-1918, he was part of a group receiving banned books about Ireland smuggled from Melbourne. The group's activities attracted SIB interest when a letter from the previously mentioned Father Prendergast was intercepted, naming Father Hourigan's presbytery and Christian Brothers College (CBC) among safe delivery points for the illegal books.[88] It is impossible to know whether those named in this letter did more than receive banned books, but some of them were under surveillance.[89] It seems unlikely that Father Hourigan's impact on *Southern Cross* policy was benign. His subsequent outspoken support for Irish freedom suggests that he likely endorsed the paper's earlier shift towards Sinn Féin.[90] By 1919, he was an experienced newspaper director and someone consistently and publicly committed to change in Ireland. His known subversive actions during the war (involvement in smuggling banned Irish material) indicate his recognition of a changing Ireland, one that required accommodation in the publishing policies of an Irish-Catholic newspaper.

The final individual who was probably most significant in what could be described as the 'conversion' of Koerner and *The Southern Cross* – that is, to accepting a Sinn Féin-dominated Ireland – was a New Zealand-born Christian Brother, David Gabriel Purton. His maternal uncle was Thomas J. Hussey, previously mentioned in relation to *The Tablet* and its editor, Dr Kelly. McNamara's discussion of Hussey provides an important if somewhat unexpected endorsement of Brother Purton's radical perspective on Ireland.[91] Joining the Christian Brothers at a young age, Brother Purton completed his education in Australia.[92] He lived in Adelaide from 1914, a teacher then headmaster at Christian Brothers College from 1920. In 1923, he was appointed as the founding head of Adelaide's second Brothers' school, Rostrevor. Although never a director of *The Southern Cross*, his prominence as an educator and principal of Christian Brothers College, his ongoing importance in the INA (he was one of the small group who precipitated its formation),[93] and his reputation as a public speaker about Irish matters,[94] all identify him as a potentially important force for changing *Southern Cross* policy in the aftermath of the First World War.

As mentioned above, from late 1917 the SIB actively monitored individuals with known links to Ireland, and from early 1918 they were instructed to keep a 'card index' on security targets.[95] When the SIB intercepted a letter from Melbourne suggesting that Sinn Féin was being established in Adelaide,[96] close attention was then paid to the 'very open sympathy' with the Sinn Féin movement expressed during the St Patrick's Day procession.[97] At the UIL St Patrick's Day dinner in 1918, Brother Purton's toast to 'Ireland a Nation' loudly reflected his admiration and support for Sinn Féin. He said it was the

> most sanely conservative movement of the century. It is a movement to conserve Ireland's ancient language and customs, it has been pre-eminently a movement to conserve the land of Ireland for Irishmen, and to maintain her claim to those ancient constitutional powers which are her inalienable right as a nation.[98]

While there is no extant evidence of SIB interest in this particular event, Brother Purton acknowledged the need to be prudent in relation to the fledgling INA, although he chaired its constitution writing group.[99] He was also identified in communications about safe locations for the delivery of banned books.[100] SIB interest continued: in June 1918, several references in surveillance files to the potential closure of Christian Brothers College and SIB's investigation of suspected information leaks suggest this could have been connected to Brother Purton's role at the school.[101] Later comments by Adelaide's archbishop suggest that the threat of closure was real; speaking in 1923, he referred to their schools being 'accused of [wartime] disloyalty, and it was a pretty strong accusation too', despite the 10,000 Christian Brothers' students who had enlisted.[102]

Brother Purton remained of interest to the SIB. In 1920, during the War of Independence, his toast to 'Ireland a Nation' at the St Patrick's Day dinner caused a public storm.[103] Accusations of a seditious speech and Irish disloyalty were dismissed by the Crown solicitor, but the SIB documented the whole process.[104] Despite the weighty evidence of Purton's deep involvement in local Irish affairs, the history of CBC concludes the chapter on 'The Purton Decade 1914–1923' somewhat disingenuously: 'Though the brothers of Irish birth must have been far from happy at the course of events in Ireland in 1916 ... they kept aloof from politics.'[105] Brother Purton was clearly not aloof; in fact, he openly challenged official views about Ireland. In addition, his unpublicised interactions with those quietly subverting wartime restrictions (at the very least, by circulating banned books) demonstrate the strength of his convictions and the nature of his associates and underline the likelihood of his influencing *Southern Cross* policy.

CONCLUSION

The unfolding situation in Ireland between April 1916 and January 1921 posed challenges for all Irish diaspora Catholic newspapers. *The New Zealand Tablet* and *The Southern Cross* faced similar logistical difficulties: distance, time delays, and issues related to censorship, both in Britain and locally. But their editors shared the benefits of a well-developed exchange system. The number of *Tablet* exchanges published in *The Southern Cross* increased from 1917, and the context in which these appeared suggests the respect with which they were viewed. While there were some differences in the operation of the censorship and surveillance systems in the two countries, the similarities seem stronger. Irish loyalty was increasingly doubted, and as the imperial war effort increased it became easier to identify Irish communities with disloyalty, sedition, or illegality.

Editorial profiles and commitment to Ireland seemed most strongly to differentiate the two newspapers. Judging from the exchanges published in *The Southern Cross*, under English-born convert J.A. Scott, *The Tablet* showed little interest in Ireland and seemed overwhelmingly negative towards the Rising. In Adelaide, F.M. Koerner was also condemnatory, but by 12 May 1916 he was acknowledging that there was 'a certain amount of sympathy with the rebels'.[106] While he was a fervent constitutional nationalist in 1914 and remained thus in 1916, in subsequent editorials and commentary his position clearly began to modify. By 1918, propelled by events in Ireland, he had moved towards full acceptance of Sinn Féin. Without any surviving records of his reasons for such a major shift, it can be argued that the input from trusted 'exchange' sources, like *The Tablet*, is likely to have been a factor.

From early 1917, under its new editor, Irish-born Dr J.J. Kelly, *The Tablet's* perspective on Ireland was strong and increasingly unambiguous – Kelly supported Sinn Féin. In the exchanges used by Koerner in *The Southern Cross*, the New Zealand periodical demonstrated more certainty about Ireland and endorsement of Sinn Féin than Koerner's editorials. Evidence suggests that Kelly's directors, far from sharing his views, regretted his outspoken comments; their concern was shared by some bishops, who took decisive action in an attempt to restrain *The Tablet's* influence.[107] While Kelly's exchanges may have assisted Koerner's gradual acceptance of Sinn Féin, *The Tablet* was identified as a problem by New Zealand authorities. Although other Irish-Catholic papers in Australia faced similar criticism, this was never the case for *The Southern Cross*. Koerner seemed to work with full directorial support; that two of the directors strongly supported Sinn Féin makes it more likely that the evolution of *Southern Cross* policy was conflict-free. Archbishop Spence does not appear to have expressed concern or issued a rebuke. It seems Koerner struggled more with interpreting the Irish situation than did his contemporary in Dunedin, and this may explain his inclusion of *Tablet* exchanges. New Zealand-born Brother Purton, closely connected to the radical Hussey family in Dunedin, may also provide a final intriguing influence that helps to explain changes to *The Southern Cross* in 1919. What is clear is that an informed understanding of the New Zealand and Australian reporting of the Rising and subsequent events by *The Tablet* and *The Southern Cross*, two of the major organs of the antipodean Catholic press, needs to take account of the exchanges that passed between them.

CHAPTER 9

'A most cruel and bitter campaign of slander and vituperation': Easter Week 1916 and the rise of the Protestant Political Association

BRAD PATTERSON
(*Victoria University of Wellington*)

In mid-February 1918, New Zealand's newspapers were agog with the news that following a political meeting in the small Manawatu town of Feilding, the Reverend Thomas Miller (Presbyterian) and the Reverend F.H. Stockwell (Methodist) had been set upon by up to a dozen men, thought to be employees of the local freezing works.[1] The well-attended meeting, called to form a branch of the newly established Protestant Political Association (PPA) and described as 'the most exciting and rowdiest in Feilding's experience',[2] had been addressed by the organisation's dominion organiser, Baptist minister the Reverend Howard Elliott, who delivered a sustained attack on the Roman Catholic Church and its adherents.[3] 'Organised Romanism', he preached, was a menace to New Zealand. It was therefore necessary for the dominion's Protestants to organise now to combat the insidious threat. Fearing trouble, the local organisers had smuggled Elliott out through a rear door, but, unfortunately, one of the assailed clergy had borne more than a passing physical resemblance to him.

Within days, a deputation from the PPA had waited upon the minister of justice, urging him to take strong action against 'the enemy at home'.[4] That such outrages could happen reflected poorly on the judiciary and a Catholic-dominated police force. In nearby Wanganui, already a PPA stronghold, an indignation meeting was organised, while nationally, Methodists and Presbyterians recorded their strong disapproval of the attack. Equally condemnatory of the violence, the Catholic Federation nevertheless registered an emphatic protest against the Reverend Elliott being permitted to stir up religious strife 'at a time when the united efforts of the community are required to combat the common enemy'.[5] When arrests were made, the Irish surnames of the accused were widely commented upon. Three were committed to trial in the Supreme Court on assault charges: two being subsequently discharged for lack of evidence, the third sentenced to two months' imprisonment. Noting that this sentence was unusually light, an Auckland journalist pleaded for the community to recognise 'the evil of the religious strife, which, although we are fighting for our own and the world's freedom, is more acute in New Zealand today than at any time for many years'.[6]

Certainly, the public mood was volatile. Hostilities had commenced in 1914 in an unreal atmosphere of optimism and enthusiasm, New Zealand's patriotic young men embarking for a grand overseas adventure. The losses at Gallipoli, then on the Western Front, brought a greater sense of reality. Parents and siblings came to dread the arrival of telegrams, conveyed by youths on bicycles. There was trepidation as households worked their way through the daily newspaper lists of the dead. Grief coupled with an unceasing stream of propaganda fostered an enervating mix of wartime hysteria and paranoia. It was natural, then, that a search for scapegoats intensified. Beginning with anti-German demonstrations, by 1916 the witch-hunt had extended to other possible 'enemies within'. It was in this environment that a simmering broth of anti-Catholic feeling was brought to near boiling point.[7] Roman Catholics accounted for no more than one-seventh of the dominion's population, with the vast majority of Irish extraction, and there were longstanding suspicions on both counts. There was also a class dimension in the strengthening prejudice, a preponderance of Catholics being working class. With the patriotism of militant labour also being questioned, a Catholic/Irish/socialist bogey took form. The tussle at Feilding in February 1918 was by no means unique. Two months earlier, Timaru's parish priest had complained publicly of 'a most cruel and bitter campaign of slander and vituperation' aimed at his flock.[8] There were to be other physical confrontations, and the abuse, freely tendered, reached alarming proportions. In the words of Auckland's Catholic prelate Henry Cleary, it was as if New Zealand was caught in a 'cycle of sectarian epilepsy'.[9]

SECTARIANISM PRIOR TO THE FIRST WORLD WAR

Sectarianism was not entirely unknown in New Zealand. While there had been doctrinal disputation since the missions period, religious animus had tended to be muted until Irish migrants began arriving in greater numbers in the 1860s and 1870s, Irish Catholics bringing with them religious commitments and political attitudes inculcated in the homeland.[10] Although the Catholic Irish spread to all parts of the colony, ensuring that New Zealand Catholicism soon acquired a distinctly ethnic tinge, tensions first became apparent where there were distinctive clusterings. On the South Island's West Coast, a number of disturbances occurred, while in Canterbury brawling followed Orange Order marches on Boxing Day 1879.[11] Such tensions had their antecedents on the other side of the world. The Protestant Irish had also landed with their own religious and cultural allegiances, and were soon joined by co-religionists. First introduced in the 1840s, the Loyal Orange Institution was flourishing by the 1870s.[12] Determined to limit Catholic influence in public affairs, Orangemen and other sympathising Protestants enthusiastically purveyed anti-Catholic literature, despite many clergy and lay leaders making it plain there was a reluctance to rekindle old antagonisms.[13] In contrast to Ireland, New Zealand was an avowedly Protestant country, over 80 per cent of the late nineteenth-century population being adherents, making it relatively easy for the Irish Protestants to merge with the predominantly Anglo-Scottish population. Conversely, the Catholic Irish tended to remain a clearly identifiable 'other'. Yet at no time did relations descend to the violence sometimes witnessed in Canada and, to a lesser extent, Australia.[14]

The issues giving rise to the greatest friction between Catholics and Protestants prior to 1914 related to education.[15] As a result of early squabbles over denominational schools, the Education Act 1877 introduced a secular system of education. This was always a compromise. Fearing that non-sectarian religious education could well mean Protestant proselytisation, Catholic authorities made strenuous attempts to establish their own schooling network while conceding that such education would not be possible for all Catholic children; *ipso facto* all state schools should remain strictly secular.[16] This stance was unyielding and was soon matched by another demand. Between 1878 and 1891, at least four cases for funding of denominational schools were advanced through private members' bills.[17] Such propositions were staunchly opposed by most Protestant churches, who also lobbied regularly for repeal of the secular clause, urging that Bible-based instruction be restored to classrooms by legislative means. From the mid-1890s, several crusading Protestant groups emerged, which, along with other social reformers such as anti-liquor campaigners, the prohibitionists, futilely sought the passage of a General Referendum Bill which would enable Bible in Schools to be put to a vote. Premier Richard Seddon, well aware that the churches were themselves divided as to the wisdom of Bible in Schools, listened but did nothing.

A number of other related issues assumed new prominence when, following the death of Seddon in June 1906, Sir Joseph Ward became prime minister, the first Irish Catholic to hold the office.[18] That Catholics were over-represented in the public service had long been maintained by Protestant groups and politicians.[19] There had been strong charges in the 1890s that the Liberals under Seddon had endeavoured to secure Catholic votes through partiality, although, ironically, a 1909 Royal Commission on the Police Force suggested that, if anything, Catholics did less well under Ward than his predecessor.[20] Alongside was the question of Irish Home Rule, a lively issue in the United Kingdom but one previously confronted with relative indifference by most New Zealand Protestants, who conceived it as the conferral of a status already accorded New Zealand.[21] Visits by Irish nationalist delegations from the 1880s had been civilly received, with Protestant opposition showing restraint. A less favourable response to a late-1906 delegation coincided with Ward's elevation to office: newspaper correspondence columns carried anti-Irish and anti-Catholic attacks, with anti-Home Rule meetings being called in several centres by the short-lived Protestant Defence Association, a front body first set up by Orange groups to protest the number of Catholics in public employment. Adding to Ward's difficulties, the papal *Ne Temere* decree of 1908 provoked an inchoate but ongoing Protestant response.[22] This decree ruled that marriages contracted by Catholics otherwise than before a priest were canonically invalid, as well as illicit. Construed by Protestants as an insult likely to give great pain to non-Catholic parties in mixed marriages, the decree legally did not challenge the law of the land, acknowledging that non-Catholics were not bound by Catholic canon law, but Protestant clergy were in no hurry to point this out. When agitation for protective local legislation failed to bring immediate action, some said it was because of the prime minister's beliefs.

The political landscape radically changed after the 1911 election, which eventually brought the first Reform government to power under Ulster Protestant William Ferguson Massey. In the lead-up to the election, the Bible-in-Schoolers had set up a combined Bible in State Schools League, primarily an Anglican and Presbyterian alliance, which embarked on a vigorous campaign for a referendum on the issue.[23] Opponents were attacked for doing all they could 'to obstruct the one thing needed to make the national schools system perfect'.[24] This new Protestant bellicosity, however, had an unanticipated outcome as Catholics also organised: the objective being a Catholic Federation whose avowed aims were 'defence of the Catholic faith, the uplifting of Catholics generally, and the removal of religious bigotry'.[25] With a Dominion Council, diocesan councils, and parish committees, the organisation was up and running by July 1913, and by early 1914 it claimed a membership of over 100,000.[26]

However, the recommencement of the Bible-in-Schools agitation also witnessed continuing aversions to the deepening antagonisms it caused. While the referendum advocates claimed a signed-up membership of 150,000, they failed to stir the grassroots within their churches, and there were clear divisions both within and between Protestant churches.[27] Most New Zealand parliamentarians were similarly lukewarm. Preoccupied with combating industrial strife, the government exhibited little inclination to become involved, despite important Reform backers. With possible reluctance, in July 1914, Education Minister Hon. James Allen introduced a Bible in Schools Referendum Bill, which was referred to a select committee that ultimately came down against any change in the existing secular education system. In August, war intervened, and it was agreed that the matter should lapse. Even so, prior to the 1914 election, the Catholic Federation sought from all candidates their position on a referendum on Bible in Schools. Only seventeen members were in favour, eleven failed to respond, while forty-eight believed no good purpose would be served.[28] The world of 1914 was not yet one that could give birth to and nourish an organisation such as the PPA.

THE PPA IN INCUBATION

Following the inconclusive 1914 general election, New Zealand eyes turned fully towards the war. The level of sectarian tension perceptibly dropped, previous disagreements seemingly being put aside. Caught up in the wave of patriotic fervour, support for the war effort was almost universally endorsed by religious denominations. Up to October 1915, 35,000 New Zealanders had volunteered for service.[29] Among them was a strong Catholic representation, *The Tablet* boasting that while 'Catholics are about 14 per cent. of the population, yet they have contributed nearly 40 per cent. of the New Zealand fighting force … a splendid illustration of the … practical character of Catholic loyalty'.[30] While a gross exaggeration, the sentiment was indicative of the Roman Catholic Church's stance at the commencement of the war. In a public lecture, Auckland's bishop Dr Henry Cleary declared that Germany had badly miscalculated if it thought the Irish would not support the British war effort.[31]

While in no way dissenting from Cleary's position, the Catholic Federation saw no good reason to follow the Bible in State Schools League's decision to go into recess. It claimed ongoing responsibility for a number of social functions, including support for new immigrants and the provision of hostels for young Catholic women.[32] More pertinently, it lent its voice to the recruitment drive, supported patriotic fundraising, provided comforts for troops, and took responsibility for the erection of buildings 'for Catholic purposes' at the major military camps.[33] If the federation had confined itself to these functions, it could have attracted little serious criticism, but by late 1915 it was again taking up the cudgels in respect of support for church schools.[34] As well as enjoining Catholic parishioners to elect suitable candidates to state school committees, representatives repeatedly hammered at the minister of education's door, raising bitter complaints that the newly formed national government was 'Sectarian and anti-Catholic'.[35] The federation also launched sustained campaigns to remove 'obnoxious and anti-Catholic works' from libraries and bookshops, called for 'kinema film censorship', and issued terse denials to early isolated suggestions of disloyal elements in Ireland.[36] The federation's assertive strain of Catholicism was arguably to have unfortunate repercussions.

Renewed Catholic activism had been observed by hard-line Protestants.[37] They were soon to find their leader and inspiration in the Reverend Howard Leslie Elliott, pastor at Mount Eden's Baptist church.[38] Suspicion of Catholics was ingrained in Elliott and, from the outbreak of war, he had been delivering sermons testifying to Vatican culpability. Born in Victoria in 1877, from the time he entered the ministry, both in Tasmania and Queensland, he achieved 'no meagre notoriety for his Protestant zeal, and became the leader in strong conflict with the Romanists'.[39] In 1909, he accepted an invitation to guide one of Auckland's largest Baptist congregations, where he enthusiastically functioned as a watchdog of public propriety, delivering powerful denunciations of alcohol, brothel-keeping, and general immorality. Concerned with contemporary social problems, for a time Elliott flirted with the idea of launching a political party. When this fell through, he turned his attention to a leadership role in the National Schools Defence League, co-operating, for perhaps the first and only time, with Catholic lobbyists in opposing a Bible in Schools referendum.[40]

Elliott's innate prejudices against 'the Catholic menace' were likely fed by a steady flow of 'no Popery' literature from the United Kingdom and the United States.[41] From the early months of 1915, his sermons focused on the Anti-Christ and Romanist plots to subvert cherished

Protestant liberties. Previously, he had attacked drink, gambling, and social wickedness with little success; now he fastened on blaming the war on the Roman Catholic Church. If the fiery rhetoric found willing listeners among Elliott's congregation, others in the local community were less enamoured, his church buildings being subjected to repeated vandalism.[42] Elliott's discourses and the destructive reaction to them were noticed by his local Orange lodge (Lodge 70, Martin Luther), and he was soon visited by Grand Master H.S. Bilby, who proposed common cause.[43] Lodge 70 was almost certainly Auckland's most militant lodge, incorporating Ulster-born Protestant police officers and several aggressively anti-Catholic nonconformist ministers.[44] It was here that Elliott found his launch pad, becoming Lodge 70's leading personality and chief driving force in escalating anti-Catholic activities. Soon he was addressing other lodges across Auckland, with copies of his addresses widely distributed through New Zealand's Orange network.

Elliott and his Lodge 70 associates were especially active in early 1916. Expressions of approval from Presbyterian and Methodist elements had seen suggestions that a Protestant Association, one 'representative of all the churches', might be formed.[45] A visit in February 1916 by the papal legate, Dr Bonaventura Cerretti, the pope's personal representative, offered another stimulus. The papacy's neutrality was condemned as pro-German, and Mayor Gunson's agreement that the legate preach a mass in the Auckland Domain was condemned as a capitulation to 'idolatrous superstition'.[46] Contrary to all evidence, Elliott claimed that Catholic clergy were actively discouraging recruitment and fundraising, that Romanist Ireland was 'seething with sedition', and that New Zealand's Catholic schools were 'seedbeds of disloyalty'.[47] He constantly expounded these themes over the next three years. Immediate reactions suggest that such extreme views were not as yet widely embraced, the Auckland City Council expressing 'in the strongest terms its disgust at the bigotry and intolerance evidenced', while newspaper columns registered lively protests.[48] For Elliott, however, they amounted to a call to arms. If the Orange Order was to serve as a vehicle for his objectives, the greater membership had to be stirred from apathy. The next step was to engage fully with the Orange leadership.

He found his chance at Easter 1916, as the Grand Lodge in New Zealand met for the eighth time in Wellington, resolving 'to organise for Civic and Political action'.[49] Although a member of the institution for less than nine months, Elliott was already acknowledged as its primary political spokesman and was at the fore of a special committee, drawn largely from the militant faction, tasked to bring recommendations to the gathering before it dispersed.[50] This committee recommended that a further Wellington-based committee be appointed to deal with pressing and unexpected developments and to monitor politicians and public servants for unacceptable views. Increased funding for the Orange journal *The Nation* was sought, alongside additional monies for the publication of propaganda. Most presciently, the appointment of 'a lecturer' (at £300 per annum – near $40,000 in 2015 dollars) to spread the message nationally was proposed, and there was little doubt as to who the appointee would be.[51] When the recommendations were agreed to, a further resolution directed that the over eighty lodges throughout the country be asked to prepare for a campaign of action.[52]

The Grand Lodge's formal proceedings concluded on 24 April. The date is significant. While it is sometimes suggested that formation of the PPA was a direct response to the 1916 Dublin Rising, news of the insurrection did not break in New Zealand newspapers until 26 April, two days later; what was at first termed 'the Dublin riot' being then dismissed as no more than a 'regrettable incident', the work of a few misguided malcontents.[53] While expressing his 'shock and disappointment … at the disturbances in Ireland', Prime Minister Massey hastened to reassure everyone that 'the huge majority of the Irish are intensely loyal, and will prove their loyalty before the trouble goes far'.[54] These sentiments were promptly echoed by other prominent citizens, including Catholic religious and community leaders. Further details were slow in coming to the fore, largely through the British imposition of military censorship, and there were no editorial leaders until the following week.[55] There can be little doubt that the traumatising events 12,000 miles away ultimately facilitated the public emergence of the PPA and helped to underpin its highly successful recruitment campaign, but the foundations for an aggressively activist pan-Protestant organisation had been successfully laid before the first Dublin shots rang out.[56]

THE EMERGENCE OF THE PPA

Putting the Grand Lodge resolutions into effect took longer than might have been anticipated. While sharing the militants' anti-Catholic sentiments, the traditional leaders remained nervous about belligerent action in war conditions. The task of spearheading the formation of an ultra-Protestant political movement was instead embraced by an informal Auckland-based Orange group, drawn from Lodge 70, the Vigilance Committee.[57] Created early in 1916, during the papal legate's visit, this existing committee was small, tight-knit, centred around Elliott (with H.S. Bilby the nuts-and-bolts man), and quite independent of the committees set up at the 1916 conference.

Funded by Orange donations, the Vigilance Committee launched its own propaganda campaign in the closing months of 1916.[58] This campaign saw Elliott expand his Auckland speaking circuit, moving to more public gatherings, as well as the mass distribution of pamphlet literature, both local and overseas-sourced. Much of the latter material was lurid in the extreme, with accounts of clergy licentiousness, but even more damaging were publications such as *Rome's Hideous Guilt in the European Carnage*, over 20,000 copies being circulated.[59] Before long, such publications were brought before the attorney general (A.L. Herdman), and in December 1916, the chief military censor was requested to scrutinise all printed matter passing through Lodge 70's postal box (Box 912), now shared by the Vigilance Committee.[60] That such official action was contemplated when the subject matter differed little from that of previously circulated publications indicates the growth of religious tensions.

In early 1917, the campaign took a new turn. Elliott, determined to further test his platform skills beyond the confines of Auckland, in January delivered addresses in Wellington, also visiting several small Taranaki towns.[61] On each occasion his discourse was on 'what caused the war', followed by the usual homilies on how Catholics were dominating the civil service, threatening the national education system, and through the Catholic Federation seeking to exercise undue influence over domestic, civil, and political life. In Eltham and Stratford, the response was subdued, with the small-town newspapers proving less than impressed, the *Eltham Argus* tartly observing that 'in this little village

community we would fain live at peace with one another ... addresses
such as last night make religious peace impossible'.[62] In a sense, however,
Elliott was achieving his aim, his statements drawing newspaper attention
beyond Auckland. *The Tablet*, predictably, dismissed them as the rantings
of 'A Prophet in Taranaki', urging the introduction of legislation curbing
such attempted rabble-rousing, but most critical was *Truth*, which
roundly condemned 'the noisy little cleric from Auckland'.[63]

It took a hectic meeting in Hamilton at the end of February 1917 to
set the Protestant campaign alight.[64] Attended by around nine hundred
people, it soon descended into uproar. Organised heckling of ferocious
proportions bore out rumours that there would be an attempt by
Catholics to break up the meeting. Before proceedings degenerated into
complete chaos, however, Elliott succeeded in retelling his version of
the war's causes, in indicating that a range of literature was available for
purchase, and in urging good Protestants to join the Orange Institution.
As the fiercely arguing attendees spilled onto the streets, only firm
police intervention prevented physical violence. For the most part, press
reaction was negative. The hitherto restrained *New Zealand Herald* felt
that firm steps should be taken to prevent any repeat: 'during war time
it is essential that ... fanaticism should not be permitted to weaken
national action by disturbing national harmony'.[65] The Catholic response
was immediate and angry, with Auckland officers of the Catholic
Federation urging the acting prime minister to take firm action.[66] Yet
beyond requesting the Auckland police to caution Elliott to be more
circumspect, the government did nothing, with its unwillingness to act
possibly interpreted as approval.[67]

With the Grand Lodge scheduled to meet again at Easter 1917, this
time in Dunedin, the issues canvassed the previous year were certain to
be readdressed.[68] Yet with the Auckland Vigilance Committee having
been far more proactive than the Orange leadership, the formation
of a Protestant Political Association with Elliott as national lecturer
had already effectively been achieved. What was now important was
conference endorsement and backing. When the delegates finally met,
over 7–10 April, all other matters were subordinate, and a resolution to
form the PPA proceeded smoothly.[69] By the end of April 1917, Elliott
had been appointed National Lecturer (soon dominion organiser) and

his close associate Bilby, dominion secretary.[70] Preparations for the public launch of the PPA occupied a further three months, but by early July, the Orange journal *The Nation* felt able to announce that the new organisation could already claim a membership of over five hundred.[71] The formal launch, in the Auckland Town Hall on 11 July 1917 – the date deliberately selected to coincide with Protestant celebrations of the Battle of the Boyne – drew over 3,500 people, with large crowds milling outside.[72] Admissions were solely by ticket. Elliott whipped his audience into a fervour, speaking indignantly of the threat posed by the Catholic Federation, the privileges being sought, the extent of Catholic influence within the civil service, and the unholy alliance between Catholics and the burgeoning labour movement.[73] At the height of the address, however, he introduced a new accusation, claiming that mail intended for the Vigilance Committee had been intercepted and censored by Catholics in the Post Office. Inflaming emotions, he proceeded to read extracts, some explosive, from a selection of letters, purportedly from anxious Protestants. In one instance, it was implied that a nun who had drowned at Taumarunui in the previous year may have been pregnant; in another, questions were raised about the body of a child supposedly buried in convent grounds. These allegations, which soon proved to be fabrications, ensured that the PPA was launched in a full blaze of publicity.

The allegations of Post Office misdeeds prompted Postmaster-General Ward to initiate a judicial inquiry under Christchurch magistrate H.W. Bishop.[74] The inquiry, which opened in August 1917, heard evidence from sixty-five witnesses. It soon became clear that the Vigilance Committee and Box 912 had indeed been under surveillance for months. To test the system, Elliott had posted a number of letters under assumed names, including the inflammatory material presented at the Auckland launch. When Bishop's report was laid before parliament in September, Elliott's argument that the mail interceptions were a Catholic plot was completely dismissed. A reading from the fabricated letters by the attorney general shocked most members, with Prime Minister Massey complaining that in all his years in the House he had never previously encountered statements more calculated to stir religious hatred.[75] A still stronger reaction came on 15 October, when Elliott was accosted by three men, knocked down, and horsewhipped.[76] The leader was a wounded returned serviceman and the brother of the drowned nun referred to at the PPA's launch. When the assailants were brought to court, they were discharged without penalty, and the presiding magistrate opined that the reverend gentleman had 'cast aside all considerations and pretence of ordinary decency'.[77] For some New Zealanders, the PPA's tactics were viewed as squalid and unbecoming of committed Christians. Outraged, *Truth* labelled Elliott 'a slimy sectarian skunk'.[78] For Catholics, the lurid smearing of religious orders engendered new levels of bitterness. An uncomfortably large, and growing, number of citizens, however, retained their faith in the Protestant seer.

THE PPA IN ACTION

The growth of the PPA from mid-1917 was unprecedented in the history of New Zealand organisations. By the end of 1917, under the slogan 'Equal rights for all, special privileges for none', the PPA claimed to have enrolled in the vicinity of 20,000, with more than forty branches formed or in the process of formation, and they confidently predicted that total membership would reach 100,000 within twelve months.[79] By April 1919, it was claimed that the membership already topped 200,000, spread over 225 branches.[80] According to Elliott, growth continued into 1920, when a membership of over 250,000 was stated, amounting to just under 21 per cent of the European population.[81] With few records of the PPA having survived, the figures are now impossible to verify, but even allowing for considerable over-exaggeration, there can be little doubt that a mass movement had been launched.[82]

The time spent planning before the PPA's formal Auckland launch was of considerable value in the recruiting drive, as was the solid organisational and financial support afforded by the district and local Orange lodges.[83] The movement's greatest asset, however, was its leader, who tirelessly stumped the country for several years and was rarely in his Wellington office. Tours and recruitment efforts advanced through the Waikato, Invercargill, Dunedin, Christchurch, Wellington, Taranaki, Wanganui, the Manawatu, and other southern North Island districts.[84]

The strategy in each case was a preliminary meeting with identified sympathisers, often clergy and Orangemen, this being followed soon after by a public meeting. The success of this strategy is evident from the reported attendances. While large numbers, occasionally in the thousands, were to be expected in the main cities, in late 1917 it was possible to attract 1,000 in Gore and around 500 in Petone; early the following year, 200 attended in tiny Leeston; twelve months later, 500 gathered in even tinier Otautau.[85] While the 225 branches by mid-1919 ranged in size from over 4,000 to less than 50 members, almost all had exhibited significant growth from mid-1917.[86] Auckland's Parnell branch, for instance, formed in December 1917 with a membership of 75, had jumped to over 750 by January 1919.[87] Rural Feilding's membership was topping 700 by the same month.

This surge in support was accompanied by the usual exposés of Catholic machinations. Catholic plots were alleged, as evident in Rome's perfidy in international affairs and prospective alliances between Catholics and the labour unions. The Catholic Federation, a constant target, was described as 'a powerfully organised body which had a distinct effect upon the Government and the politicians', and its ongoing attempts to secure education concessions were depicted as sectionally selfish when the nation's priorities were necessarily elsewhere.[88] The perceived disproportion of Catholics in the public service was resurrected as 'an invasion of the citizenship rights of all other sections of the community'.[89] Catholic members of the police force were declared to be exercising their duties in a partial manner, their laxity at PPA meetings being cited.[90] The *Ne Temere* decree, 'which placed the law of the church above the law of the state', was repeatedly denounced.[91] Dismay continued to be expressed at the government's action in prohibiting the admission and circulation of 'loyal and patriotic Protestant literature', this being seen as a 'sop to Catholic feeling'.[92] This proscription was bitterly contrasted with the freedom seemingly enjoyed by Catholic Church publications.

None of these complaints were new, but much more insidious were several issues directly related to the war effort. Sufficient time had now elapsed for the shock of the Easter Rising to be fully exploited in the public mind. A recurring platform theme became Irish disloyalty – New Zealand Catholics and nationalist Irish being equated. In truth, news of the Easter Rising had come as a shock to New Zealand Catholics.[93] Catholic leaders had been quick to denounce the rebels' actions, asserting loyalty to the Empire and insisting that the real Irish patriots were in the front lines.[94] Execution of the rebel leaders after trial by courts-martial and the harsh military repression in Ireland that followed went some way towards modifying prevailing New Zealand Catholic aspirations and Protestant thinking. If a growing number of Catholics were coming to the view that Home Rule would no longer be enough, some Protestants, further angered by writings in *The Green Ray* and *The Tablet*, now voiced strong doubts as to the wisdom of Home Rule.[95] It was but a small step to even shriller accusations that Catholics were 'shirkers' in New Zealand and the Empire's time of need, and that 'the Roman Catholic community should be compelled to take a share in the Empire's responsibility'.[96] In his address at the Auckland launch in July 1917, Elliott implied that Catholics were not enlisting in the hope that if there was an early election, the overseas absence of patriotic Protestants might enable a takeover of government.[97] The unfairness of the charges must have been deeply hurtful to the families of serving Catholics.

The issue which, more than any other, afforded the PPA traction in 1917 and 1918 was conflict over the Catholic Church's objection to aspects of the operation of military conscription.[98] Like most citizens, the Catholic hierarchy had welcomed the introduction of conscription, and when the first ballots were held in November 1916, no immediate difficulty was perceived in that Catholics constituted roughly 40 per cent of the clergy drawn for service.[99] Catholic bishops had made representations to ministers that they would strongly resist the conscription of clerics, seminarians, and religious brothers, though a compromise had seemingly been found when Defence Minister Allen agreed that the military service boards would be instructed to deal sympathetically with these appeals.[100] However, not all boards were inclined simply to fall into line, and while appeals from ordained clergy were uncontentious, the appeals of seminarians and the teaching brothers courted controversy. By 1917, Protestant theological students had volunteered in such numbers that several of their colleges had closed, and up to one-third of male teachers in state schools were enlisted. When in February 1917 the appeals of two seminarians were dismissed, this occasioned a furious church response, and, in turn, the issue became the centrepiece of PPA crusading.[101] Men with wives and families should not be called upon 'to take the places single men of the Marist and Christian Brothers should fill'.[102] Catholic schools should be required to make 'a sacrifice proportionate to that already made by public schools'.[103]

In regard to recruiting, this was in truth a minimal issue, centring on around twenty individuals. However, the strength of public ill-feeling is indicative of the sway the politics of sacrifice possessed, and state efforts to mediate these passions proved a difficult and thankless task. In the short term, the government sought to overcome the difficulty by deferring the call-ups of those whose appeals had been dismissed. Meanwhile, it considered amendments to the Military Service Act to exempt the brothers and remaining teachers in state schools; for almost the only time in his career, Ward was willing to make a special case for Catholic interests. The measure passed narrowly in the House of Representatives, but when it was rejected in the Legislative Council, a constitutional crisis threatened.[104] Politically, Ward was not prepared to push the matter further, but there was renewed pressure on the military service boards to ensure that no brothers or seminarians were forcibly inducted for military service.[105] This result stoked PPA suspicions, and while Ward was already well in the PPA sights, now Defence Minister Allen was continually accused of surrendering to the Catholic hierarchy.[106]

It would have been too much to expect that the dominion's Catholics would simply accept such canards and wild accusations. The more moderate response was that adopted by members of the Catholic Federation and its clerical supporters, who approached ministers, issued statements, and attempted to counter PPA charges in newspaper columns.[107] To be sure, public protests were periodically lodged that government inaction permitted PPA speakers free rein, but for the most part the representations were privately made. Responses emphasised the extent of Catholic contributions to the cause, and when conscription was introduced, the federation's Dominion Executive emphasised that it was 'the law of the land, and members of the Catholic Federation as law abiding subjects will loyally conform to the legislation'.[108] In September 1917, Father Ainsworth's address in Auckland's St Patrick's Cathedral replied for those Catholics serving: 'the blood of Catholic and Protestant soldiers, a common family of loyal Britishers, was at present running in a common stream'.[109] That the PPA accusations were scarcely fair was easily proven. When New Zealand went to war, the Catholic community had gone too, and with its church's blessing. By the end of July 1917, out of 77,283 men who had departed on active service, 9,731 were Catholic; at 12.6 per cent, this was only marginally less than the Catholic proportion of the New Zealand population.[110] There was possibly some slowdown in Catholic recruitment, perhaps reflecting a fraying communal solidarity. According to a December 1917 return, 22.5 per cent of unapprehended defaulters from military service had Irish names and were therefore very probably Catholic (99 out of 440).[111] At a meeting in Otautau in March 1919, Elliott claimed that of 280 deserters from military camps in New Zealand, 111, roughly 40 per cent, were Catholics.[112] The numbers, however, are small alongside those who served.[113] Perhaps Elliott's most offensive platform observation was that it might indeed be imprudent to conscript Catholics, given that they were likely to desert or, worse, bayonet comrades in the back.[114]

Unsurprisingly, other Catholic reactions were less restrained. Following the 1916 Rising, a number of Irish clubs had been established, these federating into the Maoriland Irish Society in 1917.[115] The society was a major disseminator of Irish republican sentiment until its paper, *The Green Ray*, was shut down in June 1918, with the editors jailed for sedition. Yet the most violent reactions came from a distinctly clerical source. From February 1917, *The Tablet* passed to the editorship of Wexford-born priest Dr James Kelly, nephew of the archbishop of Sydney.[116] Kelly was an ardent Irish nationalist, who came to his post determined to return fire on those who had assailed Ireland, the pope, and Catholic loyalty. For him, Irish emancipation and support for Catholic schools were more important matters than the war with Germany. His command of invective was such that after only a few issues his writing came to the attention of the solicitor general, who advised that this journal too should be suppressed and its editor prosecuted for sedition.[117] That this did not occur reflected the government's concern that such action might further antagonise Catholics and reduce their support for the war. While, undoubtedly, Kelly enjoyed considerable clerical and lay support, even the bishops realised such tactics could be counterproductive. Bishop Cleary attempted a more considered rebuttal strategy. In June 1918, he issued a direct challenge to the PPA, promising a substantial payment to the Red Cross if the organisation could disprove his statements of the Catholic position.[118] The response was at best feeble. In the following month, Cleary launched his own journal, *The Month*, but Catholic counterassaults failed significantly to offset the progress of the PPA campaign.

BANISHING 'WARDISM–ROMANISM–BOLSHEVISM'

By this point, the PPA's campaigning front had already appreciably widened. The ultra-conservative elements forming the backbone of the organisation had long supported Massey's Reform Party. Ward, it was claimed, was in thrall to his co-religionists, carrying most of his fellow Liberals with him. Conservatives had longstanding concerns about the readiness of the Liberals to co-operate with representatives of the labour movement, but so long as the movement was splintered, any danger was considered to be more potential than real. The formal establishment of the New Zealand Labour Party in July 1916, bringing together formerly competing factions, changed all that.[119] The critical stances that sections of the labour movement had already taken in regard to the conduct of the war, most evident in charges of sedition, were anathema to the PPA, and a fervent belief that the labour movement had been infiltrated by Catholics, who would exercise a controlling hand in Labour Party affairs, created an even greater – 'Wardism–Romanism–Bolshevism' – bogey.

With the launch of the PPA, all of Elliott's pre-war prejudices of Catholic influences on organised labour had been revived. It was alleged in mid-1917 that an unholy alliance was being forged in which Catholics were seizing control of the unions.[120] True Protestant working men were urged to join the PPA and ensure that all Catholics were barred from taking union office.[121] There were stinging responses, however, from Labour Party officials, who challenged Elliott to present proof, but nothing of any substance was forthcoming.[122] Further wild charges included that there was a preponderance of Irish names at the most recent Labour conferences, that priests were acting as organisers, and that not a single Labour member would hold his parliamentary seat 'in the face of Roman opposition'.[123] The exchanges continued throughout 1917 and into 1918. Significantly, while it was not, as Elliott frequently alleged, a case of an alliance being brokered between the church and Labour, there is evidence that between 1916 and 1919 the bulk of Irish Catholics did transfer their allegiance from the Liberals to Labour.[124]

From the beginning, a proclaimed objective of the PPA was to 'secure the return of approved candidates to Parliament and to civil office'.[125] At elections, it would list tickets of candidates who were in accord with its views. Yet by September 1917, Elliott was speaking of the PPA 'nominating' candidates for every seat at the next general election, confidently predicting that the PPA could capture at least forty seats, half of those in the House of Representatives.[126] Through early 1918, a more sophisticated organisational structure, one aligned to electorates, was developed and, following school committee elections in many parts of the country in April 1918, Elliott was able to report conspicuous success in the return of 'Protestant tickets'.[127] In November 1918, the Wellington Central by-election provided the PPA with an opportunity to explore just how effectively it might bid for power in its own right.[128] With the major parties pledged not to contest with each other, there was no Reform candidate in the running. Government support for Liberal candidate W.H. Hildreth, dismissed by the PPA as a 'wobbly Protestant', was lukewarm, and there was concern that the official Labour candidate, Scottish-born Peter Fraser, 'an anti-conscription Bolshevik' and 'a Red Fed', might poll well.[129] Fraser personified all that the PPA disliked. The third serious candidate, Protestant M.J. Mack, was a conservative unionist who had been a hard-line member of a military service board that had refused exemptions to seminarians. Eager to demonstrate the force of its influence, the PPA vigorously campaigned for Mack. Yet when the result was declared, Fraser was home by a long lead, attracting more than twice the votes of Mack in second place, with Hildreth a distant third.[130]

This reverse was a surprise for the PPA, Elliott predictably attributing the result to the 'sectarian and self-seeking interests of extreme Red Fedism, Liquor and Roman Catholicism'.[131] There was nevertheless a realisation that its support base was primarily drawn from the most conservative sections of the community and that if the PPA chose to contest directly with Reform candidates, there was every possibility that the conservative vote could be split in key electorates, thus enabling Labour victories. With this being more than could be countenanced, the PPA abandoned all thought of putting up its own candidates, opting instead to act as a powerful conservative pressure group with an informal understanding with the Reform Party. It was fully involved in the lead-up to the first post-war general election, scheduled for November 1919. Actively campaigning from the beginning of the year, the PPA combined its usual anti-Catholic abuse with even more savage attacks on Labour, which it linked to 'the Industrial Workers of the World (IWW), controlled from Berlin'.[132] A major election issue was Protestantism versus Catholicism. Reform won the election convincingly. It is impossible to determine precisely the impact of the PPA's campaigning, but in two seats their influence was significant. In Awarua, former prime minister Sir Joseph Ward was defeated, although other factors undoubtedly played a part, Ward having effectively been an absentee member for many years.[133] In the Bruce electorate, Sir James Allan survived, but only just, his past willingness to consider Catholic views having been repeatedly vilified.[134] Probably, the PPA's major achievements were to alter the size of some majorities and to impart a generally poisonous atmosphere to the practice of politics. Nevertheless, following the election Elliott claimed that the PPA was now the most powerful political force in the country, that 70 per cent of the new parliament's members were pledged to uphold the association's principles, and that around forty members owed their seats directly to the association's support.[135]

CONCLUSION

The PPA was an unruly and vindictive child of the stresses of war and flourished on fostered resentments. What made it stand head and shoulders above other dissonant New Zealand wartime organisations was both the extremism of its messages and the rapidity with which it transformed itself from a small, tight-knit activist pressure group into a genuine mass movement, its growth from 1917 being unprecedented in the dominion's history. Essentially, this burgeoning was made possible through the systematic exploitation of veins of religious bigotry long embedded in New Zealand society. Sectarian tensions tended to be curbed in normal conditions, but the increasing paranoia of a nerve-wracked and anxious community called for scapegoats. Giving voice to its anti-Catholic, and particularly anti-Irish Catholic, prejudices, the PPA was eager to assist in the search. Hence the Easter Rising came as a boon. From where was the PPA's supporting membership drawn? While this question remains to be more fully explored, that it was Protestant is axiomatic, with the strongest representation almost certainly from nonconformist churches. While birthed in the Orange Order, the PPA soon completely outgrew it, the greater part of the membership being from outside the lodges by early 1918. All indications are that the membership was weighted towards the lower middle and working classes and that it was equally spread in both urban and rural locations. Perhaps significantly, few individuals of acknowledged social standing chose to be closely associated.

The violent emotions that the PPA had released were not easily constrained and took nearly a decade to ebb fully. Its influence arguably was at its peak in the immediate post-war years, when it enjoyed almost unfettered access to Prime Minister Massey and his Reform cabinet, even if the nominated beneficiaries of its support were sometimes nervous of too-open acknowledgement of the linkage. It nevertheless soon won a number of concessions, including amendments to the education legislation restricting privileges to private schools; a controversial clause in the 1920 Marriage Amendment Act that made it an offence to question a lawful marriage; and, it was widely believed, influence over senior public service appointments.[136] For two further electoral cycles (1922 and 1925), the PPA remained a concerning, if diminishing, presence. The primary targets remained 'Romans and Reds', although it also forcefully advocated for 'a white New Zealand'.

However, as the community distress, which represented the lifeblood of the PPA, began to fade, electorates and congregations tired of the incessant invective. By the late 1920s, the PPA was but a shadow of the force it had once been, as its leaders and supporters drifted away. The nadir was reached in November 1928, when Reform was swept from power by the newly formed United Party, with a rejuvenated Ward at its head. Some wartime members possibly came to regret their involvement, and it may be indicative of a wider communal shift that Ward returned to power with a former senior member of the PPA alongside him in the United cabinet. Less than three months after Reform's defeat, Elliott resigned as dominion organiser, thereafter devoting himself to financial journalism and the spasmodic promotion of other conservative causes.[137] The organisation of which he had been the mainspring, in debt and hopelessly split, struggled on until 1933, when it was finally wound up.

'Too great to be unconnected with us': Reactions to the 1916 Easter Rising in the British Empire and the United States

MALCOLM CAMPBELL

(*University of Auckland*)

I n a scene from Ken Loach's film *The Wind that Shakes the Barley* (2006), Teddy O'Donovan, a Cork guerrilla leader during the War of Independence who has turned defender of the Anglo-Irish Treaty, explains to his critics the circumstances of the agreement's signing within the context of the British Empire:

> Lloyd George is in a coalition with die-hard Tories. As far as they are concerned, Ireland is this tiny dot in a much bigger picture. Do you really think they'd let him give the green light to nationalists in India, and in Africa, and the whole fuckin' Empire by giving us complete independence? It was never going to happen that way and you all know it.[1]

In the film, O'Donovan's invocation of these wider imperial concerns is greeted scornfully by most of his anti-Treaty opponents, whose focus is firmly on the significance of the recent agreement for relations between Ireland and Great Britain. They remain resolute in the belief that the Treaty constitutes a betrayal of the Irish revolution's ideals. The question of how the events in Ireland resonated in the furthest corners of the

British Empire counted little for this group of fervent women and men set on the course of fulfilling the ideals set out in the 1916 Proclamation of the Irish Republic.

The conflict between War of Independence comrades serves as a useful metaphor for a tension between local and wider imperial concerns that has long been evident in Irish historical writing. The late Keith Jeffery, who did as much as any other historian to foster recognition of the importance of that wider context, was correct when he commented in 1996 that 'the notion that the British Empire was in any way an "Irish Empire" is not one that will cut very much ice on the contemporary island of Ireland, north or south'.[2] In the period prior to the Good Friday Agreement, a focus on modern national and local history was paramount. However, since Jeffery wrote, in a reflection of changes in Ireland as well as the impact of newer historical trends internationally, Irish historians have gradually moved from a narrower focus on the nation and adopted a range of transnational and comparative approaches to the past. Inspired in no small part by Jeffery's own work, a key component of this important recalibration has been to acknowledge and incorporate more transparently Ireland's volatile relationship with the British Empire. For, as Kevin Kenny has rightly observed, 'the course of modern Irish history was largely determined by the rise, expansion, and decline of the British Empire. And the course of British imperial history, from the age of Atlantic expansion to the age of decolonisation, was moulded in part by Irish experience.'[3]

A variety of recent work has excavated key dimensions of Ireland's long relationship with the British Empire, with rich studies on India very much to the fore in this process of rewriting Ireland and the British world.[4] However, important aspects of the Irish–Empire relationship remain underexplored, particularly in regard to relative experiences of the white dominions and the remainder of the Empire during the turbulent period of the Irish revolution. In a contribution to closing the lacunae, this chapter investigates imperial reaction to the Easter 1916 Rising. First, it poses the question: what do we know of the Empire's reaction to 1916, particularly in the settler societies of New Zealand, Australia, and Canada? Second, it asks how and why did the response to the Easter Rising within the white Empire differ from that which occurred outside, especially in the United States where Irish migrants and their descendants gathered in large numbers? Finally, it asks speculatively, in what ways, if any, did New Zealanders perceive the Easter Rising as a distinctive moment of challenge to the Empire? Was the disturbance in Dublin in 1916 represented as different from other nineteenth- and twentieth-century acts of insurgency towards Great Britain and the British Empire?

Historians' interpretations of the Easter Rising's reception in the white dominions were set early and have proved to be resistant to change. Richard Davis' pioneering study *Irish Issues in New Zealand Politics*, published in 1974, identified the reflex response of New Zealand Irish Catholics to news of the events in Dublin.[5] Their initial reaction was to express alarm and disdain, with the Dunedin-based *Tablet* quick off the mark to dismiss the reprehensible attack on the Irish people as the product of German interference in Ireland's affairs.[6] More recently, Rory Sweetman has confirmed the strength of the immediate response, emphasising that Catholics of Irish birth or descent 'clamoured to condemn the rebels and to reaffirm their belief in Irish constitutionalism'.[7] In their firm and immediate reaction, New Zealand's population of Irish birth and descent echoed the wider level of impatience, anger, and dismay within their new nation at the actions of the Dublin rebels. *The New Zealand Herald*, for example, viewed the events in Dublin with remorse while highlighting the sacrifice of Irish soldiers serving on the Western Front.[8] In the midst of the First World War and with New Zealanders serving in the terrible struggle on the front lines in Europe, the sense of anger and betrayal towards the Dublin rebels was palpable.

A similar reaction occurred across the neighbouring Australian states. Sentiment among the Irish-born and their descendants was overwhelmingly against the Dublin Rising and supportive of the Irish Parliamentary Party (IPP) and its Home Rule agenda. The United Irish League in Victoria captured well the prevailing sentiment when it urgently cabled IPP leader John Redmond in Dublin to express its alarm at news reports and to reaffirm its commitment to his leadership.[9] The hierarchy of the Roman Catholic Church also strongly repudiated the rebels, with Melbourne's archbishop, Thomas Carr, firmly to the fore with his denunciation of an insurrection that he attributed to the malign forces of German aggression and Irish-American nationalism.[10] A small fringe of more republican sympathisers was located on the Australian scene, particularly in Melbourne. However, the predominantly middle-class Irish-Australian leadership in that city moved quickly and firmly to marginalise the group of so-called Sinn Féin supporters and to endorse the Home Rule party's constitutional pathway.[11]

In both New Zealand and Australia, close familiarity with Home Rule leaders and longstanding commitment to the Irish Parliamentary Party added weight to the dismissal of the Easter Rising. By 1916, the antipodean supporters of Ireland were veterans of almost a quarter of a century of propagandising for the Home Rule cause, traceable back to the pioneering mission undertaken by brothers John and William Redmond in 1883. Their success, and that of successive tours by nationalist icons including John Dillon and Michael Davitt, had been to persuade local Irish and sympathetic liberals to invest their moral energy and money in support of the Home Rule party's campaign. For example, an Australian wing of the United Irish League, inspired by William O'Brien's Irish organisation, was established in 1900, while Irish political delegations toured the newly federated Australia in 1901, 1904, 1906, 1910, and 1912.[12] Pro-Home Rule resolutions successfully passed through both houses of the Australian parliament in 1905, modelled on Canadian initiatives, calling upon the king to grant a just measure of political reform to the people of Ireland.[13]

Reactions to the Rising in Canada closely mirrored those in New Zealand and Australia. Historians Mark McGowan and Frederick McEvoy have demonstrated the intensely negative reaction of Irish-Canadian Catholics to news of the Dublin rebellion. As elsewhere throughout the white settler Empire, raw emotions, including anger, betrayal, and disbelief, were vented at the group of little-known rebels who seemed recklessly to forsake the constitutional path and long-established logic of Home Rule in favour of armed violence. Canada's largest Roman Catholic newspaper, *The Catholic Record*, pulled no punches in its denunciation of the actions of 'the bitter, unscrupulous, and vituperative enemies of Redmond's constitutional home rule movement'.[14] At least two key factors contributed to the vehemence of the reaction. One was surprise, a feeling of being blindsided by developments across the Atlantic that was shared by the antipodean Irish. The other was the ongoing war: at a time when Canadian fathers and sons of Irish birth or descent were serving and dying on the battlefields of Western Europe, the distraction of rebellion on the streets of Dublin was compromising and unwelcome in the host society.

However, there was another important factor at play. In New Zealand, Canada, and Australia, the painstakingly built case in support of Irish Home Rule that took root from the 1880s to the First World War relied heavily on the success of political and economic achievements in those three societies. Proponents of the IPP in each of the dominions argued confidently that Ireland, once freed from the excesses of the current union with Great Britain and granted a comparable level of legislative autonomy to themselves, would develop on analogous lines as a peaceful, prosperous, and loyal member of the Empire. Though the actual Home Rule bills proved much more restrictive, John Redmond's plea, initially made in New Zealand and Australia in 1883, that all Ireland sought were the same freedoms and opportunities already enjoyed by white subjects elsewhere in the Empire, took a strong hold on colonial imaginations. It received endorsement from liberals and gained widespread acceptance in the years that followed. They had provided assurances for Ireland to sceptical opponents. For the advocates of moderate Irish self-government, the actions of the Dublin rebels were illicit ones that breached this covenant. The proclamation of an Irish Republic represented more than a rejection of Redmond and the favoured Irish Parliamentary Party; it repudiated the successful models of nationhood in these nations to which Irish migrants had gone. And, in the midst of war, it was a sharp rebuke to the standing of Catholic men and women of Irish birth or descent living within and committed to the welfare of the British Empire.[15]

In all three countries, sentiment shifted in the months after the Rising. The Irish and their descendants in New Zealand, Canada, and Australia found common cause in their anger at the extreme retribution meted out to the rebels, especially in the case of James Connolly, seriously wounded in the General Post Office and shot by firing squad while strapped to a chair.[16] Tellingly, Toronto's *Catholic Register and Canadian Extension* regarded the execution of the rebellion's leaders after a secret court martial as an act at odds with the core values and practices of the Empire.[17] Catholic New Zealanders likewise became increasingly critical of the failures of British policy towards their ancestral home country that had contributed to the Rising, including the government's spineless approach in failing to stand up to unionists opposed to the implementation of Home Rule.[18] Across the Tasman Sea, Brisbane's Archbishop James Duhig, an opponent of Sinn Féin, captured the deeply held sentiments of many Australian-Irish leaders when, invoking Irish commitment to the Empire, he expressed exasperation at the Rising and the creation of new Irish martyrs.[19]

While members of the Irish diaspora within these three white dominions showed their sympathy for the Easter Rising after the execution of its leaders, Irish migrants and their descendants in the United States were, from its early stages, more inclined to show support for the armed insurrection and the proclamation of an Irish Republic. In America, home to the largest and most influential expatriate Irish-born population, the quarter century before the Easter Rising saw nationalist politics travel on a less defined and more indirect track than that in New Zealand, Canada, or Australia.[20] As early as 1884, John and William Redmond confronted scepticism and outright hostility when they arrived in America to advocate for the Irish National League and the Home Rule cause. New York's *Irish World* newspaper, edited by Patrick Ford, had strong links to the Fenian movement and was famously a stronghold of America's Irish working class. *The World* readied its readers for the Redmonds' mission by publishing a series of negative columns about the brothers' travels. In this reportage, an Australian-based correspondent advanced a message of significant disillusionment on the other side of the Pacific Ocean towards the Redmond brothers and their adulterated vision of moderate constitutional change within the context of Empire. Though these columns in fact presented a jaundiced view of the reception afforded to the Redmond brothers' Australasian mission, *The Irish World*'s large nation-wide readership watched the delegates' progress across North America with critical eyes. At a series of large rallies held on the West Coast and in the Midwest, John Redmond skilfully avoided any endorsement of the idea that physical force was the appropriate strategy to redress Ireland's wrongs. He explicitly deplored the use of violence at his meetings and argued for the merits of constitutional reform. Redmond's reluctance to sanction the use of physical force continued in Boston, where he sought to deflect his critics by emphasising that the future of the nation should be determined by the people of Ireland, not by Irish Americans. The role of the Irish abroad, Redmond stated, was to support the Irish people's strategy of securing gradual political change.[21]

It therefore came as a surprise to no one that tensions over the use of physical force spilled over upon the Redmonds' arrival in New York City. The crescendo of opposition mounted when, in a personal interview granted to *The Irish World*, William Redmond reiterated the National League's belief in the primacy of the parliamentary strategy and objection to force. The delegates' resolute unwillingness to endorse the use of physical force and the timidity of their ambiguous vision for a future self-governing Ireland within the British Empire alienated key segments of the Irish-American population. *The World*, which had once welcomed the delegates' American mission, implored its readers not to invest their energy in the Parliamentary Party's political campaign. Editorially, it made clear its preference for a strategy of physical force alongside Parnell's increasing focus on parliamentary politics. When news of a bomb blast in London broke shortly afterwards, *The Irish World* left its readers in no doubt as to its acceptance of violence in shifting British policy towards Ireland.[22]

The Redmond brothers' visit in 1884 and numerous subsequent fundraising tours by like-minded delegates highlighted a fundamental difference between intra-Empire views of Irish affairs and those of republican America, where radical agitation and hostility towards Great Britain were acceptable. However, the differences rested on more than merely local attitudes to the IPP's objectives or recourse to Ireland's history. Unlike the white dominions, the intensity of support for the Irish Home Rule campaign across the turn of the century diminished due to the way Irish Americans strengthened their embrace of the United States' revolutionary heritage and of the nation's republican traditions. During these years, as the United States struggled under the weight of nativist antipathy to digest enormous waves of new migrants from southern and eastern Europe, organisations, including the Irish American Historical Society, sought to confirm the bona fides of the Irish as true and committed Americans. They did this by invoking their ancestors' involvement in the revolution and narrating stories of the Irish contribution to the building of the republic. The commemoration of Irish leadership and heroism in the American revolutionary era aligned much more closely with the Irish republican tradition of protest that extended from the United Irishmen and 1798 through to the Fenian movement than it did with the IPP's modest proposals for political reform through campaigns in the British House of Commons.[23] Additionally, the United States' history of successful separation from Great Britain and the ideals that underpinned the new republic enabled the existence of levels of antipathy towards Great Britain that were neither present nor permissible in New Zealand, Canada, or Australia. In the years before Pearse and his comrades took to the streets, resurgent Irish organisations in the United States, such as the Clan na Gael, thoroughly anti-imperialist and at heart pro-revolutionary, might hitch their wagon to the IPP's parliamentary strategy, but they did so strategically to achieve their own goals of full separation from the Union.[24]

The outbreak of the First World War prised open more widely this notable gap between the United States and the Empire's white dominions. In contrast to the situation within an Empire at war, American neutrality in the period from August 1914 until its declaration of war with Germany in April 1917 created fertile conditions for expressions of hostility towards Britain's war effort, sympathy for Germany's war aims, and support for republicanism in Ireland. Each of these tendencies was widely in evidence in the period until President Woodrow Wilson secured congressional approval to enter the European war.[25] John Redmond's endorsement of Britain's war effort and his commitment on 20 September 1914 at Woodenbridge, County Wicklow, that Irish Volunteers would fight in the war served in the United States not as a rallying call but as motivation for many to oppose his leadership.[26] In this context, it was unsurprising that the Dublin rebels' actions in April 1916 found immediate favour among so many Irish-American republicans. *The Irish World*, which had been honing its criticism of Redmond's leadership through the first four months of 1916, excitedly recalled in its pages heroic events of 1798 and 1803 while castigating Redmond and his parliamentary supporters.[27] Though the mainstream American press continued to dismiss the Rising as an irresponsible one, both the Wilson administration and British diplomats based in America recognised the high degree of hostility towards Great Britain that prevailed. All worried that public sentiment would be alienated by the insensitivity with which the Easter Rising's aftermath was handled.[28]

Irish historian Fearghal McGarry has written, 'there is a consensus that the suppression of the rebellion was the key factor in the transformation of public opinion after the Rising'.[29] That was undoubtedly true abroad. Angered by the executions, much of the American press showed open disdain for British policy, while the United States Congress debated several resolutions that condemned the executions and demanded that the secretary of state pursue inquiries as to the condition of American citizens involved in the Rising.[30] Even once reliable American allies were angry and opposed: former president Theodore Roosevelt wrote to Hamilton Lee, parliamentary secretary to Lloyd George, regretting the British reaction.[31] The level of outrage and dismay turned to fever pitch, even among those who had been most conciliatory towards the Irish Parliamentary Party and the Home Rule objectives. In Boston, the previously moderate *Pilot* newspaper now linked the Irish in service on the battlefields of Europe and the martyrs of the Easter Rising as co-patriots.[32] Irish men and women inside and outside the British Empire, it believed, would see the necessity to rally behind the Dublin martyrs.[33] Though even in the aftermath of the Dublin uprising *The Pilot* continued to regard the venture as an ill-conceived one, the matter had moved on and dealt a crushing blow to the Home Rule cause in the United States. It was indeed the case, as one correspondent wrote grimly to John Redmond, that his life's work had been 'destroyed' by the British retribution in the aftermath of the Rising.[34]

We have so far considered the ways in which the context of Empire shaped responses to 1916 in the three dominions, limiting the repertoire of responses available to the Irish and their descendants and constraining the opportunities for open dissent. In each of those countries, the situation varied markedly from that in the United States. But what of the situation elsewhere in the Empire? Was there a genuine risk that Dublin's Easter Rising and the wider quest for independence could trigger Empire-wide consequences? Was the perspective argued by Teddy O'Donovan in Ken Loach's film, that change in Ireland had much wider imperial ramifications, actually justified in terms of the Easter Rising? In the remainder of this chapter, we can begin to explore tentatively these wider questions of Ireland's connection with Empire.

There is no doubt that late nineteenth-century Irish nationalism was truly international in reach. At the turn of the century, key leaders across the nationalist spectrum were well versed in the issues of Empire and well known around the world in person or by reputation. John and William Redmond and John Dillon were among the IPP leaders who had travelled extensively through the white colonies of settlement, and each brought these perspectives to bear in their deliberations on the future of Ireland.[35] Other leading figures also drew upon even wider experiences and connections in Asia, Africa, and the Pacific Islands. For example, in addition to a lecturing trip to New Zealand and Australia, Michael Davitt toured South Africa from March to May 1900, drawing direct parallels between the British clampdown in Africa and the aftermath of the 1798 Rebellion, as well as between the discontent of the Boers and that of the people of Ireland.[36] Davitt had also crossed the Pacific Ocean, visiting Samoa and Hawaii.[37] As a result, he was personally familiar with the competition between western powers for control of the Pacific Islands and the ways this rivalry induced political instability. His interest in imperial struggles and their effects continued after his return to London. Likewise, Arthur Griffith, the founder of Sinn Féin, travelled to South Africa in 1897 at the time of its gold rushes, and during a period of almost two years there he observed the Boer campaign for independence.[38]

These connections and a suite of others interlaced the Empire, ensuring the ricochets heard on the streets of Dublin in 1916 echoed widely through the wider British world. The Easter Rising, an act of insurgency within the United Kingdom itself, offered a message of inspiration and hope for colonised populations seeking independence. While a comprehensive study of the Rising's Empire-wide reception remains to be done, a large body of evidence already indicates its immediate impact in the 'jewel' of Empire, India. Patrick O'Leary's study of the Irish in the Punjab highlights how Michael O'Dwyer, the Tipperary-born governor of the province, drew a connection between events in Ireland in 1916 and a recent insurgency in his province that allied Punjabi nationalists and the Ghadar Mutiny. 'In the matter of Home Rule, I fear the case of Ireland, in so far as it is analogous at all, conveys to us a lesson and a warning', he wrote at the time.[39] O'Dwyer's concern over the shadow cast by the Irish Rising proved to be a prescient one, and not just in the west of India. As historian Michael Silvestri has shown, the period after 1916 also saw Bengali nationalists reorient their attention away from continental Europe and towards Ireland as the source for strategies to advance their campaign.[40] Among those figures most honoured in the decades after 1916 was Patrick Pearse, whose ideal of self-sacrifice greatly influenced a new generation of radicals at home and abroad. Yet if nationalists in Ireland and India sometimes found common cause in their objections to Empire, colonial officials in India, including Governor O'Dwyer, were determined to differentiate the Indian and Irish experiences. For the Irish-born colonial administrator, armed Irish attempts to break the Union and challenge the British Empire were of a fundamentally different historical nature than India's ongoing experience of anti-colonial agitation. Whereas Ireland sought to reaffirm a nationhood fought for by venerated historical groups, including the United Irishmen and the Young Irelanders, India had no recourse to national traditions and no comparable experience to Ireland's pre-Union legislature. On this rationale, India lacked essential experience of and capacity for nationhood and so, compared with Ireland, was ill-prepared to take up self-rule, O'Dwyer believed.[41]

More immediately, the events of 1916 and the subsequent War of Independence produced a crisis of a different sort in India. In June 1920, motivated by the British Army's actions in subduing Sinn Féin as well as Black and Tan violence, a company of Connaught Rangers serving in the Punjab disobeyed their orders and commenced a mutiny. The disturbance quickly spread to other Irish troops. Despite the initial colour and enthusiasm, the Connaught Rangers' mutiny proved to be a short-lived one, with fourteen men sentenced to death. While only one of the participants' sentences was actually carried out, Irish units in India were disbanded in reaction to the disturbance.[42]

While nationalists in India took heart from the proclamation of an Irish republic in Dublin and considered which of its actions or strategies might be transferable, there is good reason to question whether the Easter Rising really offered a viable model of action that could be replicated elsewhere. Did the Rising and its aftermath exhibit characteristics of other insurgencies against Great Britain, or were there features that set it apart from other moments of imperial crisis?

A reading of New Zealand press coverage of the Easter Rising, with reportage heavily reliant on British press accounts transmitted throughout the Empire, is suggestive of two notable characteristics about the disturbances in Dublin. The first is the unforeseen measure of understanding shown in press coverage for the motivation of the Irish insurgents and the ability of the reportage to empathise with the non-combatant population. Beyond initial feelings of shock and anger, news reports in New Zealand in 1916 exhibit from the outset a good measure of sympathy for the general population of Dublin, though not for the actions of the rebels themselves. Expressions of concern for the physical destruction of the city matched recognition of the difficulties and privations faced by Dublin's residents who endured the week-long Rising. The challenges faced by Dubliners of attending to religious duties and securing food were noted. Additionally, Chief Secretary Birrell's praise for the civilised conduct of the population of the city during the disturbance received wide coverage throughout the crisis.[43]

Reports of conditions in Dublin that humanised the Irish as victims of an urban crisis stand in stark contrast to the general tone of reporting of Irish political affairs in Great Britain and the Empire over the preceding century. Though generalisation is fraught, it would not likely be controversial to identify indifference or disdain for the Irish people and their aspirations as central features of British reporting of Irish affairs in the century after the Act of Union. This mild empathy with the plight of Dubliners also stands in stark contrast to coverage of communities in anti-colonial protests around the Empire, including the Indian rising of 1857.[44]

Secondly, reportage of the Easter Rising was largely devoid of the racial stereotypes that had characterised English reporting of Irish affairs over the course of the nineteenth century. While recourse to racial images and ideas had been particularly prevalent during the mid-century campaign for repeal and the years of the Great Famine, it survived well beyond this time and remained a feature of opposition to Fenianism in the 1860s and early Home Rule campaigns.[45] Those images and ideas spread well beyond the United Kingdom: for example, racially tinged cartoons greeted the Redmond brothers on their international tours in 1883 and 1884, while purported distinctions in character and temperament between Anglo-Saxons and Celts continued to enjoy wide circulation late in the century.[46] In 1881, for example, in essays published in Melbourne, A.M. Topp argued that Ireland's population was fundamentally different from that of other regions in the British Isles. Whereas the Welsh and Scots merged naturally with the English, he believed, race set the Irish irreconcilably apart. Irish inferiority threatened to undermine the future of the whole of the Empire, creating an imminent challenge for Great Britain itself.[47]

In contrast, while press reportage available to New Zealanders in late April and early May 1916 shows increasing acknowledgement of the gravity of the events that have unfolded in Dublin, little recourse to racial epithets is in evidence. Such physical descriptions as exist of the rebels focus on their haggard condition and worn appearance as the rebellion unfolded and not on any characteristics that might be thought innate.[48] Neither is there wider condemnation of a general Irish temperament or of the social context in which the rebellion took place, as had long been a feature of the English press stereotyping of Ireland. To the contrary, several news reports singled out for praise the good conduct of the city's inhabitants throughout the arduous ordeal. The overall impression is of an orderly rebellion, even down to the cool and careful nature of the insurgents' planning. *The New Zealand Herald* concluded from cablegrams and information in the British press that what had taken place in the city was a calculated urban insurrection, a far cry from the violent and erratic behaviour ascribed to the Irish in Empire-wide reporting throughout the preceding century.[49] Again, one suspects that this absence of racial imagery is not a general feature of British or imperial reportage of late nineteenth- and early twentieth-century acts of insurgency but is likely to be specific to the particular context of the Dublin Rising.

A challenge for future researchers is to interrogate further these observations about empathy and race and to use them as a springboard to compare and contrast the Easter Rising with a range of other acts of insurgency against the British Empire. Between the New Zealand wars of the mid-nineteenth century and the achievement of Indian independence in 1947, the Empire was under repeated challenge. Some insurgencies, such as the Boer struggle for independence, consumed large amounts of resources and military capacity; others were more modest local protests. If the case of early twentieth-century Ireland was in fact marked by unusually empathetic reportage and the absence of racialisation, this would seem to constitute an experience sharply at odds with Ireland's past history. The particular context of insurrection in the midst of an Empire at war and of Great Britain's reliance on Irish and imperial troops may provide partial explanation for the reception of the Easter Rising. However, part of the explanation surely lies in a full understanding of Ireland's unique position as part of the Empire. In 1874, C.T. Grenville famously warned that, for Great Britain, Ireland was 'too great to be unconnected with us … too near us to be dependent on a foreign state, and too little to be independent'.[50] The complex nature of Ireland's position as a constituent element of the United Kingdom, even if a reluctant one, and simultaneously as a part of the British Empire indelibly marked wider world and local reaction to the events in Dublin at Easter 1916 and affords the Easter Rising a special place in the history of insurgency against that Empire.

Notes

Introduction

1 Mark Finnane, 'The Easter Rising in Australian History and Memory', *Australasian Journal of Irish Studies*, vol. 16, 2016, pp. 30–46.

2 'Census, 1916', *AJHR*, 1917 Session I, H-39, accessed 29 November 2019, https://atojs.natlib.govt.nz/cgi-bin/atojs?a=d&d=AJHR1917-I.2.2.4.79.

3 'Principal Results of Census of 1911', p. 136, accessed 29 November 2019, https://www.ausstats.abs.gov.au/ausstats/free.nsf/0/BB0FECF534E135D2CA257AE F00164B6A/$File/13010_1901_1916%20section%204.pdf. The population of Australia in 1916 was 4,875,325 according to the Commonwealth Bureau of Census and Statistics, *Population and Vital Statistics, Bulletin No. 34. Commonwealth Demography, 1916, and Previous Years*, p. 9, accessed 29 November 2019, https://www.ausstats.abs.gov.au/ausstats/free.nsf/0/D134A2E5E3283542CA25764000176 945/$File/31410_No34_1916.pdf.

4 Michael King, *The Penguin History of New Zealand* (Auckland: Penguin, 2003), pp. 284–316.

5 For the United Kingdom's National Register, see 'The National Register: The beginning of the end of voluntary recruitment', accessed 3 December 2019, https://greatwarlondon.wordpress.com/2015/08/25/national-register/. Registration was required for every male between the ages of fifteen and sixty-five. 'While the register did not in itself make men liable to serve, the responsible minister (Walter Long) said that "it will compel them to declare that they are doing nothing to help their country in her hour of crisis."'

6 'Military Service Act 1916 (7 GEO. V. 1916, No. 8)', accessed 2 December 2019, http://www.nzlii.org/nz/legis/hist_act/msa19167gvi916n8266/.

7 'First World War Census and Conscription', accessed 2 December 2019, https://nzhistory.govt.nz/media/photo/war-census-and-conscription. Of the 208,513 men who submitted their details, 109,683 stated their willingness to serve with the New Zealand Expeditionary Force if required. A further 43,524 were willing to serve in a civil capacity only, while 34,386 declared themselves unwilling to serve in any capacity. See also 'Getting the Men to War', accessed 2 December 2019, https://nzhistory.govt.nz/war/public-service-at-war/getting-the-men-to-war#heading8.

8 Conscription is not relevant to any Canadian involvement in the 1916 Easter Rising. See Christopher Sharpe, 'Recruitment and Conscription (Canada)', last updated 22 June 2015, https://encyclopedia.1914-1918-online.net/article/recruitment_and_conscription_canada: 'Although Canada's Prime Minister, Sir Robert Borden, had asserted in December 1914 that "there has not been, there will not be compulsion

or conscription", a promise he reiterated in January 1916, the heavy losses suffered by the Canadians at Vimy Ridge on Easter Sunday 1917 faced the Government with a dilemma – either break faith with the British Government and dishonour a 1914 commitment to maintain four full-strength battalions or break faith with the Canadian people and introduce conscription to maintain troop numbers. However, while conscription was announced on 18 May 1917, the Military Service Act was not signed into law until 29 August 1917, and not enforced until 13 October 1917.'

9   See John Percy Fletcher, *Conscription under Camouflage: An account of compulsory military training in Australasia down to the outbreak of the Great War* (Glenelg, S. Aust.: J.F. Hills, 1919).

10 'Australia's Triumph Under Voluntaryism Puts New Zealand Under Conscription to Shame', accessed 3 December 2019, http://handle.slv.vic.gov.au/10381/157784. A poster used to combat conscription.

11 H.E. Holland, 'N.Z.'s Appeal to Australia. VOTE NO', accessed 3 December 2019, http://handle.slv.vic.gov.au/10381/158416. An offprint from *The Maoriland Worker*. H.E. Holland was the editor. See Chapter 5.

12 See Bryan Fitz-Gibbon and Marianne Gizycki, 'Research Discussion Paper 2001–07: A history of last-resort lending and other support for troubled financial institutions in Australia, 6. The 1890s Depression', prepared for the Reserve Bank of Australia, accessed 3 December 2019, https://www.rba.gov.au/publications/rdp/2001/2001-07/1890s-depression.html.

13 Tom Brooking, *Richard Seddon, King of God's Own: The life and times of New Zealand's longest serving prime minister* (Auckland: Penguin, 2014), pp. 284–348.

14 James Watson and Lachy Paterson (eds), *A Great New Zealand Prime Minister? Reappraising William Ferguson Massey* (Dunedin: Otago University Press, 2011). As Rory Sweetman points out in Chapter 6 of this book, Massey was not as bigoted as he is often portrayed.

15 L.F. Fitzhardinge, *William Morris Hughes: A political biography. Vol. 1: That Fiery Particle, 1862–1914* (Sydney: Angus & Robertson, 1964); L.F. Fitzhardinge, *William Morris Hughes: A political biography. Vol. 2: The Little Digger, 1914–1952* (Sydney: Angus & Robertson, 1979).

16 Noel Towell, 'Anzacs and the Easter Rising 1916: Australia's role in Ireland's past', *The Sydney Morning Herald*, 25 March 2016, https://www.smh.com.au/national/anzacs-easter-rising-and-the-20160317-gnl5oo.html.

17 Richard P. Davis, *Irish Issues in New Zealand Politics, 1868–1922* (Dunedin: Otago University Press, 1974); Barry Gustafson, *Labour's Path to Political Independence: Origins and establishment of the New Zealand Labour Party, 1900–1919* (Auckland: Auckland University Press, 1980); Brad Patterson (ed.), *The Irish in New Zealand: Historical contexts and perspectives* (Wellington: Stout Research Centre for New Zealand Studies, Victoria University of Wellington, 2002); Paul Moon, *New Zealand in the Twentieth Century: The nation, the people* (Auckland: Harper Collins, 2011), pp. 155–8. For a work-in-progress bibliography of Irish–New Zealand relations, see 'New Zealand Ireland Connection', accessed 3 December 2019, https://www.otago.ac.nz/history/nzic/bibliography.html.

18 King, *Penguin History*, pp. 316–17: 'In 1917, however, former Baptist minister Howard Elliott formed the Protestant Political Association (PPA) with the active support of the Grand Orange Lodge, of which William Massey was a member. It was opposed to "rum, Romanism and rebellion", and it used such events and issues as the 1916 Easter Rebellion in Dublin, Joseph Ward's Catholicism and Catholic opposition to the Bible-in-Schools campaign to whip up anti-Catholic feeling.'

19 James Belich, *Paradise Reforged: A history of New Zealand from the 1880s to the year 2000* (Auckland: Penguin, 2001), pp. 221–3; James Belich, *Replenishing the Earth: The settler revolution and the rise of the Anglo-World* (Oxford: Oxford University Press, 2009). James Belich's two other volumes, *The New Zealand Wars and the Victorian Interpretation of Racial Conflict* (1986) and *Making Peoples: A history of the New Zealanders from Polynesian settlement to the end of the nineteenth century* (1996), deal with earlier periods.

Chapter 1: 'The Empire Strikes Back': Anzacs and the Easter Rising 1916

1 D.P. Russell, *Sinn Fein and the Irish Rebellion* (Melbourne: Fraser & Jenkinson, 1916), p. 71. Russell's question was ironic, appearing in the text after quotations from Anzac letters that appeared to glorify the brutality with which the Rising was put down. For a detailed description of the role of the Australians in the Easter Rising, see Jeff Kildea, 'Called to Arms: Australians in the Irish Easter Rising 1916', *Journal of the Australian War Memorial*, vol. 39, 2003, https://www.awm.gov.au/journal/j39/kildea/, and Jeff Kildea, *Anzacs and Ireland* (Sydney: UNSW Press, 2007), ch. 2. For a discussion of the New Zealanders, see Rory Sweetman, *Defending Trinity College Dublin, Easter 1916: Anzacs and the Rising* (Dublin: Four Courts Press, 2019) and Hugh Keane, 'New Zealanders at Trinity College Dublin Easter Week 1916', 5 December 2012, http://theirishwar.com/new-zealanders-at-trinity-college-dublin-easter-week-1916/.

2 Although born and educated in England, Godley was of Anglo-Irish stock, from County Leitrim, and regarded himself as an Irishman. His autobiography is entitled *Life of an Irish Soldier*. He was commissioned in the Royal Dublin Fusiliers and, among his many postings, served in the Irish Guards.

3 Diary of Private George Edward Davis, AWM, Canberra, AWM PR88/203.

4 *D*, 12 July 1916, p. 4; *Glen Innes Examiner*, 10 July 1916, p. 3.

5 *BA*, 9 August 1916, p. 3.

6 *Liverpool Daily Post*, 2 May 1916, p. 5.

7 *Wanganui Herald*, 1 July 1916, p. 8. Presumably, the 'noted countess' was Countess Markievicz.

8 'Easter Week Diary of Miss Lilly Stokes', in Roger McHugh (ed.), *Dublin 1916* (London: Arlington Books, 1966), p. 66.

9 *SMH*, 15 June 1916, p. 8.

10 *1916 Rebellion Handbook* (Dublin: Mourne River Press, 1998), pp. 260–1. This work was originally published in 1916 by *The Weekly Irish Times* as the *Sinn Féin Rebellion Handbook: Easter 1916*, with an augmented edition appearing in 1917. It coincides with a list prepared by Trinity College (TCD MS 2783, p. 132).

11 In his biography of Michael Collins, Tim Pat Coogan refers to an Australian unit, but he does not name the unit or provide any details of it, nor does he cite a source for his assertion. *Michael Collins: A biography* (London: Arrow Books, 1991), p. 44.

12 Croft was a native of Glen Innes, New South Wales, and his parents lived in Dunedin. *The Ohinemuri Gazette* (Paeroa), 4 August 1916, p. 4.

13 Australians in England were not permitted to enlist in the Australian Imperial Force (*The Age* [Melbourne], 1 July 1916, p. 3). At the time of the Rising, two reserve squadrons of King Edward's Horse (KEH) were stationed at the Curragh and Longford. Accounts of individual Australian members of the KEH involved in the Rising appeared in the press; for example, those of Trooper F.M. Battye of Sydney (*The Age*, 23 September 1916, p. 20); Trooper Harry Hill Brooker of Woodville, South Australia (*The Advertiser* [Adelaide], 5 December 1917, p. 7); Sergeant Jack Crowley of West Wyalong, New South Wales (*The Mirror* [Sydney], 30 September 1916, p. 7; *Wagga Wagga Express*, 12 October 1916, p. 2); Lieutenant Walter Gordon Helpman of Warrnambool, Victoria (*A*, 4 July 1916, p. 7); Sergeant Ian Bryce MacBean of Claremont, Western Australia (*The West Australian* [Perth], 4 July 1919, p. 6).

14 Kildea, 'Called to Arms'; *A*, 15 June 1916, p. 6; *The Critic* (Adelaide), 5 July 1916, p. 17; *Port Pirie Recorder*, 5 August 1916, p. 3; *Victor Harbor Times*, 20 December 1918, p. 5; Lynn Meyers, 'Ted Marks and the Dublin Easter Rising, 1916', 30 March 2016, http://blogs.slq.qld.gov.au/ww1/2016/03/30/ted-marks-and-the-dublin-easter-rising-1916/.

15 Warre B. Wells and N. Marlowe, *A History of the Irish Rebellion of 1916* (Dublin: Maunsel, 1916), p. 154.

16 The article was republished as 'Inside Trinity College', in Roger McHugh (ed.), *Dublin 1916* (London: Arlington Books, 1966), pp. 158–74.

17 'Letter from Robert Tweedy to his Mother, 7 May 1916', accessed 3 December 2019, http://letters1916.maynoothuniversity.ie/item/910.

18 Gerard Fitzgibbon to William Hugh Blake, 10 May 1916, TCD Manuscripts, MS 11107/1.

19 Sweetman, *Defending Trinity College*, p. 78. Sweetman comments on the little attention paid to Trinity College's role in Easter Week and the neglect of 'the men who helped to save Trinity from potential disaster' (p. 18).

20 Witness Statement of Frank Thornton, BMH, WS 510, p. 14; Witness Statement of Thomas Slater, BMH, WS 263, pp. 14–15; *SMH*, 7 July 1916, p. 12; *BA*, 9 August 1916, p. 3.

21 W.J. Brennan-Whitmore, *Dublin Burning: The Easter Rising from behind the barricades* (Dublin: Gill & Macmillan, 1996), pp. 116–18. The conversation is set out in detail in Max Caulfield, *The Easter Rebellion*, 2nd edn (Dublin: Gill & Macmillan, 1995), p. 250. See also Brennan-Whitmore's account in *An tÓglach*, 6 February 1926, p. 5, and P. de Rosa, *Rebels: The Irish Rising of 1916* (New York: Ballantine Books, 1992), p. 330. Seamus Daly, who was with Brennan-Whitmore at the Custom House, refers to a New Zealand sergeant in his witness statement to the Bureau of Military History (WS 360, pp. 50–2).

22 'Inside Trinity College', p. 161.

23 Raymond M. Keogh, 'Death of a Volunteer', *Dublin Review of Books*, 16 February 2016, http://www.drb.ie/blog/dublin-stories/2016/02/16/death-of-a-volunteer.

24 *Glen Innes Examiner*, 10 July 1916, p. 3; *The Farmer and Settler* (Sydney), 18 July 1916, p. 2.

25 *AS*, 28 June 1916, p. 8. Garland also claimed that two of the despatch riders were killed, which is not corroborated by other sources.

26 Sergeant Don also mentioned the duel with the rebels in the St Andrew's spire (*BA*, 9 August 1916, p. 3).

27 *D*, 12 July 1916, p. 4.

28 '1916 Necrology 485', accessed 12 November 2019, http://www.glasnevintrust.ie/visit-glasnevin/news/1916-list/.

29 One woman who is sometimes claimed as a rebel woman fatality is Nurse Margaret Keogh, who was shot on the first day of the Rising in or near the South Dublin Union while treating a wounded Volunteer. The 1916 Necrology lists her as a civilian fatality under the name Margaret Kehoe. For a discussion of her status, see Donal Fallon, 'A Hero Nonetheless: Nurse Margaret Keogh and the Easter Rising', 12 January 2016, http://comeheretome.com/2016/01/12/a-hero-nonetheless-nurse-margaret-keogh-and-the-easter-rising/.

30 Diary of Lieutenant John Joseph Chapman of the 9th Battalion, AWM 1DRL/0197.

31 *Burra Record*, 12 July 1916, p. 4. For a description of the capture of the Mendicity Institution, see Michael Foy and Brian Barton, *The Easter Rising* (Stroud: Sutton Publishing, 2000 [1999]), p. 180.

32 Diary of Private George Edward Davis, AWM PR88/203.

33 *The Age*, 1 July 1916, p. 11.

34 Although described as an Australian, Charles was born in Canada, where his father was general manager of Dunlop Rubber Co. When Charles was a small child, the Garlands moved to Australia, where Richard set up a branch of the company (*The Australasian* [Melbourne], 29 November 1919, p. 22).

35 Canon David John Garland Papers, John Oxley Library, State Library of Queensland, Brisbane, OM71-51/13. See John A. Moses and George F. Davis, *Anzac Day Origins: Canon DJ Garland and trans-Tasman commemoration* (Canberra: Barton Books, 2013). I am grateful to Marg Powell of the John Oxley Library for bringing the typescript copy of the letter to my attention. See her article, 'Charles Garland, Easter Rising 1916', 28 March 2016, http://blogs.slq.qld.gov.au/ww1/2016/03/28/charles-garland-easter-rising-1916/. So far the original letter has not been located.

36 Both versions of the letter give the time of the patrol as 10.30 a.m., but it is clear from the activities preceding the raid that are described in the typescript version that the time should have read 10.30 p.m.

37 For details of the court martial, see *1916 Rebellion Handbook*, pp. 108–14.

38 For further information on Bowen-Colthurst, see Bryan Bacon, *A Terrible Duty: The madness of Captain Bowen-Colthurst* (n.p.: Thena Press, 2015) and James W. Taylor, *Guilty but Insane: J.C. Bowen-Colthurst – villain or victim?* (Cork: Mercier Press, 2016).

39 *1916 Rebellion Handbook*, pp. 213–31.

40 The typescript letter describes her as a 'Prussian Countess'.

41 *The Advocate* (Melbourne), 8 July 1916, p. 23.

42 *The Tribune* (Melbourne), 6 July 1916, p. 4.

43 The words 'so we shot them' are ambiguous. They could mean that Garland was a member of the firing squad or that 'we' (i.e. the military) shot the journalists, not Garland personally. But it is unlikely that such a fine distinction would have been made by the letter's critics, particularly as that meaning might better have been conveyed by 'so they shot them'.

44 *CP*, 13 July 1916, p. 17.

45 *Official Report of the Fifth Commonwealth Conference of the Australian Labor Party* (Sydney: Worker Trade Union Printery, 1912), p. 5. For an obituary, see *BA*, 4 December 1918, p. 5.

46 Russell, *Sinn Fein and the Irish Rebellion*, pp. 69–71.

47 *The Register*, 30 September 1916, p. 5.

48 *1916 Rebellion Handbook*, pp. 108–14, 213–22.

49 *The Times* (London), 1 September 1916, p. 3. The testimony as reported in *The Times* differs somewhat from that set out in the *1916 Rebellion Handbook*. When the Royal Commission began, Dobbin had been serving in France with the 2nd Royal Irish Rifles. He was brought back to give evidence to the commission. After giving his evidence, Dobbin returned to the front, where on 1 January 1918 he was awarded the Military Cross for gallantry. On 21 March 1918, he was killed during the German breakthrough that overran his battalion's position. Dobbin's service record is at The National Archives, Kew, Richmond, WO 339/55777.

50 *The Weekly Telegraph* (London), 6 May 1916, p. 7B.

51 P.J. Hally, 'The Easter 1916 Rising in Dublin: The military aspects', *Irish Sword*, vol. 7, 1965–6, pp. 313–26; *Irish Sword*, vol. 8, 1967–8, pp. 48–57; Neil Richardson, *According to Their Lights: Stories of Irishmen in the British Army, Easter 1916* (Cork: The Collins Press, 2015), ch. 1. Richardson calculates that 35 per cent of the British military fatalities in the Rising were Irishmen.

52 Timothy Bowman, *Irish Regiments in the Great War: Discipline and morale* (Manchester: Manchester University Press, 2003), pp. 127–9.

53 'In the war as a whole, on all sides, most men simply did what they conceived to be their duty ... The reasons for this lay in their sense of patriotism, duty, honour and deference to authority; all much more important concepts [then] than they are today.' John Ellis, *Eye-Deep in Hell: The Western Front, 1914–18* (London: Penguin Books, 2002), p. 190.

Chapter 2: Women of the Rising in the Australian and New Zealand Press
My thanks to Antoine Guillemette, Val Noone, and Elizabeth Malcolm. The research for this article was funded by the Australian Research Council.

1 Scrapbook of Dr Nicholas O'Donnell. My thanks to Val Noone for access to the scrapbook prior to its digitisation. The scrapbooks are now available at https://www.snac.unimelb.edu.au/collections/.

2   For the general reaction in the Australian press, see Peter Overlack, 'Easter 1916 in Dublin and the Australian Press: Background and response', *Journal of Australian Studies*, vols 54–5, 1997, pp. 188–93. See also Patrick O'Farrell, *The Irish in Australia* (Sydney: University of New South Wales Press, 1986), pp. 263–70. For the New Zealand press and Irish community reactions, see Rory Sweetman, 'Who Fears to Speak of Easter Week? Antipodean Irish-Catholic responses to the 1916 Rising', in Ruán O'Donnell (ed.), *The Impact of the 1916 Rising: Among the nations* (Dublin: Irish Academic Press, 2008), pp. 71–90.

3   Reported widely; see, for example, *Gippsland Times* (Victoria), 1 May 1916, p. 3.

4   Sweetman, 'Who Fears to Speak?', p. 76; citing *NZT*, 4 May 1916, p. 25.

5   O'Farrell, *Irish in Australia*, pp. 259–60; Elizabeth Malcolm and Dianne Hall, *A New History of the Irish in Australia* (Sydney: NewSouth Publishing, 2018); Sweetman, 'Who Fears to Speak?', pp. 71–90.

6   *The Advocate* (Melbourne), 27 July 1912, p. 23.

7   Sweetman, 'Who Fears to Speak?', p. 77.

8   *NZT*, 18 May 1916, p. 1 and cited in Sweetman, 'Who Fears to Speak?', p. 87 n. 28.

9   Sweetman, 'Who Fears to Speak?', p. 88 n. 42.

10 Terence Brown et al., 'The *Irish Times* in 1916: A newspaper in focus', *The Irish Times*, 26 March 2016, https://www.irishtimes.com/culture/heritage/the-irish-times-in-1916-a-newspaper-in-focus-1.2585762.

11 For a summary of their activities, see Sinéad McCoole, *No Ordinary Women: Irish female activists in the revolutionary years, 1900–1923* (Dublin: O'Brien Press, 2015), pp. 34–58.

12 Senia Pašeta, *Irish Nationalist Women, 1900–1918* (Cambridge: Cambridge University Press, 2013).

13 Constance Markievicz, née Gore-Booth, has been the subject of numerous biographies, including an early hostile biography by Seán O'Faoláin, *Constance Markievicz* (London: Sphere Books, 1934), and most recently a joint study of her and her husband by Lauren Arrington, *Revolutionary Lives: Constance and Casimir Markievicz* (Princeton, NJ: Princeton University Press, 2016).

14 Some of the growing literature includes Margaret Ward, *Unmanageable Revolutionaries: Women and Irish nationalism* (London: Pluto Press, 1983); McCoole, *No Ordinary Women*; Margaret Ó hÓgartaigh, *Kathleen Lynn: Irishwoman, patriot, doctor* (Dublin: Irish Academic Press, 2006); Pašeta, *Irish Nationalist Women*; Sinéad McCoole, *Easter Widows: Seven Irish women who lived in the shadow of the 1916 Rising* (Dublin: Doubleday Ireland, 2015); Lucy McDiarmid, *At Home in the Revolution: What women said and did in 1916* (Dublin: Royal Irish Academy, 2015); Mary McAuliffe and Liz Gillis, *Richmond Barracks 1916 'We were there': 77 women of the Easter Rising* (Dublin: Four Courts Press, 2016).

15 See, for example, the web archive of Twitter account @womenof1916, accessed 27 April 2018, https://twitter.com/Womenof1916.

16 *The Brisbane Courier*, 1 May 1916, p. 7; see Overlack, 'Easter 1916', p. 191.

17 Reprinted in many newspapers; see *The Northern Miner* (Charters Towers), 1 May 1916, p. 5.

18 *SMH*, 25 October 1919, p. 8.

19 See Malcolm and Hall, *A New History of the Irish in Australia*, and Dianne Hall, '"Now Him White Man": Images of the Irish in colonial Australia', *History Australia*, vol. 11, no. 2, 2014, pp. 167–95.

20 O'Donnell's Scrapbook, *A*, 16 May 1916. The deaths of civilians during the Rising has received relatively little attention from historians, although the recent centenary is promoting a wealth of new research. See Fearghal McGarry, *The Rising: Ireland: Easter 1916* (Oxford: Oxford University Press, 2010), pp. 177–8, 182–4; see also Joe Duffy, *Children of the Rising: The untold story of the young lives lost during Easter 1916* (Dublin: Hachette Books, 2016).

21 O'Donnell's Scrapbook, *A*, 20 May 1916.

22 See some of the instances: Maud Gonne described as a 'stormy petrel' in *Taranaki Herald* (New Plymouth), 7 June 1918, p. 7; *Bendigo Independent*, 23 May 1918, p. 7; and Countess Markievicz as a 'stormy petrel', *NZH*, 24 June 1916, supp.; *The Waikato Times* (Hamilton), 9 September 1916, supp.; *FS*, 28 August 1917, p. 4; *The Advertiser* (Adelaide), 3 March 1919, p. 9; *P*, 31 December 1918, p. 2.

23 McCoole, *Easter Widows*, pp. 68, 327–8, 336–7.

24 O'Donnell's Scrapbook, *A*, 1 May 1916.

25 O'Donnell's Scrapbook, *A*, 3 May 1916.

26 *The Waimate Advertiser*, 1 May 1916, p. 4.

27 *NZH*, 4 May 1916, p. 7.

28 *SMH*, 5 May 1916, p. 7. An edited version of this article was published in *The Argus*, 8 May, and collected by Nicholas O'Donnell for his scrapbook. The article was reprinted in almost its entirety in the *Hawera & Normanby Star* (Hawera), 30 May 1916, p. 3.

29 *Kalgoorlie Miner*, 19 May 1916, p. 4.

30 *NZH*, 24 June 1916, supp. 2.

31 *The Waikato Times*, 9 September 1916, supp.

32 This story was repeated almost verbatim in, among many other papers, *The Bendigo Independent*, 16 June 1916, p. 7; *A*, 15 June 1916, p. 6; *Kalgoorlie Western Argus*, 20 June 1916, p. 4; *The Darling Downs Gazette* (Queensland), 21 June 1916, p. 6; *The Brisbane Courier*, 22 June 1916, p. 8 and cited in Overlack, 'Easter 1916', p. 191.

33 *The Tuapeka Times*, 10 May 1916, p. 2.

34 *FS*, 23 May 1918.

35 *The Journal*, 21 August 1922, p. 1.

36 McCoole, *Easter Widows*, pp. 265–7.

37 *SC*, 12 May 1916, pp. 8–9; *The Advocate*, 13 May 1916, p. 23.

38 *Manawatu Times* (Palmerston North), 6 June 1916, p. 2; reprinted from *The Sun* (Sydney), 14 May 1916, p. 3.

39 The gulf between the younger generation of revolutionaries and their parents is explored in general by R.F. Foster, *Vivid Faces: The revolutionary generation in Ireland, 1890–1923* (London: Penguin, 2015), and see pp. 355–6 n. 73 for Grace and her mother.

40 *ODT*, 27 June 1916, p. 8.

41 For Moore's interview with Grace Gifford, see McCoole, *Easter Widows*, p. 267.

42 *CP*, 28 December 1916, p. 18.
43 McCoole, *Easter Widows*, pp. 285–8.
44 Louise Ryan, 'Splendidly Silent: Representing Irish republican women, 1919–23', in Ann-Maree Gallagher, Cathy Lubelska, and Louise Ryan (eds), *Re-presenting the Past: Women and history* (Harlow: Longman, 2001), pp. 23–43.
45 Orla Fitzpatrick, 'Portraits and Propaganda: Photographs of the widows and children of the 1916 leaders in *The Catholic Bulletin*', in Lisa Godson and Joanna Brück (eds), *Making 1916: The material and visual culture of the Easter Rising* (Liverpool: Liverpool University Press, 2015), pp. 82–90. On the organisations distributing these and other funds, see Caoimhe Nic Dháibhéid, 'The Irish National Aid Association and the Radicalization of Public Opinion in Ireland, 1916–1918', *The Historical Journal*, vol. 55, no. 3, 2012, pp. 705–29.
46 *FJ*, 25 December 1919, p. 3.
47 *The Advocate*, 1 November 1919, p. 12.
48 *CP*, 3 August 1916, p. 12.
49 *SC*, 19 May 1919, p. 4.
50 *The Australian Worker* (Sydney), 20 February 1919, p. 15; *A*, 1 January 1919, p. 8; *The Chronicle*, 4 January 1919, p. 4.
51 *Barrier Miner*, 11 January 1919, p. 7.
52 O'Farrell, *Irish in Australia*, pp. 289–94. For New Zealand-Irish support for the War of Independence, see Sweetman, 'Who Fears to Speak?', pp. 85–6.
53 *FJ*, 15 June 1922, p. 9. For Hanna Sheehy Skeffington, see Maria Luddy, *Hanna Sheehy Skeffington* (Dundalk: Historical Association of Ireland, 1995).
54 *The Advocate*, 23 February 1922, p. 27.
55 O'Farrell, *Irish in Australia*, p. 299.
56 Anne-Maree Whitaker, 'Linda Kearns and Kathleen Barry Irish Republican Fundraising Tour, 1924–25', *Journal of the Australian Catholic Historical Society*, vol. 37, 2016, pp. 208–11.
57 Dianne Hall, 'Irish Republican Women in Australia: Kathleen Barry and Linda Kearns' Tour in 1924–1925', *Irish Historical Studies*, vol. 43, no. 163, 2019, pp. 73–93.
58 *The Bundaberg Mail*, 26 January 1925.
59 Ryan, 'Splendidly Silent', p. 30.

Chapter 3: 'It would really … matter tremendously': New Zealand women and the 1916 Rising
1 'ANZAC Day: Commemoration Ceremonies', *ODT*, 26 April 1916, p. 2.
2 'ANZAC Day', *ODT*, 26 April 1916, p. 4.
3 For more detail on their valued work, see, for example, 'Women's Patriotic Association', *OW*, 30 August 1916, p. 43.
4 'Correspondence', *MW*, 21 June 1916, p. 3.
5 'Women's International League: Objects', *MW*, 13 December 1916, p. 12.
6 Roberta Nicholls, *The Women's Parliament: The National Council of Women in New Zealand, 1896–1920* (Wellington: Victoria University Press, 1996), p. 101.
7 Paragraph, *ODT*, 8 June 1916, p. 10; 'Street Obstruction', *AS*, 16 June 1916, p. 6.
8 'The Too-Easy British', *FS*, 19 June 1916, p. 2.

9   Nicholls, *Women's Parliament*, pp. 101–2.
10 'The Week', *OW*, 3 May 1916, p. 65.
11 'Woman's World', *D*, 4 May 1916, p. 2.
12 Irish residents in Dunedin, for example, met on 29 April to protest against 'the ill-considered and ill-timed disturbance' in Ireland. Speaking at this meeting, the Very Reverend Father James Coffey censured 'the Sinn Feiners', backed John Redmond's position on Home Rule and the war, and expressed the desire 'to show that the hearts of Irishmen throughout the Empire were sound'. 'Insurrection in Ireland', *ODT*, 1 May 1916, p. 6. For a more detailed account of Irish-Catholic reactions, see Rory Sweetman, 'Who Fears to Speak of Easter Week? Antipodean Irish-Catholic responses to the 1916 Rising', in Ruán O'Donnell (ed.), *The Impact of the 1916 Rising: Among the nations* (Dublin: Irish Academic Press, 2008), pp. 71–90.
13 Angela McCarthy, *Irish Migrants in New Zealand, 1840–1937: 'The Desired Haven'* (Woodbridge: Boydell Press, 2005), pp. 213–14, 220, 234–5.
14 Rory Sweetman, *Faith and Fraternalism: A history of the Hibernian Society in New Zealand, 1869–2000* (Wellington: Hibernian Society, 2002), p. 15.
15 Sweetman, 'Who Fears to Speak?', p. 73; 'Catholics to the Fore', *NZT*, 20 August 1914, p. 34.
16 Sweetman, *Faith and Fraternalism*, p. 15; see also a paragraph on their fundraising activities in 'Woman's World', *D*, 3 March 1916, p. 2.
17 'The Late Very Rev. Dr. Watters, S.M.', *NZT*, 1 June 1916, pp. 23, 25, 27; 'Death of Dr. Watters', *EP*, 10 May 1916, p. 7.
18 Katherine Mansfield to Laura Kate Bright, 21 September 1914, *The Collected Letters of Katherine Mansfield*, ed. Vincent O'Sullivan and Margaret Scott, vol. 1 (Oxford: Clarendon Press, 1984), p. 140; *EP*, 6 November 1914, p. 6.
19 Mansfield, *Collected Letters*, pp. 139–40.
20 Kathleen Jones, *Katherine Mansfield: The story-teller* (Edinburgh: Edinburgh University Press, 2010), pp. 237, 247–8.
21 Nicola Gordon Bowe, 'The Art of Beatrice Elvery, Lady Glenavy (1883–1970)', *Irish Arts Review Yearbook*, vol. 11, 1995, p. 171.
22 Beatrice Lady Glenavy, *'Today we will only gossip'* (London: Constable, 1964), p. 91. Many years later, Campbell was appalled when a boy from the school told her that her painting had 'inspired him "to die for Ireland"!'
23 Bowe, 'The Art of Beatrice Elvery', p. 171; Glenavy, *'Today we will only gossip'*, p. 90.
24 Glenavy, *'Today we will only gossip'*, p. 87.
25 Mansfield, *Collected Letters*, p. 260.
26 Ibid.; 'Ireland's Ordeal', *The Observer* (London), 30 April 1916, pp. 8–9. Garvin supplied information on the Sinn Féin movement, the 'feebleness' of the Irish administration, German machinations, and the traitor Casement before outlining the events of Easter Week and noting the loyalty of Irish leaders, troops, and people.
27 Glenavy, *'Today we will only gossip'*, p. 87.
28 Mansfield, *Collected Letters*, p. 260.
29 Ibid., p. 265. Campbell reproduces Mansfield's letters of 4 and 14 May in her autobiography. Interestingly though, she has cut all the sentences pertaining to Ireland and the Rising. Glenavy, *'Today we will only gossip'*, pp. 93–4, 96–7.

30 Glenavy, *'Today we will only gossip'*, p. 87.

31 Mansfield, *Collected Letters*, p. 265.

32 Ibid., pp. 265, 266 n. 3.

33 'The Tragic Bride of Joseph Plunkett, the Rebel', *The Daily Mirror*, 9 May 1916, p. 1.

34 Mansfield, *Collected Letters*, pp. 265, 266 n. 3.

35 Ibid., p. 265.

36 Ibid., pp. 269–72.

37 Ibid., p. 272. 'Sinn Féiners' had become an umbrella term for the Irish Volunteers and other militants, even though very few of them belonged to the Sinn Féin movement.

38 Charles Townshend, *Easter 1916: The Irish rebellion* (London: Penguin, 2006), pp. 278, 317–19. Most of the Irish arrested after the rebellion were deported to England and imprisoned without trial in England, Scotland, and Wales. Chaired by Sir John Sankey, the Advisory Committee would interview each detainee in order to 'comb out' the 'innocents', i.e. those who 'should never have been arrested' in the first place. Although most of the prisoners had been moved to a military internment camp at Frongoch in Wales, the committee sat in London. In July, it sat twenty-one times, 'several times disposing of more than 100 cases in a day'.

39 Ibid., pp. 318–19.

40 Mansfield, *Collected Letters*, p. 272.

41 See, for example, 'The Case for Home Rule', *ODT*, 4 July 1911, p. 4.

42 Jessie Mackay, 'The Aftermath of Seven Centuries', *OW*, 13 September 1916, p. 45.

43 Margaret Chapman, Pauline O'Leary, Ginny Talbot, Brenda Lyon, and Jean Goodwin, *Jessie Mackay: A woman before her time* (Kakahu, NZ: Kakahu WDFF [Women's Division Federated Farmers]; Geraldine, NZ: PCCL Services, 1997), n.p.

44 Ibid.; Nellie F.H. Macleod, *A Voice on the Wind: The story of Jessie Mackay* (Wellington: Reed, 1955), p. 66.

45 Macleod, *Voice on the Wind*, pp. 66–7. See, too, the series of six articles Mackay wrote for the *Otago Witness* in 1903, entitled 'The Woman of Nations'.

46 Ibid., p. 109.

47 Jessie Mackay, 'Athenry', *OW*, 24 May 1916, p. 51. On Easter Tuesday 1916, over five hundred 'Celts' assembled near Athenry. For several days, they patrolled the area, mainly 'to disrupt communications'. While police shot at some companies, there was no significant engagement, nor were there any casualties. Townshend, *Easter 1916*, pp. 228–9.

48 Mackay, 'Athenry', p. 51; 'Sinn Féin Revolt', *ODT*, 13 May 1916, p. 7.

49 'The Made-in-Germany Rebellion', *NZT*, 4 May 1916, pp. 29–31; Mackay, 'Athenry', p. 51.

50 Mackay, 'Athenry', p. 51.

51 Ibid.

52 See F.M. Mackay's criticism in 'Miss Jessie Mackay on "Athenry"', *OW*, 16 August 1916, p. 62.

53 Mackay, 'Aftermath of Seven Centuries', p. 45. The Commission of Inquiry found that 'the Irish system of government ... is anomalous in quiet times, and almost unworkable in times of crisis' (quoted in Townshend, *Easter 1916*, pp. 25, 297).

54 Mackay, 'Aftermath of Seven Centuries', p. 45. For more information on the Ulster Crisis, including the Larne gun-running and the militarism of the Ulster Volunteer Force, see Townshend, *Easter 1916*, pp. 32–6, 51–2, and D.G. Boyce, 'The Ulster Crisis: Prelude to 1916?', in Gabriel Doherty and Dermot Keogh (eds), *1916: The long revolution* (Cork: Mercier Press, 2007), pp. 45–60.

55 Clan na Gael was an Irish republican organisation in America, a sister organisation to the Irish Republican Brotherhood. Larkinites were followers of James Larkin, a trade union leader, socialist, and founder of the Irish Citizen Army.

56 Mackay, 'Aftermath of Seven Centuries', p. 45.

57 Jessie Mackay, 'Two Roads to "Union"', *OW*, 13 December 1916, p. 57.

58 Jessie Mackay, 'Two Roads to "Union"', *OW*, 22 November 1916, p. 57.

59 Ibid.; Mackay, 'Two Roads to "Union"', 13 December 1916, p. 57.

60 'An Irish Relief Fund', *NZT*, 7 September 1916, pp. 29–30.

61 'Distress in Ireland', *NZT*, 16 November 1916, p. 30.

62 *P*, 23 October 1916, p. 6.

63 'The Freedom of the Press', *The Sun*, 6 November 1916, p. 8.

64 Sweetman, *Faith and Fraternalism*, p. 19.

65 'Ireland's Rights', *EP*, 19 September 1916, p. 2.

66 'Communications', *GR*, 1 April 1917, p. 86; Eiblin ni Connor (Eileen O'Connor), 'The Irish Rising: A reply to Mr John Diggins', *GR*, 1 May 1917, pp. 100–1.

67 O'Connor, 'The Irish Rising', pp. 100–1.

68 Townshend, *Easter 1916*, pp. 65–71.

69 Quoted in ibid., p. 68.

70 Ibid., p. 73.

71 'Communications', p. 86.

72 O'Connor, 'The Irish Rising', p. 101.

73 'Sinn Fein Amain [*sic*]', *GR*, 1 August 1917, p. 149.

74 'Our Ladies', *GR*, 1 March 1918, p. 78.

75 'Our Ladies', *GR*, 1 April 1918, pp. 99–100; 1 May 1918, pp. 121–2. I do not discuss 'Nora's' second letter here because it focuses primarily on domestic politics: the upcoming election and Harry Holland's selection as Labour Party candidate.

76 For more information on the links between Irish New Zealanders and Labour, see Richard P. Davis, *Irish Issues in New Zealand Politics, 1868–1922* (Dunedin: University of Otago Press, 1974), pp. 187–212.

77 See Seán Brosnahan's discussion of Kiely and others who attempted to evade military service, in this volume.

78 'Our Ladies', *GR*, 1 June 1918, p. 147.

79 Townshend, *Easter 1916*, p. 349.

80 For more information on *The Green Ray*, see Seán Brosnahan, '"Shaming the Shoneens": *The Green Ray* and the Maoriland Irish Society in Dunedin, 1916–22', in Lyndon Fraser (ed.), *A Distant Shore: Irish migration & New Zealand settlement* (Dunedin: University of Otago Press, 2000), pp. 117–34.

Chapter 4: Play *v.* Play: *The Otago Daily Times* and the Dunedin stage as a regional New Zealand response to the Easter Rising 1916

1   Peter Kuch, 'Irish Playwrights and the Dunedin Stage in 1862: Theatre patrons performing civility', *Journal of New Zealand Studies*, vol. 15, 2013, pp. 90–100. Principally, until 1902, the Theatre Royal (capacity 1,500) and the Princess Theatre (capacity 1,330).

2   'Theatres in Australia: Mr Williamson's [*sic*] as a manager in the Antipodes', *The New York Times*, 20 April 1890, p. 17.

3   'Amusements', *ODT*, 26 April 1916, p. 3.

4   'Report on the Results of a Census of the Population of the Dominion of New Zealand Taken for the Night of the 15th October, 1916', section 2, ch. 13, accessed 3 December 2019, https://www3.stats.govt.nz/historic_publications/1916-census/Report%20on%20Results%20of%20Census%201916/1916-report-results-census%20.html#idsect2_1_4314.

5   'His Majesty's Theatre: A substantial building: its magnificent interior', *ODT*, 2 December 1902, p. 7. The seating was dress circle, 400; orchestral stalls, 200; ordinary stalls, 350; and pit, 900.

6   See Daina Pivac, Frank Stark, and Lawrence McDonald (eds), *New Zealand Film: An illustrated history* (Wellington: Te Papa, 2011) and Alistair Fox, 'New Zealand Cinema', last modified 25 October 2017, https://www.oxfordbibliographies.com/view/document/obo-9780199791286/obo-9780199791286-0227.xml.

7   Kuch, 'Irish Playwrights and the Dunedin Stage'.

8   Peter Kuch, 'Irishness on the New Zealand Stage, 1850–1930', with an appendix detailing Sara Allgood's 1916 and 1918 tours of New Zealand compiled by Dr Lisa Marr, *Journal of Irish and Scottish Studies*, vol. 4, no. 1, 2010, pp. 99–118.

9   For an early example of prejudicial reporting, see 'Emigration from Great Britain for the Last Ten Years', *OW*, 26 March 1853, p. 4.

10   'Prospectus of the *Otago Witness*', *OW*, 8 February 1851, pp. 2–3.

11   Lyndon Fraser, 'The Provincial and Gold Rush Years', p. 5, accessed 19 November 2019, https://nzhistory.govt.nz/files/documents/peopling3.pdf.

12   'The Census Returns', *OW*, 11 February 1865, p. 3.

13   'Report on the Results of a Census', section 6, chs 36–43, accessed 3 December 2019, https://www3.stats.govt.nz/historic_publications/1916-census/Report%20on%20Results%20of%20Census%201916/1916-report-results-census%20.html#idpart_1_34092.

14   Seán Brosnahan, '"Shaming the Shoneens": *The Green Ray* and the Maoriland Irish Society in Dunedin, 1916–22', in Lyndon Fraser (ed.), *A Distant Shore: Irish migration & New Zealand settlement* (Dunedin: University of Otago Press, 2000), pp. 117–34.

15   Kuch, 'Irish Playwrights and the Dunedin Stage'.

16   Other sources, such as radio, newsreels, letters and newspapers posted from Ireland and England by friends and relatives, and the Catholic news agencies (specifically *The Tablet*), are not the concern of this chapter.

17   Terence Brown, *The Irish Times: 150 years of influence* (London: Bloomsbury, 2015), p. 90.

18 Ibid., pp. 89–90.

19 'Martial Law in Dublin', *The Times* (London), 27 April 1916, p. 7. See 'Martial Law', *The Irish Times*, 27 April 1916, p. 7: 'There is little or no news (we admit frankly) in the only newspaper; that, however, is not the newspaper's fault, and it may claim, perhaps, as a merit that it comes out at all.'

20 *WC*, 25 April 1916, p. 5; *NZH*, 25 April 1916, p. 8; *AS*, 25 April 1916, p. 5; *EP*, 25 April 1916, p. 5; *Manawatu Times* (Palmerston North), 25 April 1916, p. 5; *Evening Star* (Dunedin), 25 April 1916, p. 6; *Wanganui Herald*, 25 April 1916, p. 5; *TDN*, 25 April 1916, p. 5; *Manawatu Standard* (Palmerston North), 25 April 1916, p. 5; *New Zealand Times* (Wellington), 25 April 1916, p. 5; *Greymouth Standard*, 25 April 1916, p. 3; *Taihape Daily Times*, 25 April 1916, p. 5.

21 'General Items', *ODT*, 25 April 1916, p. 5.

22 'A Raid on Ireland: German attempt to land arms', *The Times* (London), 25 April 1916, p. 4; 'Capture of Casement: His supreme vanity', *ODT*, 1 May 1916, p. 5, citing *The Daily Chronicle*.

23 'Gun Running: The Ireland sensation', *ODT*, 26 April 1916, p. 5.

24 Mark Twain, *Following the Equator: A journey around the world*, Project Gutenberg ebook, last updated 23 February 2018, http://www.gutenberg.org/files/2895/2895-0.txt.

25 'Gun Running', 'The Cabinet Crisis', 'Notes on the Cables', *ODT*, 26 April 1916, p. 5.

26 'Sedition in Ireland', *ODT*, 27 April 1916, p. 4.

27 'Riots in Dublin', *ODT*, 27 April 1916, p. 5.

28 *Oxford English Dictionary Online*, s.v. 'émeute': 'A popular rising or disturbance'.

29 'Notes on the Cables', *ODT*, 27 April 1916, p. 5. The Zeppelin raids were first reported as 'Zeppelin Raid: Over eastern counties', *ODT*, 26 April 1916, p. 5.

30 'Rebellion in Ireland', *ODT*, 28 April 1916, p. 5.

31 'The Irish Insurgents', *ODT*, 29 April 1916, p. 4.

32 'Passing Notes', *ODT*, 29 April 1916, p. 4.

33 'The Irish Rising', *ODT*, 1 May 1916, p. 4.

34 'The World's Press: How the Rising is viewed: Irish opinion in America', *ODT*, 1 May 1916, p. 5.

35 'Insurrection in Ireland: Protest in Dunedin', *ODT*, 1 May 1916, p. 6.

36 'Insurrection in Ireland', *ODT*, 2 May 1916, p. 5.

37 'Notes on the Cables', *ODT*, 29 April 1916, p. 8.

38 'Otago Quota Largely Exceeded: An enthusiastic farewell', *ODT*, 5 May 1916, p. 3.

39 James Moran, *Staging the Easter Rising: 1916 as theatre* (Cork: Cork University Press, 2006).

40 Quoted in Declan Kiberd, 'The 1916 Rising: Then and now: the Easter Rebellion: poetry or drama', accessed 3 December 2019, www.theirelandinstitute.com/wp/the-easter-rebellion-poetry-or-drama/.

41 W.B. Yeats, 'The Man and the Echo', in Peter Alt and Russell K. Alspach (eds), *The Variorum Edition of the Poems of W.B. Yeats* (New York: Macmillan, 1973), p. 632.

42 W.B. Yeats, 'Noble and Ignoble Loyalties', *The United Irishman*, 21 April 1900, rptd in John P. Frayne and Colton Johnson (eds), *Uncollected Prose by W.B. Yeats*, vol. 2 (London: Macmillan, 1975), pp. 211–13.

43 P.J. Mathews, 'A Poet's Revolt: How culture heavily influenced the Rising and its leaders', *Irish Independent*, 21 January 2016, http://www.independent.ie/irish-news/1916/rising-perspectives/a-poets-revolt-how-culture-heavily-influenced-the-rising-and-its-leaders-34379291.html.

44 'Constant Reader', 'Literature: Special reviews, and gleanings from various sources', *ODT*, 6 May 1916, p. 2.

45 'Amusements', *ODT*, 4 April 1916, p. 1; Fearghal McGarry, *The Abbey Rebels of 1916: A lost revolution* (Dublin: Gill & Macmillan, 2015), p. 8. The Abbey had advertised performances of *Cathleen ni Houlihan*, *The Mineral Workers*, and *The Spancel of Death* for Easter Week, but the Abbey manager, St John Ervine, cancelled them as soon as he heard the first shots. 'Kathleen ni Houlihan 1916 (Abbey)', accessed 19 November 2019, https://www.abbeytheatre.ie/archives/production_detail/6602/.

46 'Miss Dorothea Spinney's Recital', *ODT*, 5 April 1916, p. 3.

47 'Constant Reader', 'Literature', p. 2.

48 Maura Shaffrey, 'Sackville Street/O'Connell Street', *Irish Arts Review*, 1988, pp. 144–9. The Dublin Corporation had attempted to rename the street in 1884 but was prevented by an injunction. The official renaming did not take place until 1924.

49 'Constant Reader', 'Literature', p. 2.

50 Lionel Johnson, 'Poetry and Patriotism', in *Poetry and Ireland: Essays by W.B. Yeats and Lionel Johnson* (Churchtown, Dundrum: Cuala Press, 1908), pp. 21–54, https://archive.org/stream/poetryirelandessooyeatrich/poetryirelandessooyeatrich_djvu.txt.

51 'Empire Day', *ODT*, 13 May 1916, p. 12.

52 'Anglo-Celt', 'John Bull's Empire Party', *ODT*, 27 May 1916, p. 6. The Overseas Club's Hon. Secretary's reply is in *ODT*, 29 May 1916, p. 3.

53 'Allen Doone Season', *ODT*, 20 July 1916, p. 1; 'How O'Leary Charged the Germans', *ODT*, 14 April 1915, p. 8.

54 'Amusements', *D*, 4 July 1916, p. 7.

55 'Michael John O'Leary VC', accessed 3 December 2019, http://www.vconline.org.uk/michael-j-oleary-vc/4587805344.

56 British Pathé, 'London's Welcome – Sgt O'Leary VC', 13 April 2014, https://www.youtube.com/watch?v=TtaA2fFN4qE. For a crowd shot, see British Pathé, 'O'Leary VC', 13 April 2014, https://www.youtube.com/watch?v=D7agL8uHxIk.

57 'Dublin's Welcome to Sergeant O'Leary, V.C.', a Gaumont Graphic newsreel, was screened at the King Edward Theatre, Dunedin. See *ODT*, 21 September 1915, p. 7.

58 'A Gleam of Truth', *D*, 1 January 1916, p. 2.

59 'Amusements: The Allen Doone Company', *ODT*, 1 August 1916, p. 8; 'Princess Theatre', *ODT*, 15 November 1916, p. 7. A synopsis of *The Bold Soger Boy* is in 'Amusements: The Allen Doone Company', *ODT*, 29 July 1916, p. 10, and 'Entertainments', *D*, 14 July 1916, p. 3. *A Bit of Irish* was said to be 'vaudeville', a 'Hibernian frivolity'.

60 Paragraph, *ODT*, 5 October 1916, p. 8.

61 'Punishment of the Rebels: Appeal against undue severity' and 'General Items: Ireland's position', *ODT*, 21 October 1916, p. 7.

62 Kuch, 'Irish Playwrights and the Dunedin Stage'.

63 'Peg o' My Heart', *New Zealand Times*, 30 September 1916, p. 8. See also 'Peg o' My Heart', *ODT*, 11 November 1916, p. 10; 'Amusements', *ODT*, 8 November 1916, p. 1, which claimed '900 Performances in London, 700 Performances in New York, [and] 112 Performances in Sydney'.

64 'Peg o' My Heart: And a captivating actress', *D*, 12 October 1916, p. 3.

65 'Amusements', *ODT*, 13 November 1916, p. 3.

66 Ibid.

67 'Arrival of the "Willochra": Nearly 200 men on board: some exciting experiences', *ODT*, 29 September 1916, p. 7.

68 'Notes on the Cables', *ODT*, 14 October 1916, p. 7.

69 'Ireland and Conscription: Speech by Mr Redmond: the fatal Rising', *ODT*, 9 October 1916, p. 5.

70 'Entertainments', *D*, 14 October 1916, p. 16.

71 W.B. Yeats, 'The Irish Literary Theatre', *Daily Express* (Dublin), 14 January 1899, rptd in John P. Frayne and Colton Johnson (eds), *Uncollected Prose by W.B. Yeats*, vol. 2 (London: Macmillan, 1975), pp. 139–42.

Chapter 5: Harry Holland, *The Maoriland Worker*, and the Easter Rising

1   *MW*, 16 July 1919, p. 5.

2   P.J. O'Farrell, *Harry Holland: Militant socialist* (Canberra: ANU Press, 1964), *passim*.

3   Peter Franks and Jim McAloon, *Labour: The New Zealand Labour Party, 1916–2016* (Wellington: Victoria University Press, 2016), ch. 3.

4   O'Farrell, *Harry Holland*, pp. 92–3.

5   Barry S. Gustafson, *Labour's Path to Political Independence* (Auckland: Auckland University Press, 1980), pp. 126–7.

6   R.P. Davis, *Irish Issues in New Zealand Politics, 1868–1922* (Dunedin: Otago University Press, 1974), p. 190.

7   For a general discussion, with references, see Franks and McAloon, *Labour*, ch. 2.

8   J.J. Lee, *Ireland, 1912–1985: Politics and society* (Cambridge: Cambridge University Press, 1989), p. 32.

9   *MW*, 17 May 1916, p. 4.

10 *MW*, 5 July 1916, p. 5; 28 July 1916, p. 4; 6 September 1916, p. 2.

11 *MW*, 12 September 1913, p. 3.

12 *MW*, 22 October 1913, p. 4.

13 Ibid.

14 *MW*, 10 November 1915, p. 5.

15 *MW*, 3 May 1916, p. 4.

16 *MW*, 17 May 1916, p. 4. The attitude of the Australian labour press is briefly discussed in Dianne Hall and Elizabeth Malcolm, 'Catholic Irish Australia and the Labor Movement: Race in Australia and nationalism in Ireland, 1880s–1920s', in Greg Patmore and Shelton Stromquist (eds), *Frontiers of Labor: Comparative histories of the United States and Australia* (Urbana: University of Illinois Press, 2018), pp. 149–67.

17 *MW*, 17 May 1916, p. 4.

18 Ibid.

19 Nicholas Hoare, 'Harry Holland's "Samoan Complex"', *Journal of Pacific History*, vol. 49, no. 2, 2014, esp. p. 154.

20 V.I. Lenin, 'The Discussion on Self-Determination Summed Up', accessed 22 February 2017, https://www.marxists.org/archive/lenin/works/1916/jul/x01.htm. See also, and intriguingly, Conor Cruise O'Brien, 'The Embers of Easter 1916–1966', *New Left Review*, vol. 1, no. 37, 1966, pp. 3–14.

21 Davis, *Irish Issues*, p. 191.

22 Kevin Molloy, 'Victorians, Historians and Irish History: A reading of the *New Zealand Tablet*, 1873–1903', in Brad Patterson (ed.), *The Irish in New Zealand: Historical contexts and perspectives* (Wellington: Stout Research Centre, 2002), esp. p. 160.

23 Senia Pašeta, 'Green [née Stopford], Alice Sophia Amelia', in *Oxford Dictionary of National Biography*, accessed 23 February 2018, https://doi.org/10.1093/ref:odnb/33531. See also Sandra Holton, 'Gender Difference, National Identity and Professing History: The case of Alice Stopford Green', *History Workshop Journal*, vol. 53, 2002, p. 120.

24 James Connolly, *Labour in Irish History* (New York: Donnelly Press, 1919), p. 5.

25 R.F. Foster, *The Irish Story: Telling tales and making it up in Ireland* (London: Penguin, 2001), p. 25.

26 *MW*, 24 May 1916, p. 4.

27 *MW*, 31 May 1916, p. 1.

28 *MW*, 7 June 1916, p. 1.

29 *MW*, 14 June 1916, p. 1.

30 *MW*, 21 June 1916, p. 1.

31 See, for instance, the opening of James Connolly's *The Re-conquest of Ireland* (1915), https://www.marxists.org/archive/connolly/1915/rcoi/index.htm.

32 *MW*, 21 June 1916, p. 1.

33 Connolly, *Labour in Irish History*, pp. 14–15.

34 *MW*, 12 July 1916, p. 1.

35 *MW*, 5 July 1916, p. 1.

36 *MW*, 12 July 1916, p. 1.

37 *MW*, 19 July 1916, p. 1.

38 *MW*, 26 July 1916, p. 1.

39 *MW*, 2 August 1916, p. 1.

40 *MW*, 9 August 1916, p. 1.

41 *MW*, 16 August 1916, p. 2.

42 *MW*, 30 August 1916, p. 2.

43 *MW*, 23 August 1916, p. 2.

44 *MW*, 30 August 1916, p. 2.

45 *MW*, 6 September 1916, p. 6.

46 *MW*, 13 September 1916, p. 6.

47 *MW*, 20 September 1916, p. 6.

48 See Eugenio F. Biagini, *British Democracy and Irish Nationalism* (Cambridge: Cambridge University Press, 2007), p. 288.

49 Holland discussed the Famine in *MW*, 27 September–25 October 1916.

50 *MW*, 25 October 1916, p. 6.

51 *MW*, 8 November 1916, p. 6.

52 *MW*, 6 December 1916, p. 6.

53 Ibid.; James Connolly, 'Michael Davitt: A text for a revolutionary lecture' (1908), last updated 11 August 2003, https://www.marxists.org/archive/connolly/1908/08/davitt.htm.

54 See, for instance, *NZT*, 8 November 1895, p. 18.

55 *MW*, 3 January 1917, p. 1; 10 January 1917, p. 6; 17 January 1917, p. 6; 24 January 1917, p. 6; Francis Sheehy Skeffington, *Michael Davitt: Revolutionary, agitator, and labor leader* (Boston: Dana Estes, 1909), p. 124.

56 *MW*, 7 February 1917, p. 6.

57 *MW*, 14 February 1917, p. 6.

58 *MW*, 21 February–7 March 1917.

59 Norway's book comprised letters from Dublin to family members and was published by Smith, Elder and Co. of London later in 1916.

60 *MW*, 14 March 1917, p. 6.

61 *MW*, 4–18 April 1917.

62 *MW*, 21 March 1917, p. 6.

63 *MW*, 28 March 1917, p. 6.

64 Ibid.

65 *MW*, 2 May 1917, p. 6.

66 I am influenced here by Francis Shaw, 'The Canon of Irish History: A challenge', *Studies*, vol. 61, no. 2, 1972, pp. 113–52. Unfortunately, Shaw avoided discussing Connolly's historical writing on the grounds of space. Such a discussion would have been interesting.

67 *MW*, 2 May 1917, p. 6.

68 Anthony Coughlan, 'Ireland's Marxist Historians', in Ciaran Brady (ed.), *Interpreting Irish History: The debate on historical revisionism* (Dublin: Irish Academic Press, 1994), p. 296.

69 *MW*, 2 May 1917, p. 6.

70 Davis, *Irish Issues*, p. 209.

Chapter 6: Bishop Henry Cleary and the North King Street Murders

1 General Sir John Maxwell admitted to his wife his fears that some of the North King Street victims were 'innocent civilians' who had been 'murdered … in cold blood'. Michael Foy and Brian Barton, *The Easter Rising* (Stroud: Sutton Publishing, 2000), p. 189. This was later confirmed by Prime Minister Asquith's legal adviser. Charles Townshend, *Easter 1916: The Irish Rebellion* (London: Penguin, 2006), p. 294.

2 Adrian Gregory and Senia Pašeta (eds), *Ireland and the Great War: 'A war to unite us all'?* (Manchester: Manchester University Press, 2002).

3   'The city is full of the most horrible rumours as to wholesale murders in the various barracks, and in the houses', John Dillon told his chief, John Redmond, on 17 May 1916. F.S.L. Lyons, *John Dillon: A biography* (London: Routledge & Kegan Paul, 1968), p. 384.

4   Townshend, *Easter 1916*, p. 293.

5   Roger McHugh (ed.), *Dublin 1916* (London: Arlington Books, 1976), pp. 220–39.

6   Townshend, *Easter 1916*, pp. 205–7, 293–4; Fearghal McGarry, *The Rising: Ireland: Easter 1916* (Oxford: Oxford University Press, 2010), pp. 187–8; Foy and Barton, *The Easter Rising*, pp. 120–3. For a modern restatement of the charge that these victims were killed after the fighting had ceased, see Tim Pat Coogan, *1916: The Easter Rising* (London: Cassell, 2001), pp. 145–9.

7   Townshend, *Easter 1916*, p. 204.

8   Max Caulfield, *The Easter Rebellion* (Dublin: Gill & Macmillan, 1995), pp. 265–71. Caulfield's book was first published in 1963.

9   Katharine Tynan, *The Years of the Shadow* (London: Constable, 1919), p. 213.

10 Caulfield, *The Easter Rebellion*, p. 293.

11 Townshend, *Easter 1916*, p. 293.

12 Townshend claims that 'the killing of civilians in North King Street was perhaps inevitable in fighting of such claustrophobic intensity'. Ibid., p. 207.

13 Frank Shouldice, *Grandpa the Sniper: The remarkable story of a 1916 Volunteer* (Dublin: Liffey Press, 2015), pp. 35–53.

14 Paul O'Brien, *Blood on the Streets: 1916 and the battle for Mount Street Bridge* (Cork: Mercier Press, 2008).

15 Witness Statement of Patrick J. Kelly, BMH, WS 781.

16 Caulfield, *The Easter Rebellion*, p. 265.

17 Townshend, *Easter 1916*, p. 189.

18 Ibid., p. 270.

19 Ibid., p. 292; Patrick Maume, 'Skeffington, Francis Sheehy- (1878–1916)', in *Dictionary of Irish Biography*, vol. 8 (Cambridge: Cambridge University Press, 2009), pp. 981–3. See also James W. Taylor, *Guilty but Insane: J.C. Bowen-Colthurst: villain or victim?* (Cork: Mercier Press, 2016).

20 Townshend, *Easter 1916*, p. 294.

21 Rory Sweetman, 'Cleary, Henry William (1859–1929)', in *Dictionary of Irish Biography*, vol. 2 (Cambridge: Cambridge University Press, 2009), pp. 567–8. See also Rory Sweetman, 'New Zealand Catholicism, War, Politics and the Irish Issue, 1912–1922', PhD thesis, University of Cambridge, 1991.

22 Cyril Bryan, *Archbishop Mannix: Champion of Australian democracy* (Melbourne: Advocate Press, 1918); E.J. Brady, *Doctor Mannix: Archbishop of Melbourne* (Melbourne: Library of National Biography, 1934); Frank Murphy, *Daniel Mannix: Archbishop of Melbourne* (Melbourne: Advocate Press, 1948); Arthur H. Ryan, *Daniel Mannix, Archbishop of Melbourne* (Melbourne: Advocate Press, 1949); Niall Brennan, *Dr Mannix* (Adelaide: Rigby, 1964); Walter A. Ebsworth, *Archbishop Mannix* (Melbourne: Stephenson, 1977); B.A. Santamaria, *Daniel Mannix: The quality of leadership* (Melbourne: Melbourne University Press, 1984);

Michael Gilchrist, *Daniel Mannix: Wit and wisdom* (North Melbourne: Freedom, 2004); James Griffin, *Daniel Mannix: Beyond the myths* (Mulgrave, Vic.: Garratt Publishing, 2012); Val Noone and Rachel Naughton (eds), *Daniel Mannix: His legacy* (East Melbourne: Melbourne Diocesan Historical Commission, Catholic Archdiocese of Melbourne, 2014); Brenda Niall, *Mannix* (Melbourne: Text Publishing, 2015).

23 Patrick O'Farrell, *Vanished Kingdoms: Irish in Australia and New Zealand* (Kensington: New South Wales University Press, 1990), p. 7. A glaring example of this myopia is the erroneous claim that the First World War 'served firmly to incorporate … [the] Irish into the New Zealand nation'. Jock Phillips, 'Race and New Zealand National Identity', in Neal Garnham and Keith Jeffery (eds), *Culture, Place and Identity* (Dublin: University College Dublin Press, 2005), p. 175. See my response: 'Who Fears to Speak of Easter Week? Antipodean Irish-Catholic responses to the 1916 Rising', in Ruán O'Donnell (ed.), *The Impact of the 1916 Rising: Among the nations* (Dublin: Irish Academic Press, 2008), pp. 73–90.

24 Patrick O'Farrell, *The Catholic Church and Community in Australia* (Melbourne: Thomas Nelson, 1977), ch. 4. See also Philip Ayres, *Prince of the Church: Patrick Francis Moran, 1830–1911* (Melbourne: The Miegunyah Press, 2007).

25 The rebellion was presented as an occasion when Irish Protestants and Catholics fought together for Irish independence from English rule.

26 Henry Cleary to John Dillon, 21 December 1898, Dillon Papers MS 6771, TCD.

27 Ibid.

28 Joseph Devlin and J.T. Donovan collected more than £5,000 in their 1906–7 tour, while W.A. Redmond, Richard Hazleton, and Donovan (once again) carried off more than twice this amount in 1911. R.P. Davis, *Irish Issues in New Zealand Politics, 1868–1922* (Dunedin: University of Otago Press, 1974), pp. 126–7.

29 Henry W. Cleary, *An Impeached Nation: Being a study of Irish outrages* (Dunedin: New Zealand Tablet, 1909).

30 Diary 1917–18, CLE 6-16, Cleary Papers, Auckland Catholic Diocesan Archives (ACDA).

31 *NZT*, 3 May 1917. Cleary's 'diary' contains no reference to his furious lobbying to become the next bishop of Ferns (his native diocese) after the death of James Browne in mid-1917.

32 Rory Sweetman, 'Kelly, James Joseph (1877–1939)', in *Dictionary of Irish Biography*, vol. 5 (Cambridge: Cambridge University Press, 2009), pp. 77–8.

33 Rory Sweetman, 'Waving the Green Flag in the Southern Hemisphere: The Kellys and the Irish College, Rome', in Daire Keogh and Albert McDonnell (eds), *The Irish College Rome and Its World* (Dublin: Four Courts Press, 2008), pp. 205–24.

34 Kelly was a cousin of the Ryans of Tomcoole, a Wexford family deeply involved in advanced Irish nationalism. See R.F. Foster, *Vivid Faces: The revolutionary generation in Ireland, 1890–1923* (London: Allen Lane, 2014), pp. 17–18. 'Knowing Ireland and being in constant touch' were the credentials Kelly presented to his colonial audience for the accuracy of his interpretation of Irish political developments. *NZT*, 8 November 1917.

35 *NZT*, 22 November 1917.

36 *NZT*, 26 July 1917.

37 After only nine issues from Kelly's pen, the solicitor-general was advising that he be charged with sedition and his newspaper be suppressed. J.W. Salmond to Attorney General, 9 May 1917, Opinion Book 1917, Crown Law Office, Wellington. The National Government did not accept Salmond's advice. Alex Frame, *Salmond: Southern Jurist* (Wellington: Victoria University Press, 1995).

38 James Kelly to M.J. O'Connor, 27 June 1916, HAG 1/1916/77, Hagan Papers, Irish College Rome.

39 *NZT*, 8 March 1917.

40 *NZT*, 24 May 1917.

41 *NZT*, 3 May 1917.

42 BMH, WS 781 (Patrick J. Kelly); Witness Statement of Charles Skelly, BMH, WS 870; Witness Statement of Frank Shouldice, BMH, WS 162.

43 BMH, WS 162 (Frank Shouldice).

44 Statement of Ellen Walsh in McHugh (ed.), *Dublin 1916*, p. 231.

45 Witness Statement of Father Aloysius Travers, BMH, WS 200.

46 Tynan, *The Years of the Shadow*, p. 210.

47 Father Aloysius Travers, 'Easter Week 1916: Personal recollections', *Capuchin Annual* (Dublin, 1942), pp. 211–20. Father Albert allegedly told Patrick Kelly: 'Go forth now my child and if necessary die for Ireland as Christ died for mankind.' BMH, WS 781 (Patrick J. Kelly).

48 *NZT*, 18 May 1916; 6 July 1916. Henry Cleary to Matthew Brodie [undated], CLE 97-1, Cleary Papers, ACDA.

49 *NZT*, 3 May 1917.

50 On the broken promise to publish the inquiry results, see Coogan, *1916*, pp. 148–9.

51 *NZT*, 3 May 1917. Maxwell also 'blamed all the trouble on the Government's pusillanimity in allowing Carson to form the Ulster Volunteers, naming this as the primary cause of the Rebellion and the growing unrest which succeeded it'. Caulfield, *The Easter Rebellion*, p. 295.

52 Michael Laffan, *The Resurrection of Ireland: The Sinn Féin party, 1916–1923* (Cambridge: Cambridge University Press, 1999), pp. 77–122.

53 Reverend Dr Cleary, *Prussian Militarism at Work: A letter* (London: Barclay & Fry, 1917). See Michael Sanders and Philip M. Taylor, *British Propaganda during the First World War, 1914–18* (London: Macmillan, 1982), p. 299.

54 *NZT*, 3 May 1917.

55 Rory Sweetman, '"How To Behave Among Protestants": Varieties of Irish Catholic leadership in Colonial New Zealand', in Brad Patterson (ed.), *The Irish in New Zealand: Historical contexts and perspectives* (Wellington: Stout Research Centre for New Zealand Studies, Victoria University of Wellington, 2002), pp. 89–101.

56 Paul Baker, *King and Country Call: New Zealanders, conscription and the Great War* (Auckland: Auckland University Press, 1988).

57 H.S. Moores, 'The Rise of the Protestant Political Association: Sectarianism in New Zealand politics during World War I', MA thesis, University of Auckland, 1966.

58 Rory Sweetman, *Bishop in the Dock: The sedition trial of James Liston in New Zealand* (Dublin: Irish Academic Press, 2007).

59 Terence Denman, *A Lonely Grave: The life and death of William Redmond* (Dublin: Irish Academic Press, 1995).

60 Sweetman, '"How To Behave Among Protestants"', p. 94. Charles Townshend pithily observes that 'while shared war experience at the front sometimes eroded old prejudices, it could just as often reinforce stereotypes'. Townshend, *Easter 1916*, p. 313. See also Rory Sweetman, *Defending Trinity College Dublin, Easter 1916: Anzacs and the Rising* (Dublin: Four Courts Press, 2019), pp. 92–5.

61 Denman, *A Lonely Grave*, p. 14. John Redmond has been described as 'a kind of imperialist nationalist'. D.G. Boyce, *Ireland, 1828–1923: From ascendancy to democracy* (Oxford: Blackwell, 1992), p. 80.

62 Foster, *Vivid Faces*, pp. 98, 187.

63 Kettle lamented that the Dublin rebels would 'go down in history as heroes and martyrs, and I will go down – if I go down at all – as a bloody British officer'. J.B. Lyons, *The Enigma of Tom Kettle: Irish patriot, essayist, poet, British soldier, 1880–1916* (Dublin: Glendale Press, 1983), p. 293.

64 *NZT*, 5 June 1919.

Chapter 7: Rebel Hearts: New Zealand's fenian families and the Easter Rising

1 The small 'f' is used here to indicate a distinction from what Fenianism meant in Ireland, Britain, or America. In those places, Fenianism was an umbrella term for political organisations dedicated to the establishment of an Irish Republic. In New Zealand 'fenian' was used in a much more general sense to indicate someone with an Irish background who was in favour of Irish independence or an Irish Republic or even just opposed to British domination of Ireland. It was frequently a pejorative term used by the wider New Zealand community but also one embraced by many ethnic Irish with a sense of pride.

2 Details on Irish migration can be found at 'Irish', Te Ara: The Encyclopedia of New Zealand, http://www.TeAra.govt.nz/en/irish/.

3 See Jeff Kildea, 'What Price Loyalty? Australian Catholics in the First World War', the 2018 Knox Lecture, Catholic Theological College, Melbourne, accessed 12 November 2019, https://jeffkildea.com/wp-content/uploads/2018/05/Kildea-What-Price-Loyalty-2018.pdf.

4 The apparent lack of trans-Tasman connections between Irish nationalist organisations during the war is perhaps surprising and would merit further research. I canvassed this subject with the late Professor Patrick O'Farrell, who wrote, 'I cannot recall a New Zealand dimension of any of this stuff' in his own research material nor in Albert Dryer's papers in relation to Irish nationalist activity in Australia. Personal communication to the author, 7 October 1999. Professor O'Farrell's description of Australia's wartime Irish republican organisations as 'small, powerless and irrelevant, just visible enough to cause trouble' would apply equally, however, to New Zealand's Irish radicals. *The Irish in Australia*, rev. edn (Sydney: University of New South Wales Press, 1993), p. 254. On the attempt at co-ordination between the Wellington

Irish Republican Association and its Australian counterparts in the 1920s, see my essay, 'Parties or Politics: Wellington's IRA, 1922–1928', in Brad Patterson (ed.), *The Irish in New Zealand: Historical contexts and perspectives* (Wellington: Victoria University of Wellington, 2002), pp. 67–87.

5   New Zealand Provost Marshal's War Diary, NA.

6   Military service record, 54034, Jeremiah Griffin, NA. See also *C*, 18 April 1917.

7   Military service record, 61728, F.J. McKenna, NA. McKenna's IRA activity is corroborated by the witness statement of Captain Edward Lynch, 4th Battalion Mid-Clare Brigade, to the Irish Bureau of Military History in 1955. See Witness Statement of Edward Lynch, BMH, WS 1333, p. 3, accessed 12 November 2019, http://www.bureauofmilitaryhistory.ie/reels/bmh/BMH.WS1333.pdf#page=4.

8   Military service record (F.J. McKenna). A more elaborate account of McKenna's experiences drawing on family stories is included in a thesis prefaced as 'a work of creative non-fiction' by Kerry Casey, 'The Diggers and the IRA: A story of Australian and New Zealand Great-War soldiers involved in Ireland's War of Independence', MA thesis, University of New South Wales, 2014.

9   *The Waikato Times* (Hamilton), 8 August 1917 and *New Zealand Police Gazette*, 1917. Both men were already military defaulters. Following his release in April 1918, O'Neill was called up again and deserted. Captured in October, he went into camp and died at Trentham during the influenza pandemic in November 1918. See 'John O'Neill, Sedition', updated 6 May 2016, https://nzhistory.govt.nz/media/photo/john-oneill-sedition.

10 It has not been possible to test such claims from sources available in New Zealand. Family traditions of such involvement are therefore taken at face value here, notwithstanding the possible exaggeration or even falsification of radical pedigrees involved.

11 *GR*, April 1917. For a fuller account of *The Green Ray* and Maoriland Irish Society, see my article '"Shaming the Shoneens": *The Green Ray* and the Maoriland Irish Society in Dunedin, 1916–22', in Lyndon Fraser (ed.), *A Distant Shore: Irish migration & New Zealand settlement* (Dunedin: University of Otago Press, 2000), pp. 117–34.

12 Details on Cummins' background supplied to the author by his nephew, the late Monsignor Bryan Walsh, along with his unpublished essay about his uncle's experiences, 'Irish Felon in New Zealand', 1998.

13 Information supplied to the author by Ryan's niece, the late Shona Kinney, 1994. See also family history in Marie Purcell, *Dozens of Cousins: A story of the O'Donnell and Purcell Families, 1841–1991* (Pascoe Vale South, Vic.: M. Purcell, 1991).

14 There is no evidence to support this claim, and James Bradley is not featured in any of the standard histories of the IRB.

15 Information supplied to the author by Bradley's daughter Katherine Craig and McCarthy's son, the late Cormac McCarthy, 1994.

16 Information on Sean Tohill supplied to the author by family members, Peter and Hugh Tohill, 1995, and Tobias Tohill, 2016. These claims have not been corroborated and perhaps represent the tendency of immigrants to embellish their pedigrees in the colonies.

17 The lack of surviving evidence makes this a moot point. It is in the nature of a secret organisation not to leave behind archives. In their absence a researcher can only assess indications of what might have been. No equivalent has been found to the remarkable record of Irish political activity in Australia assembled by Dr Albert Dryer in 1956 for the Irish government's Bureau of Military History and now available online. See Witness Statement of Albert Thomas Dryer, BMH, WS 1526, p. 2, accessed 12 November 2019, http://www.bureauofmilitaryhistory.ie/reels/bmh/BMH.WS1526.pdf#page=2.

18 A useful point of comparison would be the small IRB circle that existed within the Irish National Association in Australia and held a secret military training camp in the Blue Mountains in 1916–17. See O'Farrell, *Irish in Australia*, pp. 273–4.

19 Memorandum for the Commissioner of Police from the Director of Personal Services, 26 October 1917, NA.

20 Military service record, 65251, Denis Mangan, NA.

21 Military service record, 65167, Patrick Fitzpatrick, NA.

22 This figure is based on my count of notices in the *New Zealand Police Gazette* and does not necessarily allow for subsequent cancellations and amendments to warrants. An official return of warrants outstanding as at 31 December 1918 gives a figure of 1,906. 'Personnel – Military Defaulters List – General File', NA, AD1 780.

23 Rowan Carroll and Elizabeth Plumridge, 'Section 5: Police extension of mandate and detection of resistance and non-compliance with conscription', unpublished paper, *Rethinking War* Conference, Stout Centre, 2013.

24 Military service records, 49271, William Thomas Doyle, and 51143, John Steven Doyle, NA.

25 Record of interview, Jack Doyle speaking to Patrick O'Farrell, August 1970. Personal communication to the author by the late Professor Patrick O'Farrell, 2006.

26 'When Rugby Went to War', *Manawatu Standard* (Palmerston North), 28 April 2015. See also *Manawatu Times* (Palmerston North), 14 February 1917; *FS*, 27 October 1917; *The Star* (Christchurch), 5 November 1917; *Grey River Argus* (Greymouth), 22 January 1918.

27 Personal communication to the author by Dean Parker, 2000.

28 Postal Censorship of J. to Mrs J. O'Brien, May, NA, AD10 Box 10/ 19/24. My thanks to Jared Davidson for sending me this reference, personal communication, 2016. Dan Butler's name appears on the 1919 list of Military Defaulters with the Royal Hotel, Gisborne, as his address. He had been called up in a ballot in June 1918.

29 *The Wairarapa Age* (Masterton), 8 June 1918.

30 Military service records, 62700, John Larkin, and 62701, Robert Ernest Larkin, NA. See also *AS*, 5 December 1917; *The Tuapeka Times* (Lawrence), 12 January 1918; *ODT*, 11 July 1918; and *Grey River Argus*, 20 July 1918.

31 Memo 24/188, New Zealand Military Forces Headquarters, 31 May 1917, NA, AD1 780.

32 *NZH*, 29 August 1918; *D*, 29 August 1918; and *Northern Advocate* (Whangarei), 31 August 1918.

33 Military service record, 52356, Daniel Maguire, NA.

34 Military service record, 53669, Lawrence Joseph Kirwan, NA. Additional information from Lawrence's nephew Peter Kirwan, 2016.

35 David Grant, *Field Punishment No. 1: Archibald Baxter, Mark Briggs & New Zealand's anti-militarist tradition* (Wellington: Steele Roberts, 2008), p. 110.

36 The Codys of Southland were New Zealand's most defiant Irish family during the First World War, but I have already described their efforts elsewhere so will not detail them here. See Brosnahan, '"Shaming the Shoneens"'.

37 It is worth noting how these evaders were characterised (by themselves and others) as ethnically 'Irish' regardless of whether they were Irish-born or colonials, a reminder perhaps that ethnic identity 'is a culturally constructed set of usages adopted by people in their day-to-day relationships with one another and the society around them'. Lyndon Fraser, *To Tara via Holyhead: Irish Catholic immigrants in nineteenth-century Christchurch* (Auckland: Auckland University Press, 1997), p. 3.

38 *NZ Truth* (Wellington), 14 December 1918.

39 H.E. Holland, *Armageddon or Calvary: The conscientious objectors of New Zealand and 'The process of their conversion'* (Wellington: Maoriland Worker Printing and Publishing, 1919), p. 127.

40 Photos at NA in AAYS 8638, AD1 Box 738/ 10/566 Part 2.

41 *GR*, June 1917.

42 *GR*, October 1917.

43 *GR*, January 1918. Additional information on Tim Brosnan from his great grand-daughter Veronica O'Grady, 2016. In neither case should the claim to be a 'Sinn Féiner' be seen as indicating formal membership of the Irish political organisation. Like 'fenian' before it, this term had become an epithet of abuse for republican supporters among the New Zealand Irish by the wider community. It was a notional affiliation that men like O'Sullivan and Brosnan were proud to own.

44 Censorship of correspondence, T. Brosnan to Mrs M. McCarthy, April–December, NA, AD10 Box 10/ 19/5.

45 'For Publication in Press', 9 October 1918, NA, AD1 780.

46 Tim Shoebridge, 'New Zealanders Who Resisted the First World War', updated 1 August 2016, http://www.nzhistory.net.nz/war/nzers-who-resisted-ww1.

47 See also the tabulation by Jared Davidson, 'Dissent during the First World War: By the numbers', 28 June 2016, http://blog.tepapa.govt.nz/2016/06/28/dissent-during-the-first-world-war-by-the-numbers/.

Chapter 8: Challenging Times: The Irish-Catholic press in Dunedin and Adelaide, 1916–19

1 Historians differ in the distinctions made between those newspapers printed and published in Ireland and others printed and distributed in the diaspora. Thus, some would refer to *The Southern Cross* as a diaspora Catholic newspaper. However, it is important to recognise that, from 1889 to 1927, its masthead characterised itself (with minor variations) as a 'Weekly Record [or Journal] of Catholic, Irish and General News'.

2 *SC*, 14 August 1914, p. 9.

3   For a more detailed discussion of the exchange process, see Stephanie James, "'From Beyond the Sea": The Irish Catholic press in the southern hemisphere', in Angela McCarthy (ed.), *Ireland in the World: Comparative, transnational, and personal perspectives* (New York: Routledge, 2015), pp. 86–90.

4   *The Tablet* was registered as a commercial company in 1874 and as a public company in 1886, while *The Southern Cross* was immediately registered as a limited liability company in 1889.

5   *SC*, 28 April 1916, p. 9; 24 November 1916, p. 12; 9 March 1917, p. 12.

6   *SC*, 14 August 1914, p. 9. Scott's editorial was in *The Tablet* of 30 July.

7   Heather McNamara, 'The Sole Organ of the Irish Race in New Zealand? A social and cultural history of the *New Zealand Tablet* and its readers, 1898–1923', MA thesis, University of Auckland, 2002, p. 28.

8   Emerging in 1905 after the Anglo-Boer War, Sinn Féin focused on cultural and economic independence. Its policies aimed for passive resistance. Without real success until the First World War, its opposition to recruiting endorsed its anti-British reputation, explaining why the public attributed responsibility for the Rising to Sinn Féin.

9   See James Elwick, 'Layered History: Styles of reasoning as stratified conditions of possibility', *Studies in History and Philosophy of Science*, vol. 43, no. 4, 2012, p. 620.

10 See Stephanie James, 'Deep Green Loathing? Shifting Irish-Australian loyalties in the Victorian and South Australian Irish Catholic press, 1868–1923', PhD thesis, Flinders University, 2013, in particular, ch. 5: 'Shifting Loyalty? Challenges to Irish-Australians from the Easter Rising to the end of World War One', pp. 231–70.

11 *SC*, 15 September 1916, p. 12. Cleary was editor from 1898. This item also mentioned Scott's 'distinguished academic career at a New Zealand University'.

12 *SC*, 28 April 1916, p. 9.

13 *SC*, 24 November 1916, p. 12.

14 SC, 9 March 1917, p. 12.

15 McNamara, 'The Sole Organ', p. 28.

16 Heather McNamara, 'The *New Zealand Tablet* and the Irish Catholic press worldwide, 1898–1923', *New Zealand Journal of History*, vol. 37, no. 2, 2003, p. 154.

17 McNamara, 'The Sole Organ', p. 30. McNamara quotes a letter written by Kelly to his friend John O'Hagan, rector of the Irish College in Rome on 15 May 1918. She also suggests that the paper, 'financially successful' under Cleary and initially under Scott, was by 'late 1916 … losing money and declining in circulation' (pp. 29–30).

18 Ibid., p. 34. McNamara notes that Hussey eventually joined the 'Board of Directors'.

19 Ibid., p. 35.

20 Ibid. See also Rory Sweetman, *Bishop in the Dock: The sedition trial of James Liston* (Auckland: Auckland University Press, 1997), pp. 18–19.

21 Seán Brosnahan, "'Shaming the Shoneens": *The Green Ray* and the Maoriland Irish Society in Dunedin, 1916–22', in Lyndon Fraser (ed.), *A Distant Shore: Irish migration & New Zealand settlement* (Dunedin: University of Otago Press, 2000), p. 131.

22 McNamara, 'The Sole Organ', p. 36.

23　The chairman of directors was Limerick-born T.F. O'Neill (1853–1924). Kilkenny-born Very Rev. Precentor Patrick Hurley (1862–1930) was a director for twenty-five years. Father Michael Hourigan (1859–1951) was born in Limerick.

24　The founding editor, Senator J.V. O'Loghlin, enlisted as a lieutenant colonel at sixty-two and accompanied troops travelling from Australia. His editorial successor (1896–1903), Lieutenant W.J. Denny MP, enlisted in 1915. The third lay director was J.F. Murphy JP.

25　*SC*, 3 July 1914, p. 13.

26　*SC*, 24 November 1916, pp. 10–11.

27　*SC*, 13 April 1917, p. 10.

28　See James, 'Deep Green Loathing?', pp. 61–5.

29　See Diarmaid Ferriter, *A Nation and Not a Rabble: The Irish Revolution, 1913–1923* (London: Profile Books, 2015).

30　See Kevin Molloy, 'The Politics of Reading: Identity and the Australian reading experience, 1800–1880', in Brad and Kathryn Patterson (eds), *Ireland and the Irish Antipodes: One world or worlds apart? Papers delivered at the 16th Australasian Irish Studies Conference, Massey University, Wellington, New Zealand, 9–12 July 2009* (Sydney: Anchor Books, 2010), pp. 145–61.

31　McNamara, 'The *New Zealand Tablet*', p. 158.

32　*SC*, 4 August 1916, p. 10.

33　*SC*, 22 September 1916, p. 10.

34　*SC*, 16 March 1917, p. 4.

35　*SC*, 9 July 1917, p. 14.

36　*SC*, 21 July 1916, p. 10.

37　*SC*, 5 October 1917, p. 4. Irish-born Patrick Healy was Adelaide's UIL president from 1900 to its 1920 amalgamation with the Irish National Association.

38　*SC*, 30 November 1917, p. 10.

39　*SC*, 14 December 1917, p. 8. O'Loghlin penned a weekly commentary column, '*Currente Calamo*'.

40　*SC*, 15 March 1918, pp. 4, 5, 10, 16, 19; 22 March 1918, pp. 6, 8, 10, 23; 29 March 1918, p. 4.

41　*SC*, 24 January 1919, p. 10.

42　For details of these individuals, see Stephanie James, '"The Drought Is Worrying People Here Far Worse than the War": Letters between Hamley Bridge and Ireland during the Great War', *Journal of the Historical Society of South Australia*, no. 43, 2015, pp. 5–16, and Stephanie James, 'The Evolution of Adelaide's Irish National Association, 1918–1950: From security threat to cultural force?', *Journal of the Historical Society of South Australia*, no. 45, 2017, pp. 31–45.

43　'Irish National Association', 30 May 1918, NAA (Adelaide), D1915 SA29, Pt. 1.

44　McNamara, 'The *New Zealand Tablet*', p. 160.

45　Ibid.

46　Ibid., p. 162.

47　*SC*, 24 May 1918, p. 10.

48 Kevin Fewster, 'Expression and Suppression: Aspects of military censorship in Australia during the Great War', PhD thesis, University of New South Wales, 1980, p. 213.

49 Brosnahan, '"Shaming the Shoneens"', p. 128.

50 Frank Cain, *The Origins of Political Surveillance in Australia* (Sydney: Angus & Robertson, 1983), pp. 1–43.

51 Ibid., pp. 19–20.

52 Ibid., pp. 26–7.

53 Circular 15, 17 November 1917, NAA (Adelaide), D1915 SA29 Pt. 1.

54 Cain, *Origins of Political Surveillance*, p. 26.

55 McNamara, 'The *New Zealand Tablet*', p. 163.

56 Richard P. Davis, *Irish Issues in New Zealand Politics, 1868–1922* (Dunedin: University of Otago Press, 1974), p. 199.

57 McNamara, 'The *New Zealand Tablet*', p. 159.

58 *SC*, 23 June 1916, p. 4.

59 *SC*, 3 November 1916, p. 7.

60 *SC*, 8 December 1916, p. 18.

61 The first conscription plebiscite was held on 28 October 1916.

62 *SC*, 22 December 1916, p. 20.

63 For coverage of issues relating to NZ conscription, see *SC*, 16 March 1917, p. 2; 6 April 1917, p. 19; 13 April 1917, p. 3; 20 April 1917, p. 11.

64 *SC*, 13 April 1917, p. 15.

65 *SC*, 20 July 1917, p. 7.

66 *SC*, 31 August 1917, p. 2.

67 *SC*, 14 December 1917, p. 11.

68 *SC*, 4 January 1918, p. 4.

69 *SC*, 1 March 1918, p. 4.

70 *SC*, 26 April 1918, p. 5.

71 *SC*, 17 May 1918, p. 8.

72 *SC*, 14 February 1919, p. 4.

73 *SC*, 3 November 1916, p. 7.

74 *SC*, 13 April 1917, p. 15.

75 *SC*, 4 January 1918, p. 4.

76 *SC*, 17 May 1918, p. 8.

77 *SC*, 14 February 1919, p. 4.

78 *The Catholic Bulletin* was a Catholic and nationalist paper, published from 1911 to 1939. It became more strident after the First World War, opposing the Anglo-Irish Treaty of 1921. *Nationality* was edited by Arthur Griffith.

79 15 May 1919, NAA (Adelaide), D1915 SA29 Pt. 1.

80 See, for example, *The Register* (Adelaide), 14 March 1883, p. 1 (The Redmond visit); *The Register*, 23 December 1885, p. 6 (Irish Independence); and *The Weekly Chronicle* (Adelaide), 14 May 1887, p. 6 (Mr Parnell and *The Times*).

81 The loyalty and patriotism O'Loghlin demonstrated 'as a soldier and a Senator' – he was elected to the Australian Senate in 1913 – did not protect him from censor criticism in a letter to the PM during the Irish War of Independence. 12 February 1919, NAA (Adelaide), D1915 SA29 Pt. 1.

82   *SC*, 23 March 1917, pp. 7–8.
83   See 'Sinn Fein South Australia: General reports on organisation', 30 May 1918, NAA (Canberra), A8911/219. The report was sent to the acting PM because O'Loghlin was a senator, and he was linked to Patrick Healy's letter to Morgan Jageurs, the UIL leader in Melbourne, in which Healy referred to O'Loghlin as 'one of our leading UIL members'.
84   *SC*, 9 August 1918, pp. 6–7.
85   *SC*, 10 September 1943, p. 5.
86   *SC*, 25 August 1916, p. 5.
87   SC, 31 May 1918, pp. 10–11.
88   18 June 1918, NAA (Adelaide), D1915 SA29 Pt. 1.
89   As well as watching Father Prendergast, the SIB was monitoring a convent of Irish nuns, J.J. Daly's city office (he was a young Irish-Australian lawyer prominent in the INA), and Miss Considine's Catholic bookshop, all named by Prendergast as 'trustworthy'.
90   See *SC*, 4 February 1921, p. 8, which reported Father Hourigan's address to the Irish National Foresters. See also 14 April and 9 August 1920, NAA (Adelaide), D1915 SA29 Pt. 1; in these items, his communications to the INA from Ireland were noted.
91   McNamara, 'The Sole Organ', pp. 34–6.
92   See Richard B. Healy, *The Christian Brothers of Wakefield Street, 1878–1978* (Adelaide: Lutheran Publishing House, 1978), pp. 117–23.
93   Brother Purton to Albert Dryer, 30 May 1918, NAA (Adelaide), D1915 SA29 Pt. 1. Purton wrote to Dryer, founder of Sydney's INA, urging that his name not be mentioned as founder or organiser 'for certain reasons which it were better to leave unexpressed'.
94   For dates and topics of his speeches, see James, 'Deep Green Loathing?', pp. 528–9.
95   Circular, 4 January 1918, NAA (Adelaide), D1915 SA29 Pt. 1.
96   P.F. O'Sullivan to P.E. O'Leary, 25 February 1918, NAA (Canberra), A8911/219.
97   Ibid., 25 and 28 March 1918, NAA (Adelaide), D1915 SA29 Pt. 1.
98   *SC*, 22 March 1918, pp. 8–9, 18.
99   See *SC*, 31 May 1918, for the names of seventeen committee members with Purton as chair.
100 NAA (Adelaide), D1915 SA29 Pt. 1. A series of reports followed letters between Father Prendergast and Melbourne's P.F. O'Sullivan about receiving banned books: 19 May, 8 and 21 June, 15 July, and 3 September 1918.
101 Ibid., 24 June, 1 and 15 July. The items refer to Brother Purton's enquiries into rumours of the school's closure which alerted authorities to possible information leaks from Dr A.F. Lynch, an old scholar of CBC.
102 *SC*, 11 May 1923, p. 6.
103 See *SC*, 26 March 1920, pp. 4–5, 10–11; 16 April 1920, pp. 9–10.
104 22 March 1920, NAA (Canberra), A8911/219.
105 Healy, *The Christian Brothers*, p. 116.
106 *SC*, 12 May 1916, p. 11.
107 Brosnahan, '"Shaming the Shoneens"', p. 131.

Chapter 9: 'A most cruel and bitter campaign of slander and vituperation': Easter Week 1916 and the Rise of the Protestant Political Association

An earlier version of this chapter, '"We stand for the Protestant religion, the (Protestant) King and Empire": The rise of the Protestant Political Association in World War One', was published in Steven Loveridge (ed.), *New Zealand Society at War, 1914–1918* (Wellington: Victoria University Press, 2016).

1   *NZH*, 15 February 1918, p. 4; *WC*, 15 February 1918, p. 5.

2   *C*, 19 February 1918, p. 2.

3   There has been no authoritative published account of the Protestant Political Association, but H.S. Moores, 'The Rise of the Protestant Political Association: Sectarianism in New Zealand politics during World War I' (MA thesis, University of Auckland, 1966) is a source of much information otherwise difficult to obtain. Max Satchell, 'Pulpit Politics: The Protestant Political Association in Dunedin from 1917 to 1922' (BA Hons, University of Otago, 1983) provides a unique local case study. Rory Sweetman, 'New Zealand Catholicism, War, Politics and the Irish Issue, 1912–1922' (PhD thesis, University of Cambridge, 1991) offers valuable background from a Catholic perspective.

4   *D*, 16 February 1918, p. 8.

5   *NZH*, 3 March 1917, p. 6.

6   *AS*, 18 May 1918, p. 4.

7   P.S. O'Connor, 'Sectarian Conflict in New Zealand, 1911–1920', *Political Science*, vol. 19, no. 1, 1967, pp. 3–16; P.S. O'Connor, 'Protestants, Catholics and the New Zealand Government, 1916–18', in G.A. Wood and P.S. O'Connor (eds), *W.P. Morrell: A tribute* (Dunedin: University of Otago Press, 1973), pp. 185–202; Rory Sweetman, 'New Zealand Catholicism and the Irish Issue, 1914–1922', in W.J. Shiels and Diana Wood (eds), *The Churches, Ireland and the Irish* (Oxford: Blackwell, 1989), pp. 375–84.

8   *Timaru Herald*, 9 May 1918, p. 2.

9   O'Connor, 'Protestants, Catholics and the New Zealand Government', p. 185.

10 Jock Phillips and Terry Hearn, *Settlers: New Zealand immigrants from England, Ireland and Scotland, 1800–1945* (Auckland: Auckland University Press, 2008); Terry Hearn, 'The Origins of New Zealand's Irish Settlers, 1840–1945', in Brad Patterson (ed.), *The Irish in New Zealand: Historical contexts and perspectives* (Wellington: Stout Research Centre for New Zealand Studies, Victoria University of Wellington, 2002), pp. 15–34.

11 Richard S. Hill, *The Colonial Frontier Tamed: New Zealand policing in transition, 1867–1886* (Wellington: Historical Branch, Department of Internal Affairs; GP Books, 1989), pp. 156–61; Seán Brosnahan, 'The "Battle of the Borough" and the "Saige o Timaru": Sectarian riot in colonial Canterbury', *New Zealand Journal of History*, vol. 28, no. 1, 1994, pp. 41–59.

12 Rory Sweetman, 'Towards a History of Orangeism in New Zealand', in Brad Patterson (ed.), *Ulster–New Zealand Migration and Cultural Transfers* (Dublin: Four Courts Press, 2006), pp. 154–64; Gerard Horn, 'The Orange Order in Wellington, 1874–1930: Class, ethnicity and politics', *Australasian Journal of Irish Studies*, vol. 10, 2010, pp. 55–80; P.J. Coleman, 'Transplanted Irish Institutions:

Orangeism and Hibernianism in New Zealand, 1877–1910', MA thesis, University of Canterbury, 1994.

13 Brad Patterson, '"We Love One Country, One Queen, One Flag": Loyalism in early colonial New Zealand, 1840–1880', in Allan Blackstock and Frank O'Gorman (eds), *Loyalism and the Formation of the British World, 1775–1914* (Woodbridge, UK: Boydell & Brewer, 2014), pp. 255–61.

14 For examples, see David A. Wilson (ed.), *The Orange Order in Canada* (Dublin: Four Courts Press, 2007) and Keith Amos, *The Fenians in Australia* (Sydney: New South Wales University Press, 1988).

15 Richard P. Davis, *Irish Issues in New Zealand Politics, 1868–1922* (Dunedin: University of Otago Press, 1974), pp. 71–98; Ian Breward, *Godless Schools? A study of Protestant reactions to the Education Act of 1877* (Christchurch: Presbyterian Bookroom, 1967), pp. 21–36, 47–73.

16 Davis, *Irish Issues*, pp. 78–9; Rory Sweetman, *'A Fair and Just Solution?': A History of the Integration of Private Schools in New Zealand* (Palmerston North: Dunmore Press in Association with the Ministry for Culture and Heritage and the Association of Proprietors of Integrated Schools, 2002), pp. 23–5.

17 Davis, *Irish Issues*, p. 82.

18 Michael Bassett, *Sir Joseph Ward: A political biography* (Auckland: Auckland University Press, 1993), pp. 141–55.

19 Moores, 'The Rise of the Protestant Political Association', pp. 24, 33; James Watson, 'Were Catholics Over-Represented in the Public Service during the Early Twentieth Century?', *Political Science*, vol. 42, no. 2, 1990, pp. 20–34.

20 Moores, 'The Rise of the Protestant Political Association', p. 33.

21 Davis, *Irish Issues*, pp. 144–62.

22 O'Connor, 'Sectarian Conflict', pp. 1–2; Donald Harman Akenson, *Half the World from Home: Perspectives on the Irish in New Zealand, 1860–1950* (Wellington: Victoria University Press, 1990), pp. 105–6.

23 Breward, *Godless Schools?*, pp. 52–71; D.V. MacDonald, 'The New Zealand Bible in Schools League', MA thesis, Victoria University of Wellington, 1964.

24 *NZH*, 10 December 1912, p. 9.

25 Rory Sweetman, *Faith and Fraternalism: A history of the Hibernian Society in New Zealand, 1869–2000* (Wellington: Hibernian Society, 2002), pp. 95–6.

26 *EP*, 8 January 1913, p. 2.

27 Breward, *Godless Schools?*, pp. 60–2.

28 *Manawatu Standard* (Palmerston North), 14 December 1914, p. 5.

29 James Belich, *Paradise Reforged: A history of the New Zealanders from the 1880s to the Year 2000* (Auckland: Penguin, 2001), p. 98.

30 *NZT*, 20 August 1914, p. 34; Hugh Laracy, 'Priests, People and Patriotism: New Zealand Catholics and the War, 1914–1918', *Australasian Catholic Record*, vol. 70, no. 1, 1993, p. 19.

31 *NZT*, 10 September 1914, p. 49; cited in Laracy, 'Priests, People and Patriotism', p. 21.

32 *EP*, 18 February 1914, p. 4; 24 February 1915, p. 3; 12 July 1915, p. 4.

33 *EP*, 24 February 1915, p. 3.

34 Moores, 'The Rise of the Protestant Political Association', p. 52; *EP*, 25 August 1915, p. 11; *EP*, 7 January 1916, p. 4; *AS*, 20 January 1916, p. 7.

35 *FS*, 8 September 1916, p. 2; *D*, 7 September 1916, p. 6.

36 *The Sun* (Christchurch), 19 May 1914, p. 3; *ODT*, 19 May 1914, p. 6; *EP*, 24 February 1915, p. 3; *NZH*, 19 November 1915, p. 4; *NZH*, 3 December 1915, p. 7; *EP*, 26 February 1916, p. 2; *D*, 29 February 1916, p. 9.

37 Moores, 'The Rise of the Protestant Political Association', p. 111.

38 Christopher van der Krogt, 'Elliott, Howard Leslie', in *Dictionary of New Zealand Biography, Te Ara: The Encyclopedia of New Zealand*, accessed 12 November 2019, https://www.TeAra.govt.nz/en/biographies/3e5/elliott-howard-leslie; Moores, 'The Rise of the Protestant Political Association', pp. 87–90. A small collection of papers relating to Elliott, collected by Moores, is now held in the University of Auckland Library (an inventory is available).

39 *Australasian Christian Word*, vol. 21, no. 1061, 1906; cited in Moores, 'The Rise of the Protestant Political Association', p. 88.

40 Breward, *Godless Schools?*, p. 60; Moores, 'The Rise of the Protestant Political Association', p. 108. Elliott's proposed political party was to be a 'Christian Socialist Party', a counter to the 'atheistic, materialistic socialists' then steering the labour movement. In planning this party, he flirted with rebel Liberal politician George Fowlds. Moores, 'The Rise of the Protestant Political Association', p. 103.

41 Moores, 'The Rise of the Protestant Political Association', p. 108.

42 Ibid., p. 86.

43 Ibid., p. 111. When researching his thesis, Moores had access to many involved individuals (twenty-nine interviewees), including H.S. Bilby and members of the Elliott family. He also had access to Orange Order records no longer locatable.

44 Ibid., p. 111.

45 Ibid., pp. 122–3.

46 *NZH*, 10 April 1916, p. 7; 14 April 1916, p. 7. Committee of Vigilance (Loyal Orange Lodge no. 70), *The Papal Delegate and the Mayor* (Auckland: New Zealand Mission Press, 1916).

47 Moores, 'The Rise of the Protestant Political Association', p. 116.

48 *NZH*, 20 April 1916, p. 8.

49 *EP*, 22 April 1916, p. 6; *D*, 24 April 1916, p. 9; *Report of Proceedings of Eighth Annual Session of the Grand Orange Lodge of New Zealand* (Christchurch: n.p., 1916), pp. 14–18.

50 Moores, 'The Rise of the Protestant Political Association', p. 124.

51 Ibid., p. 128. All contemporary figures calculated using the Reserve Bank's Inflation Calculator, http://www.rbnz.govt.nz.

52 In spite of a courtesy visit by Prime Minister Massey, there is no evidence that he was a party to hatching the plan. See ibid., p. 129.

53 *NZH*, 27 April 1916, p. 2.

54 *EP*, 27 April 1916, p. 7.

55 *AS*, 1 May 1916, p. 4; *D*, 2 May 1916, p. 4; *P*, 3 May 1916, p. 6.

56 G.E. Horn, 'The Irish Revolution and Protestant Politics in New Zealand 1916–1922', unpublished paper presented at the 'Irish Diaspora and Revolution' conference, NUI Maynooth, November 2012, p. 4.

57 Moores, 'The Rise of the Protestant Political Association', pp. 131–5.

58 Regular flows of donations are recorded in the minute book of the Orange Hall Trustees, Auckland, 1915–32; cited in Moores, 'The Rise of the Protestant Political Association', p. 134. The secretary of the trustees was J.J. Carnahan, influential historian of the New Zealand Orange movement.

59 Published by Free Press Print (Wm Richardson), Auckland, in 1915; *Marlborough Express*, 20 August 1917, p. 8; Moores, 'The Rise of the Protestant Political Association', p. 145.

60 *AJHR*, 1917, F-8, 'Auckland Post Office Inquiry', p. 105. See also Alex Frame, *Salmond: Southern jurist* (Wellington: Victoria University Press, 1995), pp. 175–8.

61 Moores, 'The Rise of the Protestant Political Association', p. 153.

62 Ibid.; *EP*, 27 January 1917, p. 3; *New Zealand Times* (Wellington), 1 February 1917, p. 6; *Eltham Argus*, 25 January 1917, p. 4. The *New Zealand Tablet* was a Catholic weekly, published in Dunedin from 1873; see Heather McNamara, 'The *New Zealand Tablet* and the Irish Catholic Press Worldwide, 1898–1923', *New Zealand Journal of History*, vol. 37, no. 2, 2003, pp. 153–70. The *NZ Truth* was a Wellington tabloid which between 1905 and 1922 was known for its support of radical and socialistic ideas, the primary audience being working people; see Redmer Yska, *Truth: The rise and fall of the people's paper* (Nelson: Craig Potton Publishing, 2010).

63 Cited in Moores, 'The Rise of the Protestant Political Association', p. 154; *NZ Truth*, 17 February 1917, p. 1.

64 *NZH*, 1 March 1917, p. 6; *AS*, 1 March 1917, p. 4.

65 *NZH*, 1 March 1917, p. 6.

66 *NZT*, 15 March 1917, p. 31.

67 *New Zealand Baptist*, May 1917, p. 76.

68 Moores, 'The Rise of the Protestant Political Association', p. 159.

69 *ODT*, 9 April 1916, p. 6; 10 April 1917, p. 6. *Report of Proceedings of Ninth Annual Session of the Grand Orange Lodge of New Zealand* (Wellington: n.p., 1917), pp. 22–4.

70 H.S. Bilby interview, 2 June 1965; cited in Moores, 'The Rise of the Protestant Political Association', pp. 165, 168.

71 *The Nation*, 10 July 1917, p. 10.

72 *NZH*, 12 July 1917, p. 6.

73 Ibid.

74 *AJHR*, 1917, F-8, 'Auckland Post Office Inquiry'; Moores, 'The Rise of the Protestant Political Association', pp. 174–207, focuses fully on the Post Office Inquiry.

75 *NZPD*, vol. 180, 13 September 1917, pp. 108–9, 133.

76 *D*, 16 October 1917, p. 5; *MW*, 24 October 1917, p. 4.

77 *NZH*, 3 November 1917, p. 8; *P*, 3 November 1917, p. 8.

78 *NZ Truth*, 10 November 1917, p. 1.

79 *EP*, 12 December 1917, p. 3.

80 *C*, 16 April 1919, p. 1.

81 *P*, 20 August 1920, p. 8.

82 The lack of primary documentation precludes precise determination of just what sort of people made up PPA membership. That they were Protestants is axiomatic; indications being that Methodists, Baptists, and other nonconformist churches were most strongly represented. Moores, 'The Rise of the Protestant Political Association', pp. 221–3.

83   Ibid., pp. 209–12.

84   *The Nation*, 10 September 1917, p. 4; 10 October 1917, pp. 12–13.

85   *The Nation*, 10 October 1917, p. 10; *EP*, 12 December 1917, p. 3; *Ellesmere Guardian*
     (Southbridge), 20 March 1918, p. 3; *Otautau Standard and Wallace County
     Chronicle*, 4 March 1919, p. 3. By early 1918, it had become readily apparent that
     an increasing proportion of the PPA membership was drawn from outside the
     ranks of the lodges and that an adjustment was required in the relationship with
     the Loyal Orange Institution. When attempts to paper over the differences were
     unsuccessful, it was agreed at the April 1918 meeting of the Grand Lodge that
     separation was inevitable. *EP*, 18 June 1919, p. 6; *Report of Proceedings of Tenth
     Annual Session of the Grand Orange Lodge of New Zealand* (Wellington: n.p.,
     1918), p. 9; Moores, 'The Rise of the Protestant Political Association', pp. 241–6.

86   *EP*, 18 June 1919, p. 6.

87   *AS*, 19 February 1919, p. 7.

88   *P*, 21 September 1917, p. 5.

89   *Wairarapa Age* (Masterton), 20 February 1918, p. 4.

90   *D*, 24 April 1918, p. 6.

91   *NZH*, 28 August 1918, p. 9.

92   Ibid.

93   Rory Sweetman, 'Who Fears to Speak of Easter Week? Antipodean Irish-Catholic
     responses to the 1916 Rising', in Ruán O'Donnell (ed.), *The Impact of the 1916
     Rising: Among the nations* (Dublin: Irish Academic Press, 2008), pp. 74–7.

94   *NZT*, 4 May 1916; cited in Sweetman, 'Who Fears to Speak?', p. 76.

95   *The Green Ray* was an overtly Irish nationalist publication launched in Dunedin in
     1916 and forcibly closed because of its militancy two years later; see Seán Brosnahan
     '"Shaming the Shoneens": *The Green Ray* and the Maoriland Irish Society in
     Dunedin, 1916–22', in Lyndon Fraser (ed.), *A Distant Shore: Irish migration & New
     Zealand settlement* (Dunedin: University of Otago Press, 2000), pp. 117–34.

96   *TDN*, 12 February 1918, p. 5.

97   *NZH*, 12 July 1917, p. 6.

98   P.S. O'Connor, 'Storm over the Clergy: New Zealand, 1917', *Journal of Religious
     History*, vol. 4, no. 2, 1966, pp. 129–48; Paul Baker, *King and Country Call: New
     Zealanders, conscription and the Great War* (Auckland: Auckland University Press,
     1988).

99   *EP*, 11 December 1916, p. 8; Laracy, 'Priests, People and Patriotism', pp. 21–2.

100 *NZH*, 27 February 1917, p. 6.

101 *D*, 22 February 1917, p. 6; O'Connor, 'Storm over the Clergy', pp. 132–5.

102 *WC*, 18 July 1917, p. 5.

103 *P*, 21 September 1917, p. 5.

104 Bassett, *Sir Joseph Ward*, pp. 229–30.

105 *EP*, 12 December 1917, p. 3; *AS*, 28 August 1918, p. 6.

106 O'Connor, 'Sectarian Conflict', p. 9.

107 *Timaru Herald*, 9 May 1918, p. 2.

108 *EP*, 11 December 1916, p. 8.

109 *NZH*, 17 September 1917, p. 6.

110   *AJHR*, 1917, H-19D, 'Return Showing the Number of Adherents of Each Religious Denomination Embarked on Active Service up to and Including the 28th Reinforcements.'

111   *AJHR*, 1917, H-19K, 'Defaulters from Military Service Not Found by Police up to 17 October 1917.'

112   *Otautau Standard and Wallace County Chronicle*, 4 March 1919, p. 3.

113   *ODT*, 7 May 1918, p. 7.

114   O'Connor, 'Sectarian Conflict', p. 9.

115   Brosnahan, '"Shaming the Shoneens"', pp. 117–34.

116   Sweetman, 'Who Fears to Speak?', pp. 81–6; see also Rory Sweetman, 'Kelly, James Joseph', in *Dictionary of New Zealand Biography, Te Ara: The Encyclopedia of New Zealand*, accessed 12 November 2019, https://www.TeAra.govt.nz/en/biographies/3k6/kelly-james-joseph.

117   Sweetman, 'Who Fears to Speak?', p. 82.

118   Laracy, 'Priests, People and Patriotism', pp. 21–4; Moores, 'The Rise of the Protestant Political Association', pp. 218–19.

119   Barry Gustafson, *Labour's Path to Political Independence: The origins and establishment of the New Zealand Labour Party, 1900–19* (Auckland: Auckland University Press, 1980), pp. 89–94.

120   *WC*, 18 July 1917, p. 5.

121   *EP*, 25 April 1918, p. 4.

122   *EP*, 15 December 1917, p. 4; 1 January 1918, p. 2.

123   *EP*, 1 January 1918, p. 2.

124   Catholic confidence in Ward had been severely eroded because of his failure to advance state aid for denominational schools, his inability to secure exempting legislation for conscripted clergy, and his relative silence on Irish issues. Labour came to win the support of the Catholic bishops concerned at the economic and social problems confronting working-class Catholics. However, the Labour leadership, while including a sprinkle of practising Catholics, had as many or more who were committed Protestants or claimed no religion at all. Moores, 'The Rise of the Protestant Political Association', p. 273; R.P. Davis, 'The New Zealand Labour Party's "Irish Campaign", 1916–1921', *Political Science*, vol. 19, no. 2, 1967, pp. 13–23; Gustafson, *Labour's Path*, p. 120.

125   Moores, 'The Rise of the Protestant Political Association', p. 216.

126   *EP*, 26 September 1917, p. 3; *NZ Truth*, 6 October 1917, p. 1.

127   Moores, 'The Rise of the Protestant Political Association', p. 251; *D*, 24 April 1918, p. 3; *Hawera & Normanby Star*, 17 August 1918, p. 5.

128   Moores, 'The Rise of the Protestant Political Association', pp. 287–310; Michael Bassett and Michael King, *Tomorrow Comes the Song: A life of Peter Fraser* (Auckland: Penguin, 2000), pp. 82–6; *NZ Truth*, 28 September 1918, p. 1.

129   *EP*, 28 September 1918, p. 3.

130   *D*, 4 October 1918, p. 6.

131   *The Nation*, October 1918, pp. 2–3.

132   *Hastings Standard*, 31 January 1919, p. 6.

133 *NZ Truth*, 17 January 1920, p. 5; *D*, 25 February 1920, p. 5; Bassett, *Sir Joseph Ward*, pp. 246–9.
134 *TDN*, 22 December 1919, p. 5; 3 January 1919, p. 11.
135 *TDN*, 5 June 1920, p. 4.
136 *D*, 13 May 1920, p. 8; *P*, 4 August 1920, p. 6; *EP*, 8 September 1920, p. 8; *P*, 14 September 1920, p. 6; *P*, 18 September 1920, p. 8; P.S. O'Connor, 'Mr Massey and the PPA: A suspicion confirmed', *Journal of Public Administration*, vol. 28, no. 2, 1966, pp. 69–74.
137 *NZH*, 6 February 1929, p. 12.

Chapter 10: 'Too great to be unconnected with us': Reactions to the 1916 Easter Rising in the British Empire and the United States
1   Ken Loach (dir.), *The Wind that Shakes the Barley* (Paris: Pathé Distribution, 2006).
2   Keith Jeffery, 'Introduction', in Keith Jeffery (ed.), *'An Irish Empire': Aspects of Ireland and the British Empire* (Manchester: Manchester University Press, 1996), p. 1.
3   Kevin Kenny, *Ireland and the British Empire* (Oxford: Oxford University Press, 2004), p. xix.
4   For example, Barrie Crosbie, 'Networks of Empire: Linkage and reciprocity in nineteenth-century Irish and Indian history', *History Compass*, vol. 7, 2009, pp. 993–1007. See also Barrie Crosbie, *Irish Imperial Networks: Migration, social communication and exchange in nineteenth-century India* (Cambridge: Cambridge University Press, 2011); Kate O'Malley, *Ireland, India, and Empire: Indo-Irish radical connections, 1919–64* (Manchester: Manchester University Press, 2008); Michael Silvestri, *Ireland and India: Nationalism, empire and memory* (New York: Palgrave Macmillan, 2009); Patrick O'Leary, *Servants of the Empire: The Irish in Punjab, 1881–1921* (Manchester: Manchester University Press, 2011); and Michael and Denis Holmes (eds), *Ireland and India: Connections, comparisons, contrasts* (Dublin: Folens, 1997).
5   Richard P. Davis, *Irish Issues in New Zealand Politics, 1868–1922* (Dunedin: Otago University Press, 1974), p. 191.
6   *NZT*, 4 May 1916.
7   Rory Sweetman, 'Who Fears to Speak of Easter Week? Antipodean Irish-Catholic responses to the 1916 Rising', in Ruán O'Donnell (ed.), *The Impact of the 1916 Rising: Among the nations* (Dublin: Irish Academic Press, 2008), p. 76.
8   *NZH*, 1 May 1916.
9   *A*, 1 May 1916, 2 May 1916; Albert Thomas Dryer, 'The Independence of Ireland: Source material for the history of the movement in Australia', Dryer Papers, National Library of Australia, MS 6610 Box 1, Folder 11; *The Irish Rebellion and Australian Opinion* (Melbourne: Critchley Parker, 1916), pp. 1–30.
10 *CP*, 4 May 1916, 11 May 1916.
11 Val Noone (ed.), *Nicholas O'Donnell's Autobiography* (Ballarat: Ballarat Heritage Services, 2017), p. 298.
12 Dryer, 'Independence of Ireland'.
13 Commonwealth of Australia, *Parliamentary Debates*, XXVIII (Session 1905), House of Representatives, pp. 3807–18 (19 October 1905), Senate, pp. 3761–81 (19 October 1905).

14 Frederick J. McEvoy, 'Canadian Catholic Press Reaction to the Irish Crisis, 1916–1921', in David A. Wilson (ed.), *Irish Nationalism in Canada* (Montreal: McGill-Queen's University Press, 2009), p. 122. See also Mark G. McGowan, 'Between King, Kaiser and Canada: Irish Catholics in Canada and the Great War, 1914–1918', in Wilson (ed.), *Irish Nationalism in Canada*, p. 98.

15 See Malcolm Campbell, 'John Redmond and the Irish National League in Australia and New Zealand, 1883', *History*, vol. 86, 2001, pp. 348–62; McEvoy, 'Canadian Catholic Press Reaction', p. 124.

16 On the aftermath and executions, see Fearghal McGarry, *The Rising: Ireland: Easter 1916* (Oxford: Oxford University Press, 2010), pp. 274–6.

17 Quoted in McEvoy, 'Canadian Catholic Press Reaction', p. 123.

18 Sweetman, 'Who Fears to Speak?', pp. 77–8.

19 *A*, 16 May 1916; *FJ*, 11 May 1916; T.P. Boland, *James Duhig* (St Lucia: University of Queensland Press, 1986), pp. 128–39.

20 See David Brundage, *Irish Nationalists in America: The politics of exile, 1798–1998* (New York: Oxford University Press, 2016), pp. 119–26.

21 *IW*, 16 February 1884; *The Pilot* (Boston), 9 February 1884; Michael Funchion, *Chicago's Irish Nationalists, 1881–1890* (New York: Arno Press, 1976), pp. 56–104.

22 *IW*, 8 March 1884.

23 Malcolm Campbell, *Ireland's New Worlds: Immigrants, politics, and society in the United States and Australia, 1815–1922* (Madison: University of Wisconsin Press, 2007), pp. 154–6.

24 For the turn of the century period, see Campbell, *Ireland's New Worlds*, pp. 132–58; Francis M. Carroll, 'America and the 1916 Rising', in Gabriel Doherty and Dermot Keogh (eds), *1916: The long revolution* (Cork: Mercier Press, 2007), pp. 124–30.

25 Brundage, *Irish Nationalists in America*, pp. 143–5; David M. Kennedy, *Over Here: The First World War and American society* (New York: Oxford University Press, 1980), pp. 3–44.

26 *IW*, 3 October 1914, 10 October 1914.

27 *IW*, 6 May 1916; F.M. Carroll, *American Opinion and the Irish Question, 1910–1923* (Dublin: Gill & Macmillan, 1978), pp. 66–9.

28 Bernadette Whelan, 'The Wilson Administration and the 1916 Rising', in Ruán O'Donnell (ed.), *The Impact of the 1916 Rising: Among the nations* (Dublin: Irish Academic Press, 2008), pp. 97–8.

29 McGarry, *The Rising*, p. 264.

30 Carroll, *American Opinion*, pp. 62–3.

31 Ibid., pp. 57–63; Alan J. Ward, *Ireland and Anglo-American Relations, 1899–1921* (London: Weidenfeld & Nicolson, 1969), pp. 111–13.

32 *The Pilot*, 13 May 1916.

33 Ibid., 3 June 1916.

34 Carroll, *American Opinion*, pp. 64–5.

35 See Campbell, 'John Redmond', pp. 348–62.

36 Michael Davitt, *The Boer Fight for Freedom* (Johannesburg: Scripta Africana, 1902), pp. 544, 582; Carla King, *Michael Davitt after the Land League, 1882–1906* (Dublin: University College Dublin Press, 2016), pp. 465–92; Keith Jeffery, 'The Irish

Military Tradition and the British Empire', in Keith Jeffery (ed.), *'An Irish Empire':*
Aspects of Ireland and the British Empire (Manchester: Manchester University Press,
1996), p. 95.

37 Malcolm Campbell, 'Michael Davitt's Pacific World', *Journal of Irish and Scottish*
Studies, vol. 4, 2010, pp. 131–44.

38 Henry Boylan, *Dictionary of Irish Biography* (New York: St Martin's Press, 1988),
p. 137.

39 Quoted in O'Leary, *Servants of the Empire*, p. 205.

40 Michael Silvestri, '"The Sinn Féin of India": Irish nationalism and the policing
of revolutionary terrorism in Bengal', *Journal of British Studies*, vol. 39, 2000, pp.
466–7. See also Richard Davis, 'The Influence of the Irish Revolution on Indian
Nationalism: The evidence of the Indian press, 1916–22', *South Asia: Journal of*
South Asian Studies, vol. 9, 1986, pp. 55–68, and H.V. Brasted, 'Irish Models and the
Indian National Congress, 1870–1922', *South Asia: Journal of South Asian Studies*,
vol. 8, 1985, pp. 24–85.

41 O'Leary, *Servants of the Empire*, p. 205.

42 Michael Silvestri, 'Commemoration: Nationalism, empire and memory: the
Connaught Rangers mutiny, June 1920', *History Ireland*, vol. 18, 2010, https://
www.historyireland.com/20th-century-contemporary-history/commemoration
nationalism-empire-and-memory-the-connaught-rangers-mutiny-june-1920/.

43 Extensive coverage of events in Dublin appears in major New Zealand newspapers,
especially from 1 May. International news reports featured prominently. On Birrell's
praise of Dublin's population, see *NZH*, 2 May 1916, p. 7, drawing on interviews
with English journalists.

44 A comprehensive survey of New Zealand press coverage of the so-called Indian
'mutiny' is in progress. Samplings of earliest reactions include reportage in *The*
New Zealander, 10 June 1857. A strong racial dimension is present in subsequent
coverage, some sourced from the Australian press and repeated in different New
Zealand newspapers, including *The Nelson Examiner and New Zealand Chronicle*,
12 August 1857, and *The Daily Southern Cross*, 4 August, 7 August, and 29 September
1857.

45 Michael de Nie, *The Eternal Paddy: Irish identity and the British press, 1798–1882*
(Madison: University of Wisconsin Press, 2004); L. Perry Curtis Jr, *Apes and Angels:*
The Irishman in Victorian caricature (Washington, DC: Smithsonian Institution
Press, 1997).

46 Cian T. McMahon, *The Global Dimensions of Irish Identity: Race, nation, and the*
popular press, 1840–1880 (Chapel Hill: University of North Carolina Press, 2015).

47 A.M. Topp, 'English Institutions and the Irish Race', *Melbourne Review*, vol. VI,
1881, pp. 9–10.

48 *C*, 3 May 1916.

49 *NZH*, 1 May 1916, p. 4.

50 Quoted in Brian Jenkins, *Irish Nationalism and the British State from Repeal to*
Revolutionary Nationalism (Montreal: McGill-Queen's University Press, 2006),
p. 334.

Bibliography

'1916 Necrology 485', http://www.glasnevintrust.ie/visit-glasnevin/news/1916-list/ [accessed 12 November 2019]

1916 Rebellion Handbook (Dublin: Mourne River Press, 1998)

Akenson, Donald Harman, *Half the World from Home: Perspectives on the Irish in New Zealand, 1860–1950* (Wellington: Victoria University Press, 1990)

Amos, Keith, *The Fenians in Australia* (Sydney: New South Wales University Press, 1988)

Arrington, Lauren, *Revolutionary Lives: Constance and Casimir Markievicz* (Princeton, NJ: Princeton University Press, 2016)

'Australia's Triumph Under Voluntaryism Puts New Zealand Under Conscription to Shame', http://handle.slv.vic.gov.au/10381/157784 [accessed 3 December 2019]

Ayres, Philip, *Prince of the Church: Patrick Francis Moran, 1830–1911* (Melbourne: The Miegunyah Press, 2007)

Bacon, Bryan, *A Terrible Duty: The madness of Captain Bowen-Colthurst* (n.p.: Thena Press, 2015)

Baker, Paul, *King and Country Call: New Zealanders, conscription and the Great War* (Auckland: Auckland University Press, 1988)

Bassett, Michael, *Sir Joseph Ward: A political biography* (Auckland: Auckland University Press, 1993)

Bassett, Michael, and Michael King, *Tomorrow Comes the Song: A life of Peter Fraser* (Auckland: Penguin, 2000)

Belich, James, *Making Peoples: A history of the New Zealanders from Polynesian settlement to the end of the nineteenth century* (London: Allen Lane, 1996)

Belich, James, *The New Zealand Wars and the Victorian Interpretation of Racial Conflict* (Auckland: Auckland University Press, 1986)

Belich, James, *Paradise Reforged: A history of New Zealand from the 1880s to the year 2000* (Auckland: Penguin, 2001)

Belich, James, *Replenishing the Earth: The settler revolution and the rise of the Anglo-world* (Oxford: Oxford University Press, 2009)

Biagini, Eugenio F., *British Democracy and Irish Nationalism* (Cambridge: Cambridge University Press, 2007)

Boland, T.P., *James Duhig* (St Lucia: University of Queensland Press, 1986)

Bowe, Nicola Gordon, 'The Art of Beatrice Elvery, Lady Glenavy (1883–1970)', *Irish Arts Review Yearbook*, vol. 11, 1995, pp. 169–75

Bowman, Timothy, *Irish Regiments in the Great War: Discipline and morale* (Manchester: Manchester University Press, 2003)

Boyce, D.G., *Ireland, 1828–1923: From ascendancy to democracy* (Oxford: Blackwell, 1992)

Boyce, D.G., 'The Ulster Crisis: Prelude to 1916?', in Gabriel Doherty and Dermot Keogh (eds), *1916: The long revolution* (Cork: Mercier Press, 2007), pp. 45–60

Boylan, Henry, *Dictionary of Irish Biography* (New York: St Martin's Press, 1988)

Brady, E.J., *Doctor Mannix: Archbishop of Melbourne* (Melbourne: Library of National Biography, 1934)

Brasted, H.V., 'Irish Models and the Indian National Congress, 1870–1922', *South Asia: Journal of South Asian Studies*, vol. 8, 1985, pp. 24–85

Brennan, Niall, *Dr Mannix* (Adelaide: Rigby, 1964)

Brennan-Whitmore, W.J., *Dublin Burning: The Easter Rising from behind the barricades* (Dublin: Gill & Macmillan, 1996)

Breward, Ian, *Godless Schools? A study of Protestant reactions to the Education Act of 1877* (Christchurch: Presbyterian Bookroom, 1967)

British Pathé, 'London's Welcome – Sgt O'Leary VC', https://www.youtube.com/watch?v=TtaA2fFN4qE [accessed 23 March 2020]

British Pathé, 'O'Leary VC', https://www.youtube.com/watch?v=D7agL8uHxIk [accessed 23 March 2020]

Brooking, Tom, *Richard Seddon: King of God's Own: The life and times of New Zealand's longest serving prime minister* (Auckland: Penguin, 2014)

Brosnahan, Seán, 'The "Battle of the Borough" and the "Saige o Timaru": Sectarian riot in colonial Canterbury', *New Zealand Journal of History*, vol. 28, no. 1, 1994, pp. 41–59

Brosnahan, Seán, 'Parties or Politics: Wellington's IRA, 1922–1928', in Brad Patterson (ed.), *The Irish in New Zealand: Historical contexts and perspectives* (Wellington: Victoria University of Wellington, 2002), pp. 67–87

Brosnahan, Seán, '"Shaming the Shoneens": *The Green Ray* and the Maoriland Irish Society in Dunedin, 1916–22', in Lyndon Fraser (ed.), *A Distant Shore: Irish migration & New Zealand settlement* (Dunedin: University of Otago Press, 2000), pp. 117–34

Brown, Terence, *The Irish Times: 150 years of influence* (London: Bloomsbury, 2015)

Brown, Terence, et al., 'The *Irish Times* in 1916: A newspaper in focus', *The Irish Times*, 26 March 2016, https://www.irishtimes.com/culture/heritage/the-irish-times-in-1916-a-newspaper-in-focus-1.2585762 [accessed 23 March 2020]

Brundage, David, *Irish Nationalists in America: The politics of exile, 1798–1998* (New York: Oxford University Press, 2016)

Bryan, Cyril, *Archbishop Mannix: Champion of Australian democracy* (Melbourne: Advocate Press, 1918)

Cain, Frank, *The Origins of Political Surveillance in Australia* (Sydney: Angus & Robertson, 1983)

Campbell, Malcolm, *Ireland's New Worlds: Immigrants, politics, and society in the United States and Australia, 1815–1922* (Madison: University of Wisconsin Press, 2007)

Campbell, Malcolm, 'John Redmond and the Irish National League in Australia and New Zealand, 1883', *History*, vol. 86, 2001, pp. 348–62

Campbell, Malcolm, 'Michael Davitt's Pacific World', *Journal of Irish and Scottish Studies*, vol. 4, 2010, pp. 131–44

Carroll, Francis M., 'America and the 1916 Rising', in Gabriel Doherty and Dermot Keogh (eds), *1916: The long revolution* (Cork: Mercier Press, 2007), pp. 124–30

Carroll, Francis M., *American Opinion and the Irish Question, 1910–1923* (Dublin: Gill & Macmillan, 1978)

Carroll, Rowan, and Elizabeth Plumridge, 'Section 5: Police extension of mandate and detection of resistance and non-compliance with conscription', unpublished paper, *Rethinking War* conference, Stout Centre, 2013

Casey, Kerry, 'The Diggers and the IRA: A story of Australian and New Zealand Great-War soldiers involved in Ireland's War of Independence', MA thesis, University of New South Wales, 2014

Caulfield, Max, *The Easter Rebellion*, 2nd edn (Dublin: Gill & Macmillan, 1995)

Chapman, Margaret, Pauline O'Leary, Ginny Talbot, Brenda Lyon and Jean Goodwin, *Jessie Mackay: A woman before her time* (Kakahu, NZ: Kakahu WDFF [Women's Division Federated Farmers]; Geraldine, NZ: PCCL Services, 1997)

Cleary, Henry W., *An Impeached Nation: Being a study of Irish outrages* (Dunedin: New Zealand Tablet, 1909)

Cleary, Henry W., Papers, Auckland Catholic Diocesan Archives

Cleary, Henry W., *Prussian Militarism at Work: A letter* (London: Barclay & Fry, 1917)

Coleman, P.J., 'Transplanted Irish Institutions: Orangeism and Hibernianism in New Zealand, 1877–1910', MA thesis, University of Canterbury, 1994

Committee of Vigilance (Loyal Orange Lodge no. 70), *The Papal Delegate and the Mayor* (Auckland: New Zealand Mission Press, 1916)

Commonwealth Bureau of Census and Statistics, *Population and Vital Statistics, Bulletin No. 34: Commonwealth demography, 1916, and previous years*, https://www.ausstats.abs.gov.au/ausstats/free.nsf/0/D134A2E5E3283542CA2576400017 6945/$File/31410_No34_1916.pdf [accessed 29 November 2019]

Commonwealth of Australia, *Parliamentary Debates*, vol. XXVIII, 1905

Connolly, James, *Labour in Irish History* (New York: Donnelly Press, 1919)

Connolly, James, 'Michael Davitt: A text for a revolutionary lecture' (1908), https://www.marxists.org/archive/connolly/1908/08/davitt.htm [accessed 23 March 2020]

Connolly, James, *The Re-conquest of Ireland* (1915), https://www.marxists.org/archive/connolly/1915/rcoi/index.htm [accessed 23 March 2020]

Coogan, Tim Pat, *1916: The Easter Rising* (London: Cassell, 2001)

Coogan, Tim Pat, *Michael Collins: A biography* (London: Arrow Books, 1991)

Coughlan, Anthony, 'Ireland's Marxist Historians', in Ciaran Brady (ed.), *Interpreting Irish History: The debate on historical revisionism* (Dublin: Irish Academic Press, 1994), pp. 288–305

Crosbie, Barrie, *Irish Imperial Networks: Migration, social communication and exchange in nineteenth-century India* (Cambridge: Cambridge University Press, 2011)

Crosbie, Barrie, 'Networks of Empire: Linkage and reciprocity in nineteenth-century Irish and Indian history', *History Compass*, vol. 7, 2009, pp. 993–1007

Curtis, L. Perry Jr, *Apes and Angels: The Irishman in Victorian caricature* (Washington, DC: Smithsonian Institution Press, 1997)

Davidson, Jared, 'Dissent during the First World War: By the numbers', http://blog.tepapa.govt.nz/2016/06/28/dissent-during-the-first-world-war-by-the-numbers/ [accessed 23 March 2020]

Davis, Richard P., 'The Influence of the Irish Revolution on Indian Nationalism: The evidence of the Indian press, 1916–22', *South Asia: Journal of South Asian Studies*, vol. 9, 1986, pp. 55–68

Davis, Richard P., *Irish Issues in New Zealand Politics, 1868–1922* (Dunedin: Otago University Press, 1974)

Davis, Richard P., 'The New Zealand Labour Party's "Irish Campaign", 1916–1921', *Political Science*, vol. 19, no. 2, 1967, pp. 13–23

Davitt, Michael, *The Boer Fight for Freedom* (Johannesburg: Scripta Africana, 1902)

De Nie, Michael, *The Eternal Paddy: Irish identity and the British press, 1798–1882* (Madison: University of Wisconsin Press, 2004)

de Rosa, P., *Rebels: The Irish Rising of 1916* (New York: Ballantine Books, 1992)

Denman, Terence, *A Lonely Grave: The life and death of William Redmond* (Dublin: Irish Academic Press, 1995)

Dháibhéid, Caoimhe Nic, 'The Irish National Aid Association and the Radicalization of Public Opinion in Ireland, 1916–1918', *The Historical Journal*, vol. 55, no. 3, 2012, pp. 705–29

Dryer, Albert, Papers, National Library of Australia

Duffy, Joe, *Children of the Rising: The untold story of the young lives lost during Easter 1916* (Dublin: Hachette Books, 2016)

Ebsworth, Walter A., *Archbishop Mannix* (Melbourne: Stephenson, 1977)

Ellis, John, *Eye-Deep in Hell: The Western Front, 1914–18* (London: Penguin Books, 2002)

Elwick, James, 'Layered History: Styles of reasoning as stratified conditions of possibility', *Studies in History and Philosophy of Science*, vol. 43, no. 4, 2012, pp. 619–27

Fallon, Donal, 'A Hero Nonetheless: Nurse Margaret Keogh and the Easter Rising', http://comeheretome.com/2016/01/12/a-hero-nonetheless-nurse-margaret-keogh-and-the-easter-rising/ [accessed 23 March 2020]

Ferriter, Diarmaid, *A Nation and Not a Rabble: The Irish Revolution, 1913–1923* (London: Profile Books, 2015)

Fewster, Kevin, 'Expression and Suppression: Aspects of military censorship in Australia during the Great War', PhD thesis, University of New South Wales, 1980

Finnane, Mark, 'The Easter Rising in Australian History and Memory', *Australasian Journal of Irish Studies*, vol. 16, 2016, pp. 30–46

'First World War Census and Conscription', https://nzhistory.govt.nz/media/photo/war-census-and-conscription [accessed 2 December 2019]

Fitz-Gibbon, Bryan, and Marianne Gizycki, 'Research Discussion Paper 2001–07: A history of last-resort lending and other support for troubled financial institutions in Australia, 6. The 1890s depression', prepared for the Reserve Bank of Australia, https://www.rba.gov.au/publications/rdp/2001/2001-07/1890s-depression.html [accessed 3 December 2019]

Fitzhardinge, L.F., *William Morris Hughes: A political biography, Vol. 1: That fiery particle, 1862–1914* (Sydney: Angus & Robertson, 1964)

Fitzhardinge, L.F., *William Morris Hughes: A political biography, Vol. 2: The little digger, 1914–1952* (Sydney: Angus & Robertson, 1979)

Fitzpatrick, Orla, 'Portraits and Propaganda: Photographs of the widows and children of the 1916 leaders in *The Catholic Bulletin*', in Lisa Godson and Joanna Brück (eds), *Making 1916: The material and visual culture of the Easter Rising* (Liverpool: Liverpool University Press, 2015), pp. 82–90

Fletcher, John Percy, *Conscription under Camouflage: An account of compulsory military training in Australasia down to the outbreak of the Great War* (Glenelg, S. Aust.: J.F. Hills, 1919)

Foster, R.F., *The Irish Story: Telling tales and making it up in Ireland* (London: Penguin, 2001)

Foster, R.F., *Vivid Faces: The revolutionary generation in Ireland, 1890–1923* (London: Allen Lane, 2014)

Foster, R.F., *Vivid Faces: The revolutionary generation in Ireland, 1890–1923* (London: Penguin, 2015)

Fox, Alistair, 'New Zealand Cinema', https://www.oxfordbibliographies.com/view/document/obo-9780199791286/obo-9780199791286-0227.xml [accessed 23 March 2020]

Foy, Michael, and Brian Barton, *The Easter Rising* (Stroud: Sutton Publishing, 2000)

Frame, Alex, *Salmond: Southern jurist* (Wellington: Victoria University Press, 1995)

Franks, Peter, and Jim McAloon, *Labour: The New Zealand Labour Party, 1916–2016* (Wellington: Victoria University Press, 2016)

Fraser, Lyndon, 'The Provincial and Gold Rush Years', https://nzhistory.govt.nz/files/documents/peopling3.pdf [accessed 19 November 2019]

Fraser, Lyndon, *To Tara via Holyhead: Irish Catholic immigrants in nineteenth-century Christchurch* (Auckland: Auckland University Press, 1997)

Funchion, Michael, *Chicago's Irish Nationalists, 1881–1890* (New York: Arno Press, 1976)

Garland, Canon David John, Papers, John Oxley Library, State Library of Queensland, Brisbane

'Getting the Men to War', https://nzhistory.govt.nz/war/public-service-at-war/getting-the-men-to-war#heading8 [accessed 2 December 2019]

Gilchrist, Michael, *Daniel Mannix: Wit and wisdom* (North Melbourne: Freedom, 2004)

Glenavy, Beatrice Lady, *'Today We Will Only Gossip'* (London: Constable, 1964)

Grant, David, *Field Punishment No. 1: Archibald Baxter, Mark Briggs & New Zealand's anti-militarist tradition* (Wellington: Steele Roberts, 2008)

Gregory, Adrian, and Senia Pašeta (eds), *Ireland and the Great War: 'A war to unite us all'?* (Manchester: Manchester University Press, 2002)

Griffin, James, *Daniel Mannix: Beyond the myths* (Mulgrave, Vic.: Garratt Publishing, 2012)

Gustafson, Barry, *Labour's Path to Political Independence: Origins and establishment of the New Zealand Labour Party, 1900–1919* (Auckland: Auckland University Press, 1980)

Hagan, John, Papers, Irish College Rome

Hall, Dianne, 'Irish Republican Women in Australia: Kathleen Barry and Linda Kearns' tour in 1924–1925', *Irish Historical Studies*, vol. 43, no. 163, 2019, pp. 73–93

Hall, Dianne, '"Now Him White Man": Images of the Irish in colonial Australia', *History Australia*, vol. 11, no. 2, 2014, pp. 167–95

Hall, Dianne, and Elizabeth Malcolm, 'Catholic Irish Australia and the Labor Movement: Race in Australia and nationalism in Ireland, 1880s–1920s', in Greg Patmore and Shelton Stromquist (eds), *Frontiers of Labor: Comparative histories of the United States and Australia* (Urbana: University of Illinois Press, 2018), pp. 149–67

Hally, P.J., 'The Easter 1916 Rising in Dublin: The military aspects', *Irish Sword*, vol. 7, 1965–6, pp. 313–26

Hally, P.J., 'The Easter 1916 Rising in Dublin: The military aspects', *Irish Sword*, vol. 8, 1967–8, pp. 48–57

Healy, Richard B., *The Christian Brothers of Wakefield Street, 1878–1978* (Adelaide: Lutheran Publishing House, 1978)

Hearn, Terry, 'The Origins of New Zealand's Irish Settlers, 1840–1945', in Brad Patterson (ed.), *The Irish in New Zealand: Historical contexts and perspectives* (Wellington: Stout Research Centre for New Zealand Studies, Victoria University of Wellington, 2002), pp. 15–34

Hill, Richard S., *The Colonial Frontier Tamed: New Zealand policing in transition, 1867–1886* (Wellington: Historical Branch, Department of Internal Affairs; GP Books, 1989)

Hoare, Nicholas, 'Harry Holland's "Samoan Complex"', *Journal of Pacific History*, vol. 49, no. 2, 2014, pp. 151–69

Holland, H.E., *Armageddon or Calvary: The conscientious objectors of New Zealand and 'The process of their conversion'* (Wellington: Maoriland Worker Printing and Publishing, 1919)

Holland, H.E., 'N.Z.'s Appeal to Australia. VOTE NO', http://handle.slv.vic.gov.au/10381/158416 [accessed 3 December 2019]

Holmes, Michael, and Denis Holmes (eds), *Ireland and India: Connections, comparisons, contrasts* (Dublin: Folens, 1997)

Holton, Sandra, 'Gender Difference, National Identity and Professing History: The case of Alice Stopford Green', *History Workshop Journal*, vol. 53, 2002, pp. 118–27

Horn, G.E., 'The Irish Revolution and Protestant Politics in New Zealand, 1916–1922', unpublished paper presented at *The Irish Diaspora and Revolution* conference, NUI Maynooth, November 2012

Horn, Gerard, 'The Orange Order in Wellington, 1874–1930: Class, ethnicity and politics', *Australasian Journal of Irish Studies*, vol. 10, 2010, pp. 55–80

'Irish', Te Ara: The Encyclopedia of New Zealand, http://www.teara.govt.nz/en/irish/ [accessed 23 March 2020]

The Irish Rebellion and Australian Opinion (Melbourne: Critchley Parker, 1916)

James, Stephanie, 'Deep Green Loathing? Shifting Irish-Australian loyalties in the Victorian and South Australian Irish Catholic press, 1868–1923', PhD thesis, Flinders University, 2013

James, Stephanie, '"The Drought Is Worrying People Here Far Worse than the War": Letters between Hamley Bridge and Ireland during the Great War', *Journal of the Historical Society of South Australia*, no. 43, 2015, pp. 5–16

James, Stephanie, 'The Evolution of Adelaide's Irish National Association, 1918–1950: From security threat to cultural force?', *Journal of the Historical Society of South Australia*, no. 45, 2017, pp. 31–45

James, Stephanie, '"From Beyond the Sea": The Irish Catholic press in the southern hemisphere', in Angela McCarthy (ed.), *Ireland in the World: Comparative, transnational, and personal perspectives* (New York: Routledge, 2015), pp. 81–109

Jeffery, Keith, 'Introduction', in Keith Jeffery (ed.), *'An Irish Empire': Aspects of Ireland and the British Empire* (Manchester: Manchester University Press, 1996), pp. 1–24

Jeffery, Keith, 'The Irish Military Tradition and the British Empire', in Keith Jeffery (ed.), *'An Irish Empire': Aspects of Ireland and the British Empire* (Manchester: Manchester University Press, 1996), pp. 94–122

Jenkins, Brian, *Irish Nationalism and the British State from Repeal to Revolutionary Nationalism* (Montreal: McGill-Queen's University Press, 2006)

'John O'Neill, Sedition', https://nzhistory.govt.nz/media/photo/john-oneill-sedition [accessed 23 March 2020]

Johnson, Lionel, 'Poetry and Patriotism', in *Poetry and Ireland: Essays by W.B. Yeats and Lionel Johnson* (Churchtown, Dundrum: Cuala Press, 1908), pp. 21–54, https://archive.org/stream/poetryirelandessooyeatrich/poetryirelandessooyeatrich_djvu.txt [accessed 23 March 2020]

Jones, Kathleen, *Katherine Mansfield: The story-teller* (Edinburgh: Edinburgh University Press, 2010)

'Kathleen ni Houlihan 1916 (Abbey)', https://www.abbeytheatre.ie/archives/production_detail/6602/ [accessed 19 November 2019]

Keane, Hugh, 'New Zealanders at Trinity College Dublin Easter Week 1916', 5 December 2012, http://theirishwar.com/new-zealanders-at-trinity-college-dublin-easter-week-1916/ [accessed 23 March 2020]

Kennedy, David M., *Over Here: The First World War and American society* (New York: Oxford University Press, 1980)

Kenny, Kevin, *Ireland and the British Empire* (Oxford: Oxford University Press, 2004)

Keogh, Raymond M., 'Death of a Volunteer', *Dublin Review of Books*, 16 February 2016, http://www.drb.ie/blog/dublin-stories/2016/02/16/death-of-a-volunteer [accessed 23 March 2020]

Kiberd, Declan, 'The Easter Rebellion: Poetry or drama?', www.theirelandinstitute.com/wp/the-easter-rebellion-poetry-or-drama/ [accessed 3 December 2019]

Kildea, Jeff, *Anzacs and Ireland* (Sydney: UNSW Press, 2007)

Kildea, Jeff, 'Called to Arms: Australians in the Irish Easter Rising 1916', *Journal of the Australian War Memorial*, vol. 39, 2003, https://www.awm.gov.au/journal/j39/kildea/ [accessed 23 March 2020]

Kildea, Jeff, 'What Price Loyalty? Australian Catholics in the First World War', the 2018 Knox Lecture, Catholic Theological College, Melbourne, https://jeffkildea.com/wp-content/uploads/2018/05/Kildea-What-Price-Loyalty-2018.pdf [accessed 12 November 2019]

King, Carla, *Michael Davitt after the Land League, 1882–1906* (Dublin: University College Dublin Press, 2016)

King, Michael, *The Penguin History of New Zealand* (Auckland: Penguin, 2003)

Kuch, Peter, 'Irish Playwrights and the Dunedin Stage in 1862: Theatre patrons performing civility', *Journal of New Zealand Studies*, vol. 15, 2013, pp. 90–100

Kuch, Peter, 'Irishness on the New Zealand Stage, 1850–1930', with an appendix detailing Sara Allgood's 1916 and 1918 tours of New Zealand compiled by Dr Lisa Marr, *Journal of Irish and Scottish Studies*, vol. 4, no. 1, 2010, pp. 99–118

Laffan, Michael, *The Resurrection of Ireland: The Sinn Féin party, 1916–1923* (Cambridge: Cambridge University Press, 1999)

Laracy, Hugh, 'Priests, People and Patriotism: New Zealand Catholics and the war, 1914–1918', *Australasian Catholic Record*, vol. 70, no. 1, 1993, pp. 14–26

Lee, J.J., *Ireland, 1912–1985: Politics and society* (Cambridge: Cambridge University Press, 1989)

Lenin, V.I., 'The Discussion on Self-Determination Summed Up', https://www.marxists.org/archive/lenin/works/1916/jul/x01.htm [accessed 22 February 2017]

'Letter from Robert Tweedy to His Mother, 7 May 1916', http://letters1916.maynoothuniversity.ie/item/910 [accessed 3 December 2019]

Loach, Ken (dir.), *The Wind that Shakes the Barley* (Paris: Pathé Distribution, 2006)

Luddy, Maria, *Hanna Sheehy Skeffington* (Dundalk: Historical Association of Ireland, 1995)

Lyons, F.S.L., *John Dillon: A biography* (London: Routledge & Kegan Paul, 1968)

Lyons, J.B., *The Enigma of Tom Kettle: Irish patriot, essayist, poet, British soldier, 1880–1916* (Dublin: Glendale Press, 1983)

MacDonald, D.V., 'The New Zealand Bible in Schools League', MA thesis, Victoria University of Wellington, 1964

Macleod, Nellie F.H., *A Voice on the Wind: The story of Jessie Mackay* (Wellington: Reed, 1955)

Malcolm, Elizabeth, and Dianne Hall, *A New History of the Irish in Australia* (Sydney: NewSouth Publishing, 2018)

Mansfield, Katherine, *The Collected Letters of Katherine Mansfield*, ed. Vincent O'Sullivan and Margaret Scott, vol. 1 (Oxford: Clarendon Press, 1984)

Mathews, P.J., 'A Poet's Revolt: How culture heavily influenced the Rising and its leaders', *Irish Independent*, 21 January 2016, http://www.independent.ie/irish-news/1916/rising-perspectives/a-poets-revolt-how-culture-heavily-influenced-the-rising-and-its-leaders-34379291.html [accessed 23 March 2020]

Maume, Patrick, 'Skeffington, Francis Sheehy- (1878–1916)', in *Dictionary of Irish Biography*, vol. 8 (Cambridge: Cambridge University Press, 2009), pp. 981–3

McAuliffe, Mary, and Liz Gillis, *Richmond Barracks 1916 'We were there': 77 women of the Easter Rising* (Dublin: Four Courts Press, 2016)

McCarthy, Angela, *Irish Migrants in New Zealand, 1840–1937: 'The desired haven'* (Woodbridge: Boydell Press, 2005)

McCoole, Sinéad, *Easter Widows: Seven Irish women who lived in the shadow of the 1916 Rising* (Dublin: Doubleday Ireland, 2015)

McCoole, Sinéad, *No Ordinary Women: Irish female activists in the revolutionary years, 1900–1923* (Dublin: O'Brien Press, 2015)

McDiarmid, Lucy, *At Home in the Revolution: What women said and did in 1916* (Dublin: Royal Irish Academy, 2015)

McEvoy, Frederick J., 'Canadian Catholic Press Reaction to the Irish Crisis, 1916–1921', in David A. Wilson (ed.), *Irish Nationalism in Canada* (Montreal: McGill-Queen's University Press, 2009), pp. 121–39

McGarry, Fearghal, *The Abbey Rebels of 1916: A lost revolution* (Dublin: Gill & Macmillan, 2015)

McGarry, Fearghal, *The Rising: Ireland: Easter 1916* (Oxford: Oxford University Press, 2010)

McGowan, Mark G., 'Between King, Kaiser and Canada: Irish Catholics in Canada and the Great War, 1914–1918', in David A. Wilson (ed.), *Irish Nationalism in Canada* (Montreal: McGill-Queen's University Press, 2009), pp. 97–120

McHugh, Roger (ed.), *Dublin 1916* (London: Arlington Books, 1976)

McMahon, Cian T., *The Global Dimensions of Irish Identity: Race, nation, and the popular press, 1840–1880* (Chapel Hill: University of North Carolina Press, 2015)

McNamara, Heather, 'The *New Zealand Tablet* and the Irish Catholic press worldwide, 1898–1923', *New Zealand Journal of History*, vol. 37, no. 2, 2003, pp. 153–70

McNamara, Heather, 'The Sole Organ of the Irish Race in New Zealand? A social and cultural history of the *New Zealand Tablet* and its readers, 1898–1923', MA thesis, University of Auckland, 2002

Meyers, Lynn, 'Ted Marks and the Dublin Easter Rising, 1916', http://blogs.slq.qld.gov.au/ww1/2016/03/30/ted-marks-and-the-dublin-easter-rising-1916/ [accessed 23 March 2020]

'Michael John O'Leary VC', http://www.vconline.org.uk/michael-j-oleary-vc/4587805344 [accessed 3 December 2019]

'Military Service Act 1916 (7 GEO. V. 1916, No. 8)', http://www.nzlii.org/nz/legis/hist_act/msa19167gv1916n8266/ [accessed 2 December 2019]

Molloy, Kevin, 'The Politics of Reading: Identity and the Australian reading experience, 1800–1880', in Brad and Kathryn Patterson (eds), *Ireland and the Irish Antipodes: One world or worlds apart? Papers delivered at the 16th Australasian Irish Studies Conference, Massey University, Wellington, New Zealand, 9–12 July 2009* (Sydney: Anchor Books, 2010), pp. 145–61

Molloy, Kevin, 'Victorians, Historians and Irish History: A reading of the *New Zealand Tablet*, 1873–1903', in Brad Patterson (ed.), *The Irish in New Zealand: Historical contexts and perspectives* (Wellington: Stout Research Centre, 2002), pp. 153–70

Moon, Paul, *New Zealand in the Twentieth Century: The nation, the people* (Auckland: Harper Collins, 2011)

Moores, H.S., 'The Rise of the Protestant Political Association: Sectarianism in New Zealand politics during World War I', MA thesis, University of Auckland, 1966

Moran, James, *Staging the Easter Rising: 1916 as theatre* (Cork: Cork University Press, 2006)

Moses, John A., and George F. Davis, *Anzac Day Origins: Canon DJ Garland and trans-Tasman commemoration* (Canberra: Barton Books, 2013)

Murphy, Frank, *Daniel Mannix: Archbishop of Melbourne* (Melbourne: Advocate Press, 1948)

'The National Register: The beginning of the end of voluntary recruitment', https://greatwarlondon.wordpress.com/2015/08/25/national-register/ [accessed 3 December 2019]

'New Zealand Ireland Connection', https://www.otago.ac.nz/history/nzic/bibliography.html [accessed 3 December 2019]

Niall, Brenda, *Mannix* (Melbourne: Text Publishing, 2015)

Nicholls, Roberta, *The Women's Parliament: The National Council of Women in New Zealand, 1896–1920* (Wellington: Victoria University Press, 1996)

Noone, Val (ed.), *Nicholas O'Donnell's Autobiography* (Ballarat: Ballarat Heritage Services, 2017)

Noone, Val, and Rachel Naughton (eds), *Daniel Mannix: His legacy* (East Melbourne: Melbourne Diocesan Historical Commission, Catholic Archdiocese of Melbourne, 2014)

O'Brien, Conor Cruise, 'The Embers of Easter, 1916–1966', *New Left Review*, vol. 1, no. 37, 1966, pp. 3–14

O'Brien, Paul, *Blood on the Streets: 1916 and the battle for Mount Street Bridge* (Cork: Mercier Press, 2008)

O'Connor, P.S., 'Mr Massey and the PPA: A suspicion confirmed', *Journal of Public Administration*, vol. 28, no. 2, 1966, pp. 69–74

O'Connor, P.S., 'Protestants, Catholics and the New Zealand Government, 1916–18', in G.A. Wood and P.S. O'Connor (eds), *W.P. Morrell: A tribute* (Dunedin: University of Otago Press, 1973), pp. 185–202

O'Connor, P.S., 'Sectarian Conflict in New Zealand, 1911–1920', *Political Science*, vol. 19, no. 1, 1967, pp. 3–16

O'Connor, P.S., 'Storm over the Clergy: New Zealand 1917', *Journal of Religious History*, vol. 4, no. 2, 1966, pp. 129–48

O'Faoláin, Seán, *Constance Markievicz* (London: Sphere Books, 1934)

O'Farrell, Patrick, *The Catholic Church and Community in Australia* (Melbourne: Thomas Nelson, 1977)

O'Farrell, Patrick, *Harry Holland: Militant socialist* (Canberra: ANU Press, 1964)

O'Farrell, Patrick, *The Irish in Australia* (Sydney: University of New South Wales Press, 1986)

O'Farrell, Patrick, *The Irish in Australia*, rev. edn (Sydney: University of New South Wales Press, 1993)

O'Farrell, Patrick, *Vanished Kingdoms: Irish in Australia and New Zealand* (Kensington: New South Wales University Press, 1990)

Official Report of the Fifth Commonwealth Conference of the Australian Labor Party (Sydney: Worker Trade Union Printery, 1912)

Ó hÓgartaigh, Margaret, *Kathleen Lynn: Irishwoman, patriot, doctor* (Dublin: Irish Academic Press, 2006)

O'Leary, Patrick, *Servants of the Empire: The Irish in Punjab, 1881–1921* (Manchester: Manchester University Press, 2011)

O'Malley, Kate, *Ireland, India, and Empire: Indo-Irish radical connections, 1919–64* (Manchester: Manchester University Press, 2008)

One of the Garrison, 'Inside Trinity College', in Roger McHugh (ed.), *Dublin 1916* (London: Arlington Books, 1966), pp. 158–74

Overlack, Peter, 'Easter 1916 in Dublin and the Australian Press: Background and response', *Journal of Australian Studies*, vols 54–5, 1997, pp. 188–93

Pašeta, Senia, 'Green [née Stopford], Alice Sophia Amelia', in *Oxford Dictionary of National Biography*, https://doi.org/10.1093/ref:odnb/33531 [accessed 23 February 2018]

Pašeta, Senia, *Irish Nationalist Women, 1900–1918* (Cambridge: Cambridge University Press, 2013)

Patterson, Brad (ed.), *The Irish in New Zealand: Historical contexts and perspectives* (Wellington: Stout Research Centre for New Zealand Studies, Victoria University of Wellington, 2002)

Patterson, Brad, '"We Love One Country, One Queen, One Flag": Loyalism in early colonial New Zealand, 1840–1880', in Allan Blackstock and Frank O'Gorman (eds), *Loyalism and the Formation of the British World, 1775–1914* (Woodbridge, UK: Boydell & Brewer, 2014), pp. 255–61

Phillips, Jock, 'Race and New Zealand National Identity', in Neal Garnham and Keith Jeffery (eds), *Culture, Place and Identity* (Dublin: University College Dublin Press, 2005), pp. 161–78

Phillips, Jock, and Terry Hearn, *Settlers: New Zealand immigrants from England, Ireland and Scotland, 1800–1945* (Auckland: Auckland University Press, 2008)

Pivac, Daina, Frank Stark and Lawrence McDonald (eds), *New Zealand Film: An illustrated history* (Wellington: Te Papa, 2011)

Powell, Marg, 'Charles Garland, Easter Rising 1916', http://blogs.slq.qld.gov.au/wwi/2016/03/28/charles-garland-easter-rising-1916/ [accessed 23 March 2020]

'Principal Results of Census of 1911', https://www.ausstats.abs.gov.au/ausstats/free.nsf/0/BB0FECF534E135D2CA257AEF00164B6A/$File/13010_1901_1916%20section%204.pdf [accessed 29 November 2019]

Purcell, Marie, *Dozens of Cousins: A story of the O'Donnell and Purcell families, 1841–1991* (Pascoe Vale South, Vic.: M. Purcell, 1991)

Report of Proceedings of Eighth Annual Session of the Grand Orange Lodge of New Zealand (Christchurch: n.p., 1916)

Report of Proceedings of Ninth Annual Session of the Grand Orange Lodge of New Zealand (Wellington: n.p., 1917)

Report of Proceedings of Tenth Annual Session of the Grand Orange Lodge of New Zealand (Wellington: n.p., 1918)

'Report on the Results of a Census of the Population of the Dominion of New Zealand Taken for the Night of the 15th October, 1916', https://www3.stats.govt.

nz/historic_publications/1916-census/Report%20on%20Results%20of%20
Census%201916/1916-report-results-census%20.html#idsect2_1_4314 [accessed 3
December 2019]

Richardson, Neil, *According to Their Lights: Stories of Irishmen in the British Army,
Easter 1916* (Cork: The Collins Press, 2015)

Russell, D.P., *Sinn Fein and the Irish Rebellion* (Melbourne: Fraser & Jenkinson, 1916)

Ryan, Arthur H., *Daniel Mannix, Archbishop of Melbourne* (Melbourne: Advocate
Press, 1949)

Ryan, Louise, 'Splendidly Silent: Representing Irish republican women, 1919–23', in
Ann-Maree Gallagher, Cathy Lubelska and Louise Ryan (eds), *Re-presenting the
Past: Women and history* (Harlow: Longman, 2001), pp. 23–43

Sanders, Michael, and Philip M. Taylor, *British Propaganda during the First World War,
1914–18* (London: Macmillan, 1982)

Santamaria, B.A., *Daniel Mannix: The quality of leadership* (Melbourne: Melbourne
University Press, 1984)

Satchell, Max, 'Pulpit Politics: The Protestant Political Association in Dunedin from
1917 to 1922', BA Hons, University of Otago, 1983

Shaffrey, Maura, 'Sackville Street/O'Connell Street', *Irish Arts Review*, 1988, pp. 144–9

Sharpe, Christopher, 'Recruitment and Conscription (Canada)', https://encyclopedia.
1914-1918-online.net/article/recruitment_and_conscription_canada [accessed 23
March 2020]

Shaw, Francis, 'The Canon of Irish History: A challenge', *Studies*, vol. 61, no. 2, 1972, pp.
113–52

Sheehy Skeffington, Francis, *Michael Davitt: Revolutionary, agitator, and labor leader*
(Boston: Dana Estes, 1909)

Shoebridge, Tim, 'New Zealanders Who Resisted the First World War', http://www.
nzhistory.net.nz/war/nzers-who-resisted-ww1 [accessed 23 March 2020]

Shouldice, Frank, *Grandpa the Sniper: The remarkable story of a 1916 volunteer* (Dublin:
Liffey Press, 2015)

Silvestri, Michael, 'Commemoration: Nationalism, empire and memory: The Connaught
Rangers mutiny, June 1920', *History Ireland*, vol. 18, 2010, https://www.historyireland.
com/20th-century-contemporary-history/commemorationnationalism-empire-
and-memory-the-connaught-rangers-mutiny-june-1920/ [accessed 23 March 2020]

Silvestri, Michael, *Ireland and India: Nationalism, empire and memory* (New York:
Palgrave Macmillan, 2009)

Silvestri, Michael, '"The Sinn Féin of India": Irish nationalism and the policing of
revolutionary terrorism in Bengal', *Journal of British Studies*, vol. 39, 2000, pp.
454–86

Stokes, Lilly, 'Easter Week Diary of Miss Lilly Stokes', in Roger McHugh (ed.), *Dublin
1916* (London: Arlington Books, 1966), p. 66.

Sweetman, Rory, *Bishop in the Dock: The sedition trial of James Liston* (Auckland:
Auckland University Press, 1997)

Sweetman, Rory, 'Cleary, Henry William (1859–1929)', in *Dictionary of Irish Biography*,
vol. 2 (Cambridge: Cambridge University Press, 2009), pp. 567–8

Sweetman, Rory, *Defending Trinity College Dublin, Easter 1916: Anzacs and the Rising* (Dublin: Four Courts Press, 2019)

Sweetman, Rory, *'A Fair and Just Solution?': A history of the integration of private schools in New Zealand* (Palmerston North: Dunmore Press in Association with the Ministry for Culture and Heritage and the Association of Proprietors of Integrated Schools, 2002)

Sweetman, Rory, *Faith and Fraternalism: A history of the Hibernian Society in New Zealand, 1869–2000* (Wellington: Hibernian Society, 2002)

Sweetman, Rory, '"How To Behave Among Protestants": Varieties of Irish Catholic leadership in Colonial New Zealand', in Brad Patterson (ed.), *The Irish in New Zealand: Historical contexts and perspectives* (Wellington: Stout Research Centre for New Zealand Studies, Victoria University of Wellington, 2002), pp. 89–101

Sweetman, Rory, 'Kelly, James Joseph', in *Dictionary of New Zealand Biography, Te Ara: The Encyclopedia of New Zealand*, https://www.TeAra.govt.nz/en/ biographies/3k6/kelly-james-joseph [accessed 12 November 2019]

Sweetman, Rory, 'Kelly, James Joseph (1877–1939)', in *Dictionary of Irish Biography*, vol. 5 (Cambridge: Cambridge University Press, 2009), pp. 77–8

Sweetman, Rory, 'New Zealand Catholicism and the Irish Issue, 1914–1922', in W.J. Shiels and Diana Wood (eds), *The Churches, Ireland and the Irish* (Oxford: Blackwell, 1989), pp. 375–84

Sweetman, Rory, 'New Zealand Catholicism, War, Politics and the Irish Issue, 1912–1922', PhD thesis, University of Cambridge, 1991

Sweetman, Rory, 'Towards a History of Orangeism in New Zealand', in Brad Patterson (ed.), *Ulster–New Zealand Migration and Cultural Transfers* (Dublin: Four Courts Press, 2006), pp. 154–64

Sweetman, Rory, 'Waving the Green Flag in the Southern Hemisphere: The Kellys and the Irish College, Rome', in Daire Keogh and Albert McDonnell (eds), *The Irish College Rome and Its World* (Dublin: Four Courts Press, 2008), pp. 205–24

Sweetman, Rory, 'Who Fears to Speak of Easter Week? Antipodean Irish-Catholic responses to the 1916 Rising', in Ruán O'Donnell (ed.), *The Impact of the 1916 Rising: Among the nations* (Dublin: Irish Academic Press, 2008), pp. 71–90

Taylor, James W., *Guilty but Insane: J.C. Bowen-Colthurst: Villain or victim?* (Cork: Mercier Press, 2016)

Topp, A.M., 'English Institutions and the Irish Race', *Melbourne Review*, vol. VI, 1881, pp. 9–10

Towell, Noel, 'Anzacs and the Easter Rising 1916: Australia's role in Ireland's past', *The Sydney Morning Herald*, 25 March 2016, https://www.smh.com.au/national/ anzacs-easter-rising-and-the-20160317-gnl500.html [accessed 23 March 2020]

Townshend, Charles, *Easter 1916: The Irish rebellion* (London: Penguin, 2006)

Travers, Fr Aloysius, 'Easter Week 1916: Personal recollections', *Capuchin Annual*, Dublin, 1942, pp. 211–20

Twain, Mark, *Following the Equator: A journey around the world*, Project Gutenberg ebook, http://www.gutenberg.org/files/2895/2895-0.txt [accessed 23 March 2020]

Tynan, Katharine, *The Years of the Shadow* (London: Constable, 1919) van der Krogt, Christopher, 'Elliott, Howard Leslie', in *Dictionary of New Zealand Biography, Te Ara: The Encyclopedia of New Zealand*, https://www.TeAra.govt.nz/en/biographies/3e5/elliott-howard-leslie [accessed 12 November 2019]

War Office Records, The National Archives, Kew, Richmond

Ward, Alan J., *Ireland and Anglo-American Relations, 1899–1921* (London: Weidenfeld & Nicolson, 1969)

Ward, Margaret, *Unmanageable Revolutionaries: Women and Irish nationalism* (London: Pluto Press, 1983)

Watson, James, 'Were Catholics Over-Represented in the Public Service during the Early Twentieth Century?', *Political Science*, vol. 42, no. 2, 1990, pp. 20–34

Watson, James, and Lachy Paterson (eds), *A Great New Zealand Prime Minister? Reappraising William Ferguson Massey* (Dunedin: Otago University Press, 2011)

Wells, Warre B., and N. Marlowe, *A History of the Irish Rebellion of 1916* (Dublin: Maunsel, 1916)

Whelan, Bernadette, 'The Wilson Administration and the 1916 Rising', in Ruán O'Donnell (ed.), *The Impact of the 1916 Rising: Among the nations* (Dublin: Irish Academic Press, 2008), pp. 91–118

Whitaker, Anne-Maree, 'Linda Kearns and Kathleen Barry Irish Republican Fundraising Tour, 1924–25', *Journal of the Australian Catholic Historical Society*, vol. 37, 2016, pp. 208–11

Wilson, David A. (ed.), *The Orange Order in Canada* (Dublin: Four Courts Press, 2007)

Yeats, W.B., 'The Irish Literary Theatre', *Daily Express* (Dublin), 14 January 1899, rptd in John P. Frayne and Colton Johnson (eds), *Uncollected Prose by W.B. Yeats*, vol. 2 (London: Macmillan, 1975), pp. 139–42

Yeats, W.B., 'The Man and the Echo', in Peter Alt and Russell K. Alspach (eds), *The Variorum Edition of the Poems of W.B. Yeats* (New York: Macmillan, 1973), p. 632.

Yeats, W.B., 'Noble and Ignoble Loyalties', *The United Irishman*, 21 April 1900, rptd in John P. Frayne and Colton Johnson (eds), *Uncollected Prose by W.B. Yeats*, vol. 2 (London: Macmillan, 1975), pp. 211–13

Yska, Redmer, *Truth: The rise and fall of the people's paper* (Nelson: Craig Potton Publishing, 2010)

Index